Criminal Procedure

Aspen College Series

Criminal Procedure

From the Courtroom to the Street

Roger Wright

Professor
School of Criminal Justice
University of Cincinnati

 Wolters Kluwer

To contact Customer Service, e-mail customer.service@wolterskluwer.com, call 1-800-234-1660, fax 1-800-901-9075, or mail correspondence to:

Wolters Kluwer
Attn: Order Department
PO Box 990
Frederick, MD 21705

Printed in the United States of America.

1 2 3 4 5 6 7 8 9 0

ISBN 978-1-4548-4773-1

Library of Congress Cataloging-in-Publication Data

Wright, Roger, 1953- author.
Criminal procedure : from the courtroom to the street / Roger Wright,
Professor, School of Criminal Justice, University of Cincinnati.
pages cm. — (Aspen college series)
Includes index.
ISBN 978-1-4548-4773-1 (alk. paper)
1. Criminal procedure — United States--Outlines, syllabi, etc. I. Title.

KF9619.85.W75 2015
345.73'05 — dc23

2014048584

About Wolters Kluwer Law & Business

Wolters Kluwer Law & Business is a leading global provider of intelligent information and digital solutions for legal and business professionals in key specialty areas, and respected educational resources for professors and law students. Wolters Kluwer Law & Business connects legal and business professionals as well as those in the education market with timely, specialized authoritative content and information-enabled solutions to support success through productivity, accuracy and mobility.

Serving customers worldwide, Wolters Kluwer Law & Business products include those under the Aspen Publishers, CCH, Kluwer Law International, Loislaw, ftwilliam.com and MediRegs family of products.

CCH products have been a trusted resource since 1913, and are highly regarded resources for legal, securities, antitrust and trade regulation, government contracting, banking, pension, payroll, employment and labor, and healthcare reimbursement and compliance professionals.

Aspen Publishers products provide essential information to attorneys, business professionals and law students. Written by preeminent authorities, the product line offers analytical and practical information in a range of specialty practice areas from securities law and intellectual property to mergers and acquisitions and pension/benefits. Aspen's trusted legal education resources provide professors and students with high-quality, up-to-date and effective resources for successful instruction and study in all areas of the law.

Kluwer Law International products provide the global business community with reliable international legal information in English. Legal practitioners, corporate counsel and business executives around the world rely on Kluwer Law journals, looseleafs, books, and electronic products for comprehensive information in many areas of international legal practice.

Loislaw is a comprehensive online legal research product providing legal content to law firm practitioners of various specializations. Loislaw provides attorneys with the ability to quickly and efficiently find the necessary legal information they need, when and where they need it, by facilitating access to primary law as well as state-specific law, records, forms and treatises.

ftwilliam.com offers employee benefits professionals the highest quality plan documents (retirement, welfare and non-qualified) and government forms (5500/PBGC, 1099 and IRS) software at highly competitive prices.

MediRegs products provide integrated health care compliance content and software solutions for professionals in healthcare, higher education and life sciences, including professionals in accounting, law and consulting.

Wolters Kluwer Law & Business, a division of Wolters Kluwer, is headquartered in New York. Wolters Kluwer is a market-leading global information services company focused on professionals.

Summary of Contents

Contents

Section II
Search and Seizure

Chapter 5: Search and Seizure of Persons   53

Chapter 6: Stop and Frisk   73

Chapter 7: Investigative Detentions and Searches   87

Chapter 8: Search and Seizure Evidence   99

Section III
Self-Incrimination

Section IV
Constitutional Issues

Chapter 14: The Right to Trial   189

Chapter 15: Double Jeopardy   203

Chapter 16: The Right to Counsel   211

Preface

The objective of this text is to assist the student in understanding how the law is actually applied in the field and in the courtroom. It is designed to take the law to the street. The criminal justice professional wants to be able to make the correct legal decision when making an arrest, collecting evidence, or conducting an interrogation. The paralegal student must be able to examine a case and determine the admissibility of evidence. With the assistance of this book, the instructor should be able to provide students with the legal skills to make those decisions.

After teaching criminal law and procedure courses for undergraduates for over 30 years, I concluded that most of the available textbooks were written for law students or lawyers. Yet, virtually all undergraduate criminal justice and paralegal programs offer a criminal procedure course. The important question should be the following: Why are the students taking a criminal procedure course? The answer is diverse, yet simple. They are simply working toward their dreams. They want to be law enforcement officers, paralegals, or probation or parole officers, or they may be interested in pursuing advanced degrees in criminal justice or law.

The title, *From the Courtroom to the Street*, is indicative of my objective. I want the student reader to understand how the complicated decisions of courts and legislators are actually applied to the real streets. A key component of the text is the "On the Street" stories that are designed to help the student understand how the law works in the real world. The stories, mostly hypothetical, are designed for that objective. They are also presented in "street" language. It is safe to say that not all educators or researchers in higher education will approve of my use of less than formal language. If so, I have succeeded. This book is designed to help the student reader learn the law, not to cater to those in academic ivory towers. The text, of course, also presents the key appellate cases that provide the foundation for the rules of criminal procedure. But as with the entire text, these cases are presented in a style that should provide a practical understanding of the law.

Prior to my career in higher education, I served as a police officer, a paralegal and a practicing criminal defense attorney. These experiences provided my impetus for developing a textbook that would assist the undergraduate.

The textbook is divided into four main sections. The Introductory section lays out the foundational material for criminal procedure, the criminal justice process, the role of the appellate courts, the impact of due process, and the history and development of the exclusionary rule.

Section II addresses the more defined rules of search and seizure. The student will examine the concepts of reasonable expectation of privacy, the rules of arrests, and the many justifications for search. Those considerations will include warrants, plain view, incidental to arrest, probable cause, area within immediate control, consent, border searches, and vehicle searches.

The issues surrounding the spoken word as evidence will be discussed in Section III. The landmark case of *Miranda v. Arizona* sets the stage for a detailed look at the implications and applications surrounding interrogations, confessions, and other settings that result in incriminating statements. The section also examines the rules directed at pretrial identifications such as lineups, showups, and photographic arrays.

Section IV delves into several constitutional issues that impact how criminal procedure unfolds in the courtroom. The chapters cover double jeopardy, the right to fair trial, the right to counsel, protection from excessive bail, and the laws surrounding sentencing. The impact of the Eighth Amendment on the death penalty is studied in the last chapter.

This textbook is designed with the undergraduate classroom in mind. It should assist in preparing a student for the "real-life" workplace that is impacted by the rules of criminal procedure. It should also provide undergraduate criminal procedure instructors with a solid textbook with which to supplement their classroom teaching.

Acknowledgments

I would like to express my gratitude to my project editor Elizabeth Kenny. Without her guidance and encouragement, this project would not have been possible. Thanks are also due to the many reviewers who offered wise and valuable insight. Special thanks to Aspen's David Herzig who was kind enough to reach out to me concerning this book. It is impossible to adequately express my appreciation and love for my family; Janis Walter, Peter Wright, and Emma Wright. Professor Walter, also an author, lawyer, and professor, served as my coach and confidante through the entire process. Thanks also go to Stacy and Sharon Roberts who allowed me to hide out in their houseboat while writing much of the book.

About the Author

Roger Wright is a professor of Criminal Justice at the University of Cincinnati. He earned his Juris Doctorate from Chase College of Law and his Bachelor of Science in Criminal Justice from Memphis State University. He attended law school at Oxford University in England. He has served as a police officer in Memphis, Tennessee, and has additional experience in juvenile corrections. Wright is currently a partner in the Wright Law Group. At the University of Cincinnati, he is primarily responsible for legal courses such as Criminal Law and Criminal Procedure. Wright serves as the mentor for the doctoral teaching assistants and adjuncts who teach undergraduate courses. He has provided training and promotional exams for many local law enforcement agencies. He has received the University College Excellence in Teaching Award and most recently was honored as the University of Cincinnati Order of Omega Professor of the Year. In 2012 he was named as one of the most interesting people in Cincinnati by Cincy Magazine. Wright's interests beyond the law and academia include guitar and tennis.

Criminal Procedure

Section I
Foundations of Criminal Procedure

"The police pulled me over and asked if they could search my car. Do I have to say yes?"

"The cops asked me a bunch of questions. They didn't advise me of rights. Is that cool?"

"There's a helicopter flying over my house. What if they see my marijuana garden?"

"I don't have any money. Do I still have a right to an attorney?"

"A witness picked me out of a lineup. Was that fair?"

What Is Criminal Procedure?

Criminal procedure involves the rules that determine how criminal law is applied. It provides the rules that police, lawyers, and judges must follow in enforcing criminal law. Police have the duty to investigate criminal activity, to apprehend suspects, and to discover and obtain evidence to successfully prosecute those who are responsible for a crime. Prosecuting attorneys must present evidence in court in an effort to bring criminals to justice. Defense attorneys have the responsibility of protecting the rights of the accused and to ensure that the government proceeds in a constitutional manner. Judges preside over the trial and appellate processes to assure that the law is followed. Criminal procedure impacts all of these duties. Prosecutors, defense attorneys, witnesses, law enforcement officers, judges, and juries must follow the rules of criminal procedure.

If the police were able to investigate crime without any constitutional restrictions, their jobs would be much easier. But they cannot.

They cannot break into your home in order to search for evidence without legal justification. They cannot arrest you without a legal reason. They cannot beat a suspect until he confesses to a crime. Guilt does not matter. The fact that a suspect is guilty of a crime does not relieve the participants in the criminal justice system from following the rules. As a nation, we have decided that the process by which we reach justice is just as important as the outcome.

The study of criminal procedure addresses those rules and answers many questions. It addresses the issues affecting search and seizure, interrogation, and investigation. When must the *Miranda* rights be given? When may the police search a person's car? When can the police pull over a car? Does a person have to give consent to a search if asked? Why does the Transportation Security Administration search your bags at the airport? Criminal procedure also examines the constitutional rights provided by the **Bill of Rights** in the U.S. Constitution. Those rights, such as right to jury trial, the right to confront one's accusers, the right to counsel, protection against self-incrimination, and protection from cruel and unusual punishment, all impact the administration of justice. However, questions will undoubtedly remain as technology and society evolve.

Universities, police academies, and law schools typical distinguish criminal law from criminal procedure. Most criminal law courses address substantive criminal law. The study of substantive criminal law examines the elements of crime. The student of criminal law must determine what behaviors constitute criminal behavior. What is robbery? What is murder? What is theft? The study of criminal procedure addresses the methods by which those laws are enforced.

For students' consideration, this textbook provides various hypothetical situations in "On the Street" scenarios that present realistic issues impacted by the study material. While hypothetical, most scenarios are based in part on real-life events. Some of the street stories will also provide an answer while others require readers to reach their own conclusions.

On the Street

Criminal procedure or substantive criminal law?

The police, suspecting that Jeremy is manufacturing methamphetamine, break into his mobile home by prying open the front door. They do not have a search warrant or any other legal justification. They do not find any evidence of a meth lab, but while searching Jeremy's bedroom, they discover a large marijuana plant growing in a clay pot. When Jeremy returns home, the police arrest him for illegal possession of marijuana, a controlled substance.

Jeremy asks the trial court judge to throw out the marijuana evidence, arguing that the police violated his rights by searching his home without a warrant. Is that a criminal procedure issue? Yes. If the court excludes the evidence, the case would likely be dismissed and Jeremy would go free. Did he have an illegal marijuana plant? Of course. However, in the American criminal justice system, the procedure by which evidence is obtained is also important. Determining whether evidence was obtained legally is a criminal procedure issue. The issue of guilt or innocence is substantive law issue. ∎

The chapters in Section I address the sources of law and the steps in the criminal justice process from arrest to sentencing. While these issues are often addressed during introductory criminal justice courses, they are discussed here because they are critical to understanding criminal procedure. Chapter 2 describes the role of appellate courts in developing the rules of criminal procedure. Chapter 3 addresses the constitutional right to due process and its impact on criminal procedure. Finally, Chapter 4 looks at the complex issues surrounding the exclusionary rule and its exceptions.

Chapter 1
Introduction to Criminal Procedure

Chapter 1 examines the various sources of law that impact the study of criminal procedure. The chapter also outlines and explains the steps involved in the criminal justice process from investigation to sentencing.

Sources of Law

Where does criminal law come from? Who wrote the rules of criminal procedure? Why? In this chapter you will examine the various sources of criminal law and procedure. Again, the distinction between substantive criminal law and the rules of criminal procedure must be recognized.

The U.S. Constitution and Bill of Rights

Criminal procedure
The body of laws and rules that determine how police, lawyers, judges and courts enforce and apply criminal law.

Bill of Rights
The first ten amendments to the U.S. Constitution. Ratified in 1791.

The U.S. Constitution is the primary source for **criminal procedure**. The original document was ratified in 1787. Four years later, the **Bill of Rights** was added to ensure that the citizens of the United States were apprised of certain basic rights. Included are those rights that directly impact the administration of criminal justice such as the right to jury trial, the right to speedy trial, and the protections against unreasonable search and seizure and self-incrimination. As you work through this textbook you will examine the impact of those individual rights on the procedures used by police and the courts. The U.S. Supreme Court looks to the U.S. Constitution to make its decisions regarding the rules of criminal law and procedure.

State Constitutions

Every state in the union has its own state constitution. State laws and procedures must comply with their own state constitutions, and they must comply with the provisions of the U.S. Constitution. State constitutions may provide more protection of individual rights than required by the U.S. Constitution but never less. One vivid example is the implementation of the death penalty. Though the U.S. Supreme Court has determined that death is an appropriate punishment in certain cases, some states do not allow it. Likewise, a state might adopt a law requiring that a parent must be present during the interrogation of a juvenile. Even though that is not required by the U.S. Constitution, a state could mandate it within its jurisdiction.

Appellate Courts

Appellate court
A court charged with reviewing the decision of a lower court.

The specific rules of criminal procedure are developed primarily by **appellate courts**. An appellate court examines the proceedings that occur during investigation, arrest, and trial of a criminal defendant to determine if proper procedure was followed. The appellate courts must base their decisions on the U.S. Constitution as well as the applicable state constitution. They must also follow the previous decisions of higher appellate courts which are similar to the case at hand. An appellate court does not determine the accuracy of facts or the guilt or innocence of a defendant. That is the role of the trial court. If a losing party appeals to an appellate court, that court will then examine the record and determine if all proceedings were proper. Generally speaking, any court that is charged with reviewing the decision of a lower court is acting as an appellate court. In some jurisdictions, a trial court will hear appeals from administrative law hearings as well as minor local courts such as mayor's courts. Each jurisdictional system has its own appellate court system. The ultimate and final appellate court is the U.S. Supreme Court.

In most circumstances, the U.S. Supreme Court interprets and applies the U.S. Constitution. There are also situations in which state appellate courts apply their own state constitutions. It is common for state legislatures to codify the rules set by the appellate courts. A rule is codified when it is approved and included in the written laws of the **jurisdiction**.

Jurisdiction
The authority of a court system to hear cases, and a government's power to enact laws; determined by geographical areas or subject matter.

While most of the rules of criminal procedure result from decisions of the U.S. Supreme Court, state legislatures may enact rules that are specific to their state. This is permissible so long as the rule of law does not infringe on the U.S. Constitution. For example, the U.S. Supreme Court has identified criteria for determining whether one's Sixth Amendment right to speedy trial has been violated. Yet some individual states have enacted specific statutory time limits. That is acceptable as long as the state rule complies with the Supreme Court criteria. Chapter 2 will provide a detailed examination of the role of appellate decisions in developing criminal procedure.

The U.S. Supreme Court

The highest appellate court in the land is the U.S. Supreme Court. The Court consists of nine justices including the Chief Justice. Its members are appointed by the president of the United States with the advice and consent of the U.S. Senate. The Supreme Court Building is in Washington, D.C., directly behind the U.S. Capitol. Once confirmed, a Supreme Court Justice serves a lifetime appointment, only leaving the judgeship if he or she resigns, retires, dies, or is impeached. When the President must replace a justice, it usually results in massive media coverage and political gamesmanship. The Supreme Court generally acts as the ultimate and last appellate court. In the rare instances of a civil lawsuit between state governments, between the federal government and a state, and those involving a foreign minister or counsel, the Court serves as the original trial court. The Chief Justice also serves as the presiding judge if the U.S. Senate must hold a trial regarding the **impeachment** of the President of the United States.

Impeachment
The process for the involuntary removal of a public official from office.

Statutory Law

Criminal laws are drafted by local, state, and federal legislatures. These representative bodies decide what behaviors should be considered criminal in their particular jurisdiction. The elected representatives may determine that using a gun to rob a store should be a crime. They then would write and approve the appropriate language and enact it into law. Such laws are referred to as **statutory law**. The federal government, every state, and many local jurisdictions have statutory criminal laws. As mentioned previously, legislative bodies may also codify the rules of criminal procedure. This type of rulemaking is usually in response to decisions of appellate courts, and the legislative body simply includes the rules in the state or local statutes. Many legislators claim to be in favor of strong enforcement of criminal laws as they run for office. Thus, it would be unusual for a politician running for a legislative office to advocate rules of criminal procedure that would inhibit law enforcement's ability to fight crime.

Statutory law
Law written and enacted by legislative bodies such as state legislature or the U.S. Congress.

A criminal statute could be determined to be unconstitutional. For example, it would be acceptable for a city to enact a criminal statute prohibiting residential yard sales. However, if statute provided a punishment of life in prison, the statute would be considered unconstitutional because it violates the Eighth Amendment's protection against cruel and unusual punishment. The punishment would be excessive for the crime.

State Versus Federal Procedure

The Tenth Amendment to the U.S. Constitution states the following:

> The powers not delegated to the United States by the Constitution, nor prohibited by it to the states, are reserved to the states respectively, or to the people.

Dual sovereignty
The principle that both the federal and state governments exercise jurisdiction over specific legal issues.

As a result, the U.S. criminal justice system operates under a system of **dual sovereignty**. States generally have the right to regulate and administer the criminal laws within their jurisdiction. However, the rules in the Bill of Rights guaranteeing citizens' individual rights and protection against governmental intrusion cannot be taken away by any state government. The Fourteenth Amendment states that citizens of the United States cannot be deprived of their due process of law. As a result, while states may enact their own rules of criminal procedure, they cannot infringe on the guaranteed rights of the Bill of Rights.

All American jurisdictions must guarantee those rights, but they are permitted to enact substantive criminal laws unique to their specific jurisdiction. As previously indicated, the death penalty provides one of the most dramatic examples. The U.S. Supreme Court allows death as a punishment but still requires that its administration comply with the requirements of the Eighth Amendment protection from cruel and unusual punishment. In some cases, a criminal behavior will be a violation of multiple jurisdictions. For example, if an individual robbed a federally insured bank in Louisville, Kentucky, that person could be prosecuted by both the Commonwealth of Kentucky and the federal government. The ability of both jurisdictions to prosecute the offense is referred to as **concurrent jurisdiction.**

Criminal Versus Civil Law

The laws that regulate behaviors and provide social controls by imposing criminal sanctions and punishment are considered criminal laws. Such laws are designed to protect civilized society from harm and to maintain the public peace. A violation of a criminal law is considered a crime against society and the government. It is not only an act against an individual. **Civil laws** protect and regulate private and business interests such as contracts, domestic relations, property rights, and inheritance. Violations of civil laws do provide for incarceration. The remedies for civil wrongs usually involve the payment of money or compliance with a contract or court order. A civil order might mandate that an estate passes to a particular heir or that a property line is established at a specific location. The determination of child custody would be a civil issue. Some behaviors may be both criminal and civil. An action that violates a criminal law while also giving rise to a civil lawsuit would be considered both. Assault is one of the most common situations. If an individual hit another person with a baseball bat, the offender could, of course, be prosecuted criminally and jailed as punishment. The victim of the assault would also be able to file a civil lawsuit against the offender requesting monetary damages to compensate him or her for the injuries.

Concurrent jurisdiction
When a criminal behavior is a violation of the laws of more than one jurisdiction at the same time.

Civil laws
Laws and procedures that regulate noncriminal issues such as contracts, domestic relations, real estate, and personal injury civil lawsuits; violations do not include incarceration.

On the Street

Criminal or civil?

Conrad writes an article for the company newsletter claiming that Dusty has been stealing money from the company by filing false travel expense reports. Conrad's allegations are not true. He wrote the article because his girlfriend has started dating Dusty. Dusty sues Conrad for $140,000 claiming that he has been falsely defamed. Is this civil or criminal? ■

Burden of proof
The amount of proof necessary to prove a case; in a criminal case the burden of proof is proof beyond any reasonable doubt.

There are some significant distinctions between criminal and civil procedure. In a criminal case, a defendant must be proven guilty beyond any reasonable doubt. That standard, called the **burden of proof**, is the level of probability of which the judge or

Preponderance of evidence
The burden of proof required in most civil cases. A fact is proven by a preponderance of evidence if it is considered more likely than not to be true.

jury must be convinced in order to find the defendant guilty. In most civil cases, the winner must prove his or her case by a **preponderance of evidence** that requires only that the judge or jury find that it is more likely than not that the wrong occurred. The Fifth Amendment protection against self-incrimination does not apply to civil trials, so a civil defendant could be required to testify. However, a criminal defendant cannot be compelled to testify against himself or herself. There are many distinctions in the rules of evidence as well.

The Criminal Justice Process: Investigation to Sentencing

The rules of criminal procedure affect virtually all steps of the criminal justice process. The study of criminal procedure requires an understanding of those steps and where they occur in the process. Law enforcement officers must comply with the Bill of Rights during the initial stages of a criminal investigation, the collection of evidence, arrest, and all stages leading to trial. Judges, prosecutors, and defense attorneys must be aware of the proper procedures in order to ensure a fair trial. This section identifies the sequential steps in the criminal justice process from investigation to sentencing.

Investigation

A criminal case usually begins with the discovery of a crime. The police may become aware of the existence of a criminal act in a variety of ways. Often, the victim or a witness to the offense calls the police for assistance or to report the crime. A couple returns home only to discover their home has been burglarized. Someone calls the police because they are being threatened in a domestic violence situation. A third party observes a crime in progress and calls the police. In all of these situations, law enforcement responds and begins their investigation. The police often have a variety of roles upon the arrival of a crime scene. In addition to providing assistance to the victim, they must also preserve evidence, interview witnesses, and coordinate other investigative functions. There are also, of course, circumstances in which the police arrest a suspect during their initial response. The investigation of a criminal case does not end with the initial police response. In many cases, the investigation continues all the way to trial. The rules of criminal procedure apply during all steps of the investigation. If the evidence is not obtained in a proper manner, it could result in exclusion in court. The discovery and investigation of a crime does not always result in an arrest or prosecution. In many situations, the perpetrator is never determined or there is not sufficient evidence to continue the case. In those situations, the investigation may be suspended or terminated.

Arrest
Physical seizure of a person with the intention of accusing them of a criminal offense.

Arrest

An **arrest** is the physical seizure of a person with the intention of accusing them of a criminal offense. That seizure may be obtained through physical force or voluntary submission. An arrest must be supported by sufficient proof that would lead a reasonable person to believe that the defendant has committed a crime. That standard of proof is probable cause. The physical arrest of an individual is his or her introduction into the criminal process. The defendant will be transported to a jail or the police station for booking. Booking involves identification procedures such as taking fingerprints and photographs and entering the arrest information into the court system. In some situations, the defendant may also be subjected to a lineup or other form of identification procedure. Once arrested, the defendant must be brought before the court within a reasonable period of time. If the arrest was made without a warrant, the defendant must receive a judicial probable cause hearing within 48 hours or the prosecution must prove it was an emergency situation [*County of Riverside v. McLaughlin*, 500 U.S. 44 (1991)]. In most jurisdictions, the first opportunity for the court appearance will be the following morning. If the arrest occurs on a weekend or in early morning hours, it may be the following day. Many large jurisdictions hold court for initial appearances on Saturdays and holidays to ensure a speedy appearance after arrest. Some local court systems allow the issuance of a citation to appear in court in lieu of a physical arrest.

Initial Appearance/Bail Hearing/Arraignment

In cases involving only **misdemeanor** charges, the first appearance in court is the **arraignment**. At arraignment, the defendant must enter a plea of guilty or not guilty. Some jurisdictions allow no contest pleas as well. If the charge is a **felony**, then the initial appearance is not considered an arraignment. At a felony initial appearance, the charges will be read. The defendant will not enter a formal plea at this point, but the court may address other collateral issues at this point such as the determination of **bail**, appointment of counsel, and the scheduling of the preliminary hearing. Bail is the amount of money or other security that the defendant posts in order to guarantee his or her return to court if released from jail. In some instances, courts may release a defendant upon his or her **own recognizance**, meaning the defendant is not required to post bail. The court may also determine if the defendant has the financial means to hire an attorney. If not, the court will consider the defendant to be **indigent** and appoint a public defender.

Initial appearances and misdemeanor arraignments occur in the court of lower jurisdictions. These courts hear only misdemeanor and preliminary felony issues. All other felony stages such as trial, the acceptance of pleas, and sentencing must be handled in the higher court. In most situations, if the defendant is charged with both misdemeanor and felony offenses, all charges will be transferred to felony court.

Preliminary Hearing

Preliminary hearings also occur in the lower court jurisdiction. The purpose of the preliminary hearing is to determine if sufficient probable cause exists in order to bind

Misdemeanor
Offense generally considered less serious.

Arraignment
Court hearing in which formal charges are read to the defendant, and the defendant enters a plea.

Felony
A criminal offense for which the possible punishment is incarceration of one year or more.

Bail
The amount of money or other security that the defendant posts in order to guarantee his or her return to court if released from jail.

Own recognizance
Pretrial release of a defendant without the requirement of money or property as bail; defendant is released based upon his or her own reputation and circumstances.

Indigent
A criminal defendant who is unable to afford an attorney.

Preliminary hearings
Held to determine if sufficient probable cause exists in order to bind the case over to the grand jury.

Grand jury
Body of citizens selected to examine evidence in a criminal case and to determine if probable cause exists; upon determination of probable cause, they issue an indictment.

Prosecutor
Lawyer who represents the government in a criminal case.

Double jeopardy
Legal principle that prohibits a criminal defendant from being tried twice for the same offense.

the case over to the **grand jury**. The **prosecutor** must present sufficient evidence to establish probable cause. The case does not have to be proved beyond any reasonable doubt at this point. The defense may cross-examine the witnesses. They may also present witnesses on their own behalf although that is not often done at this stage. If the judge determines that probable cause exists, then the case will be bound over to the grand jury. The judge may dismiss the case if there is insufficient evidence to prove probable cause. However, dismissal at the preliminary hearing is not considered **double jeopardy**, and the prosecution may refile the case.

Rapid indictment systems are now used by many local court jurisdictions. In those systems, felony cases may be presented directly to a grand jury immediately after the initial appearance. If an indictment is issued, then there is no need or constitutional requirement for a preliminary hearing. Many large urban cities use rapid indictment as it reduces expenses and restricts the defense opportunity to cross-examine witnesses prior to trial.

Grand Jury

The members of the grand jury must determine if probable cause exists to believe the accused has committed a crime and, if so, to determine the formal charges. The grand jury consists of a body of citizens selected from the general population of the jurisdiction. They listen to witnesses, examine evidence, and then render a decision. The evidence is presented by a prosecutor. Neither a judge nor a defense attorney is present. Though the hearing is primarily conducted by a prosecutor, the grand jury has the power to subpoena witnesses on their own. They can also subpoena a defendant, but that is unusual. The defendant, though required to appear if subpoenaed, does not have to testify because of his or her Fifth Amendment rights. Grand jury hearings are secret, and the transcript is sealed except under extraordinary circumstances. If the members of the grand jury determine that probable cause exists, then they return a **true bill** and issue an **indictment**. The indictment is considered the formal charge. If they do not believe that probable cause exists, they return a "no true bill," which results in dismissal of the case. However, just like a preliminary hearing, dismissal by a grand jury does not result in double jeopardy. The prosecutor could present the charges at a later date if additional evidence was available.

True bill
Determination by a grand jury that probable cause exists to issue an indictment.

Indictment
The formal charging instrument issued by a grand jury in a felony criminal case.

Information
A written charging document prepared and presented by the prosecutor.

The majority of states also provide for charges to be filed by **information**. The prosecutor prepares a written document formally charging the defendant and files it with the clerk of courts. This procedure allows the prosecutor to bypass the grand jury. Though allowed by law, most prosecutors' offices prefer to use the grand jury process as it provides a more neutral and detached examination of the evidence.

Felony Arraignment

The arraignment for felony charges will be conducted by a judge in the court of felony jurisdiction. Once formally charged by either indictment or information, the defendant must appear for arraignment. The formal charges are presented, and the defendant must enter a plea of guilty, not guilty, or no contest.

- *Guilty:* The defendant agrees that the charges are true and that he has committed the crime.
- *Not guilty:* The defendant denies that he is guilty of the charges.
- *No contest:* The defendant agrees that the facts alleged are true but does not agree that the facts constitute a violation of the law. The judge must rule on whether the defendant's actions actually constitute a violation of the law.

As previously mentioned, not all jurisdictions allow no contest pleas. They are allowed in federal cases.

Pretrial Motions

There are a number of issues that may have to be determined before the actual trial begins. Those concerns are handled in hearings and conferences that take place prior to trial.

- *Pretrial scheduling:* The judge meets with the attorneys and examines issues such as the anticipated length of the trial, preparation time, special technology needs, and likelihood of a plea bargaining. They may also discuss whether jury sequestration will be necessary and if there are any witness availability issues. Often these questions are resolved through informal discussions. If not, the judge may hold hearings on the specific issues.
- *Competency hearing:* This is a hearing to determine if the defendant is competent to stand trial. This is not a determination of the insanity defense. It is to decide if the defendant has the capacity to understand and assist in his or her own defense.
- *Motions to suppress:* These motions determine the admissibility of specific evidence prior to trial. If the judge determines that evidence will not be allowed, the attorneys may not present it or discuss it during the trial.
- *Motion to change venue:* In the event that pretrial publicity has made it unlikely to provide a fair and impartial trial, the court may decide to move the case to another venue.

Plea Bargaining

Plea bargaining
Negotiation between the defense and prosecution in a criminal case.

Plea bargaining is the negotiation that occurs between the prosecution and defense in an effort to reach a resolution without going to trial. Such agreements might include pleading guilty to reduced charges or to some of the charges in exchange for others being dismissed. Plea bargains may also include an agreement to a less severe punishment. In some cases, the defendant agrees to cooperate in an investigation or provide testimony against others in exchange for a reduction or dismissal of charges. Local courts take a variety of views toward plea bargaining. In some, judges do not allow the

Alford plea
A criminal defendant pleads guilty to an offense while contending that he or she did not commit the act constituting the crime.

prosecution and defense to negotiate the sentence. Some states, but not all, allow the entry of an ***Alford* plea**.

An *Alford* plea allows the defendant to enter a plea of guilty while also contending that he or she did not commit the crime. The judge upon accepting the plea makes a finding of guilty. In *North Carolina v. Alford* 400 U.S. 25 (1970), the defendant, Alford, was charged with first-degree murder and was facing the death penalty if convicted. He agreed to plead guilty to second-degree murder with a penalty of 30 years in prison. He contended that he only agreed to plead guilty because he believed that he was likely to be convicted. He stated to the judge when he entered his plea: "Yes, sir. I plead guilty on . . . from the circumstances that he [Alford's attorney] told me." Alford attempted to have his conviction overturned arguing that he was coerced because he was in fear of the death penalty. The U.S. Supreme Court allowed his plea and upheld his conviction. They said that Alford made a voluntary and knowledgeable decision by accepting the plea to the reduced charge in order to avoid the death penalty. However, in some jurisdictions, trial judges will only accept a guilty plea if the defendant states that he or she has committed the crime.

Trial

The trial is the proceeding in which a determination of guilt or innocence is made. In most cases involving the possibility of incarceration, the defendant has a right to trial by jury. If the defendant waives the right, the trial may be heard solely by the judge. In a jury trial, it is the judge's responsibility to preside over the trial, rule on admissibility of evidence, instruct the jury on their duties, and ensure a fair and impartial process. The jury must listen to the evidence and determine whether the defendant has violated the law. If the trial is solely to the judge, it is called a bench trial. In a bench trial, the judge is also responsible for determining the verdict and, if guilty, the punishment. Some states provide for trials before a panel of judges in special circumstances. In the event of an **acquittal** or not guilty verdict, the process is over. If convicted, the trial proceeds to the sentencing phase.

Acquittal
Determination by a judge or jury that a criminal defendant is not guilty of a crime.

Sentencing

In the event the defendant is found guilty of any of the charges, the judge must determine the appropriate sentence. In some states, the jury is responsible for recommending the sentence to the judge, while in others sentencing is the sole responsibility of the judge. In those states, the jury is not informed of the possible sentence. The role of the jury in death penalty cases is considerably different from other felony and misdemeanor cases. Even though individual jurisdictions have the right to determine the sentencing structure for their specific criminal offenses, those punishments must comply with the requirements of the Eighth Amendment's prohibition against cruel and unusual punishment and the restrictive procedures for death penalty cases. Those issues are discussed in subsequent chapters.

What is the sequence of events in the criminal justice system?

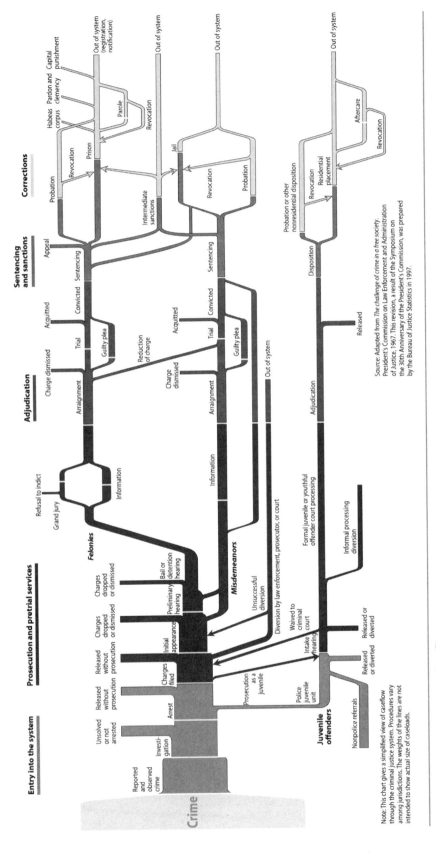

Note: This chart gives a simplified view of caseflow through the criminal justice system. Procedures vary among jurisdictions. The weights of the lines are not intended to show actual size of caseloads.

Source: Adapted from *The challenge of crime in a free society.* President's Commission on Law Enforcement and Administration of Justice, 1967. This revision, a result of the Symposium on the 30th Anniversary of the President's Commission, was prepared by the Bureau of Justice Statistics in 1997.

Figure 1-1 Criminal Justice Process

Misdemeanor Trial Process

The criminal process for misdemeanor-only cases varies somewhat from the felony track. The first appearance for a misdemeanor defendant is the arraignment. That occurs in a court of lower jurisdiction. Some courts have special courts such as municipal courts, mayor's courts, or city courts that handle only misdemeanor cases. Some systems provide courts that handle only traffic cases or other specific crimes such as domestic violence. Misdemeanor cases may require pretrial motions and conferences similar to those described in the felony track process. There are no preliminary hearings to determine probable cause. The charges are presented by formal complaint forms rather than information or indictment. Trials are conducted in the same manner. In the federal system, adult misdemeanor defendants are entitled to a right to a jury trial if they are facing the possibility of six months or more of incarceration. Some states provide for a jury trial if the defendant is facing any incarceration.

The U.S. Department of Justice provides a comprehensive flowchart that outlines the entire criminal justice process, as shown in Figure 1-1.

Summary

The American Criminal Justice system is complex in both its structure and application. Lawmakers and courts are continually wrestling with those complexities in an effort to protect the nation's citizens while ensuring a fair and equitable system. The balancing of these principles in an effort to attain justice never ends, and lawmakers are continually seeking ways to provide effective social controls while also protecting the privacy rights of citizens. Criminal laws are written in order to create those social controls. The rules of criminal procedure provide a framework in which those laws are enforced. As mentioned in the Section I introduction, we do not simply seek justice at all costs. Our right as citizens to live our own lives with minimal governmental interference is also important. So important, in fact, that the constitutional forefathers wrote a Bill of Rights to protect us from the government.

As you worked through this chapter, you studied the origins of criminal law and procedures. The rules of procedure are based on constitutional foundations and then interpreted and applied by the courts and criminal justice professionals. Chapter 1 also examined the structure of the courts and how a case travels through the criminal justice system. As you continue your adventure through this book, you will examine how those laws and rules are applied.

Review Questions

1. Why are individual states allowed to enact their own criminal statutes?
2. How are the justices of the U.S. Supreme Court selected?
3. Explain the differences between civil law and criminal law.

4. Explain the difference between statutory law and case law.
5. What is dual sovereignty?
6. What are some of the advantages of plea bargaining?
7. At what stage of the criminal justice process may bail be considered?
8. What is the purpose of a preliminary hearing?
9. What are the advantages of a rapid indictment system?

Legal Terminology

Acquittal	Grand jury
Alford plea	Impeachment
Appellate court	Indictment
Arraignment	Indigent
Arrest	Information
Bail	Jurisdiction
Bill of Rights	Misdemeanors
Burden of proof	Own recognizance
Civil law	Plea bargaining
Concurrent jurisdiction	Preliminary hearings
Criminal procedure	Preponderance of evidence
Double jeopardy	Prosecutor
Dual sovereignty	Statutory law
Felony	True bill

References

County of Riverside v. McLaughlin, 500 U.S. 44 (1991).
Criminal Justice Flow Chart, Bureau of Justice Statistics, Office of Justice Programs. Retrieved January 2014 from http://bjs.ojp.usdoj.gov/content/largechart.cfm

Chapter 2
The Appellate Process

It is the duty of appellate courts to review the decisions of lower courts. The most common situation occurs when a criminal defendant is found guilty at trial and appeals the conviction. The appellate court does not review the finding of guilt or innocence but rather the procedures that were involved in reaching that verdict. They might examine the trial judge's determination of whether evidence was admissible. They also might examine whether a search conducted by the police complied with the Fourth Amendment or whether an interrogation was conducted properly. If the trial judge committed an error that unfairly impacted the outcome of a criminal trial, the appellate court could overturn the decision and send the case back for a new trial that must then be conducted according to their ruling. Only trials from **courts of record** may be appealed to courts of appeal. A court of record is a trial court that records and documents their official proceedings. Some jurisdictions may have lower courts such as mayor's courts or small claims which are not considered courts of records. Many jurisdictions also provide for referee hearings or administrative hearings. These non-record courts are usually appealed to a local trial court and then only a decision from that court can be appealed to a traditional court of appeals. As you will see, a decision of an appellate court may be appealed to a higher appellate court such as a state supreme court or the U.S. Supreme Court. When that occurs, the higher appellate court is examining the previous appellate decision.

An appellate court may agree with the decision of the lower court by affirming the decision. If they overturn the decision, the process of sending a case back to the trial court is called a **remand**. The remand will include the court's reasoning for the reversal which then serves as instructions for the lower court. The reasoning of the appellate court is also instructive to law enforcement, judges, and attorneys for future cases. In a sense, it is how we learn criminal procedure. For example, law enforcement now knows to advise custodial suspects of certain rights before conducting an interrogation. They know because of the reasoning and instruction provided by the U.S. Supreme Court in *Miranda v. Arizona*.

Courts of record
A trial court that officially records its proceedings, and renders final decisions.

Remand
When an appellate court rules on a case and refers it back to the lower court with instructions to correct the error.

On the Street

How does an appeal work?

Alonzo was arrested for kidnapping. When the police questioned him, they failed to advise him of his right to counsel and right to remain silent as required by the U.S. Supreme Court in *Miranda v. Arizona*. He confessed to the kidnapping. At trial, Alonzo asked the trial judge to exclude his confession from evidence arguing that it was obtained illegally. The judge refused and allowed the jury to hear the confession. Alonzo is convicted so he decides to appeal. The appellate court would determine that the trial judge erred in allowing the evidence. They would likely overturn Alonzo's conviction and remand the case for a new trial. At the new trial, Alonzo's confession could not be presented into evidence. ▨

If a defendant is found not guilty, the prosecutor cannot appeal. The Fifth Amendment to the U.S. Constitution provides that a criminal defendant cannot be twice put in jeopardy for the same offense. The protection from double jeopardy prevents the retrial of a defendant for the same charge if the defendant has been found not guilty even if new evidence is discovered. A not guilty verdict means the case is over. Double jeopardy, which is discussed in more detail in Chapter 15, does not prevent a defendant from being prosecuted for a different offense. An acquittal by the judge has the same result as a not guilty verdict. As a result, only the defendant may appeal a trial court verdict in a criminal case. The prosecutor cannot appeal. However, either party, prosecutor or defense, may appeal an appellate court's decision to a higher appellate court.

So why is it not double jeopardy for an appellate court to order a new trial? It is the defendant that is asking for the new trial so he or she is waiving protection against double jeopardy.

Interlocutory appeal
An appeal in a criminal case prior to the verdict. It occurs when there is a critical legal issue that must be decided before the trial continues.

In rare circumstances, a prosecutor may appeal a decision of a trial court judge before a verdict has been reached. This is referred to as an **interlocutory appeal**. It occurs if a legal dispute arises prior to the verdict that must be decided before the trial can continue. For example, if the trial judge ruled in a pretrial motion to suppress that certain evidence could not be presented, the prosecutor might file an interlocutory appeal to have the issue determined prior to the case being presented to the jury. Otherwise, the case could be lost and the prosecutor would never have an opportunity to argue the issue before an appeals court.

The lawyers on both sides of a criminal procedure issue play an important role in the appellate process. When they file an appeal, they must file a written memorandum called a brief which provides the court with their claims of errors in the lower court and the reasoning for their arguments. In most appellate courts, the lawyers will also have the opportunity to appear in front of the panel of judges and orally argue their positions.

The Federal Appellate Court Structure

The federal system and most state systems provide a two-tiered appellate process that allows an appeal to an intermediate appellate court. In the federal system, criminal trials are conducted in the U.S. District Courts. A defendant who has been found guilty has the opportunity to appeal to the U.S. Court of Appeals. Criminal defendants have a first right of appeal meaning that they are guaranteed one review by an appeals court. The reason for the appeal does not have to meet specific criteria. It may be of great constitutional significance or it may be frivolous. The Court of Appeals must review the case and render a decision. The prosecution or defense may then appeal to the U.S. Supreme Court. However, the U.S. Supreme Court is a court of discretion. They are not required to review the case. The appealing party must first file a **writ of certiorari** which is a request to have the court consider the case. If the court refuses, then that acts the same as an affirmance of the lower court decision.

Writ of certiorari
A petition asking an appellate court to review a case. When an appellant wants the U.S. Supreme Court to review his or her case, the appellant would file a writ of certiorari.

The Federal Trial Courts

Criminal offenses which are violations of the U.S. Code are usually tried in the U.S. District Courts. The District Courts are geographically disbursed throughout the country. Most major cities have U.S. District Courts. The federal system also includes specialty courts that serve as trial courts. These courts include U.S. Court of Claims, U.S. Tax Courts, Military Tribunals, and the Courts of International Trade. Decisions of the specialty courts and the U.S. District Courts are appealed to the U.S. Court of Appeals.

U.S. Court of Appeals

The first intermediate appellate court in the federal system is the U.S. Court of Appeals. There are 12 separate U.S. Courts of Appeal disbursed through 12 geographical regions called circuits. One of those circuits serves the District of Columbia, Washington, D.C. There is an additional U.S. Court of Appeals for the Federal Circuit which has national jurisdiction but only handles appeals based on subject matter. Decisions of the federal specialty courts are appealed to this circuit. A convicted defendant from the U.S. District Court would appeal to the U.S. Court of Appeals in the circuit in which the trial court sits. As previously indicated, the U.S. Court of Appeals serves as the first right of appeal in a federal case. The number of judges assigned to each court is determined by the U.S. Code. It varies because of the caseload discrepancies in the regions. The judges are nominated by the President of the United States and then affirmed by the U.S. Senate. They serve lifetime appointments.

En banc
All of the judges on an appellate court review the case.

Most decisions by the Court of Appeals are made by a panel of three judges. The judges rotate among all of the judges who serve in the particular circuit. Occasionally, all of the judges assigned to a circuit will participate in a decision. This occurrence is considered **en banc**.

U.S. Supreme Court

The U.S. Supreme Court consists of nine justices. As with the Courts of Appeal, the members are appointed by the President with advice and consent of the Senate. In today's partisan political environment, the public confirmation hearings for a Supreme Court nominee are often contentious. Once confirmed, they also have lifetime tenure and can be removed only by resignation, retirement, death, or impeachment. The U.S. Supreme Court is the court of last resort for both state and federal appeals. As a court of discretion, they only select cases of considerable constitutional significance. All final decisions of the court are en banc. They will typically decide about one hundred cases per year. They begin each year's term in October and work until the following June. Court hearings are open to the public but seating and access are limited.

State Appellate Structure

The large majority of criminal cases in our country involve violations of state laws. State charges such as murder, robbery, theft, and drunk driving are prosecuted in state trial courts. State and municipal cases are appealed through the appropriate state

Figure 2-1   Supreme Court Justices
Steve Petteway, Collection of the Supreme Court of the United States

appellate system. Each state has the right to determine its own appellate structure based on the individual state constitution. Most states utilize a two-tiered appellate system similar to the federal courts. Generally decisions of the trial courts are appealed to a state court of appeals where a first right of appeal is provided. Appeals from those courts are then appealed to a state supreme court, usually courts of discretion. There are a number of variances across the country. For example, a few states do not have an intermediate appellate court and have only a single-level supreme court. The names of the courts, while fairly consistent, may vary slightly. The State of New York refers to its trial courts as supreme courts, while its highest appeals court is called the New York Court of Appeals.

Most state appellate courts operate in a similar fashion as the federal system. They typically have a number of geographical circuits on which several judges sit. Not all of the judges will decide each case unless they decide to sit en banc. In most states, both courts of appeals judges as well as Supreme Court justices are elected by popular vote, but not all. The appellate judges in New York are appointed.

In the two-tiered state systems, the supreme courts are courts of discretion. They are generally not required to review any particular case. The appellant must request that the Supreme Court consider the appeal. Like the federal system, a decision not to review the case acts as an affirmance of the previous lower court. Some states, however, require mandatory review of all death penalty cases. In Ohio, death penalty cases skip the intermediate appeals court and go directly to the Ohio Supreme Court. Also, like the U.S. Supreme Court, all of the members of the State Supreme Courts participate in the decisions, sitting en banc.

The state appellate courts must apply the state laws and the state constitution. They must ensure that the U.S. Constitution is followed. State supreme courts often also have the duty of regulating attorney qualifications, bar exams, and attorney discipline within their state.

State Appeals to the U.S. Supreme Court

In criminal cases, the losing party in a state appeal may appeal from the state supreme court to the U.S. Supreme Court. As previously discussed, the U.S. Supreme Court does not have to review the case. The appellant from the state supreme court must file a writ of certiorari to request review. If the U.S. Supreme Court refuses to review the case, the decision of the state supreme court stands. Because they hear only a relatively few appeals, they accept only those cases that have important constitutional significance. The U.S. Supreme Court Web site indicates they receive over 10,000 writs of certiorari annually and accept oral arguments in less than a hundred. The Court often adheres to an unwritten standard referred to as the Rule of Four. The practice allows four justices, rather than a majority, to decide to accept a case for review. The rule thus prevents a majority of justices from setting the court's agenda.

The U.S. Supreme Court may agree to examine a state criminal case because there are issues that involve application of the U.S. Constitution. As you will see in the subsequent discussion of due process, there are often constitutional concerns in criminal cases.

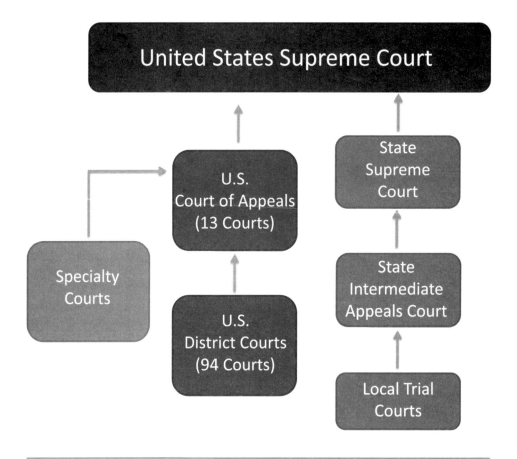

Figure 2-2   Federal and State Courts

The Role of the Executive Branch

Pardon
An order by a state governor or the President of the United States forgiving the conviction of a criminal defendant or excusing a criminal act that may have been committed by an individual.

Commutation
An order by a state governor or the President of the United States reducing the sentence of a convicted criminal defendant.

There are three branches of governments in the United States: executive, legislative, and judicial. The U.S. Supreme Court sits at the top of the judicial branch. It is the duty of that court to interpret and apply the Constitution of the United States. They are the court of last resort, and there is no further appeal. However, a convicted criminal may seek a **pardon** or **commutation** of sentence from the executive branch of the jurisdiction in which he or she was prosecuted. That is not considered an appeal. A pardon is an act of the executive branch which forgives the conviction. If the defendant is incarcerated, he or she would be released. A pardon from a state conviction can only be granted by the governor of the state in which the defendant was convicted. In some states, the governor is advised or assisted by a board that examines applications for pardons and commutations. If the conviction is from a federal court, only the President of the United States may grant a pardon. A commutation does not eradicate the conviction. A commutation is an act that reduces the sentence. It could result in the release of an inmate or in a shortening of the prison term. For example, a commutation might reduce a death penalty to life in prison.

While pardons and commutation are granted periodically, they often receive media scrutiny when an official leaves office. It is not unusual for a governor or president to grant pardons immediately before the end of the term. Pardons are often criticized because the executive branch is, in a sense, superseding the action of the judicial branch.

Notable Pardons and Commutations

■ In 1972, President Richard Nixon resigned from office in the wake of the Watergate scandal. His successor, President Gerald Ford, pardoned President Nixon for all crimes which he may have committed during his time in office.

■ Rick Hendrick, an automobile dealer and the owner of several championship NASCAR racing teams, including Jeff Gordon and Jimmy Johnson, was convicted in 1997 of mail fraud. The conviction arose from allegations of bribes paid to American Honda Motor Company. Three years later, he was pardoned by President William Clinton.

■ President George W. Bush commuted the 30-month sentence of Lewis "Scooter" Libby after he was convicted of perjury and obstruction of justice. As it was a commutation, Libby's record of conviction stood and he was required to pay the fines and continue on probation. Libby's conviction resulted from the investigation of the leak of the identity of CIA agent Valerie Plame.

Habeas Corpus

Habeas corpus
A legal proceeding in which a government agency responsible for detaining an individual must appear in court to show cause as to why the detention is legal.

A writ of **habeas corpus** also provides a type of review. It involves a legal proceeding in which a government agency responsible for detaining an individual must be brought before a court to show cause as to why the detention is legal. It is seldom used today because preliminary hearings, grand juries, and the state and federal appeal systems provide adequate judicial review. It is occasionally used as a remedy to bring a constitutional issue from the state to federal two-tiered system. It is fairly common for death penalty issues to be brought before the federal system via writs of habeas corpus. As part of an effort to reform the use of habeas corpus actions, the U.S. Congress passed the Antiterrorism and Death Penalty Act of 1966 (AEDPA). The Act, codified as 28 U.S.C. §2254, banned successive writs by one individual and narrowed the grounds upon which a writ could be based.

The U.S. Supreme Court and Criminal Procedure

It is the responsibility of the U.S. Supreme Court to interpret and apply the U.S. Constitution. When reviewing a case, they must examine the procedures used by legislatures, courts, lawyers, police, and judges and determine if they have complied with the U.S. Constitution and the Bill of Rights. In doing so, they provide reasoning and instruction. The Bill of Rights provides the foundation for their decisions. Their decisions are designed to ensure that procedures are consistent with the fundamental principles such as the protection against unreasonable search and seizure, double jeopardy, self-incrimination, excessive bail, the right to jury trial, effective counsel, and confrontation of witnesses. Criminal procedure decisions often require the Supreme Court to balance the actions of government and law enforcement against our desire for individual freedom and the right to privacy.

How Does the U.S. Supreme Court Develop a Rule of Criminal Procedure?

When a criminal case is prosecuted in the United States, there may be a number of events that are impacted by the Bill of Rights. Evidence may be discovered as a result of a search. A defendant may be interrogated and, as a result, provide incriminating statements. The police might conduct a lineup in which a witness identifies a perpetrator. Jury members will be questioned and selected. The judge will determine the admissibility of testimony and evidence at trial and provide instructions to the jury. There may be other concerns such as pretrial publicity or double jeopardy. All of these issues are addressed by the individual rights set forth in the Bill of Rights. The defendant, of course, may appeal if convicted arguing that any one of these constitutional rights have been violated. If the U.S. Supreme Court reviews the case, they will determine if the procedures of the police and courts that led to the conviction comply with the Bill of Rights. In doing so, they may actually provide instruction as to how the matter should have been handled. In the famous case of *Miranda v. Arizona*, the Court decided the police must advise a suspect of certain constitutional rights if a suspect is subjected to a custodial interrogation. All law enforcement officers in the nation must now comply with that rule. In *Miranda*, the Court examined the procedures involved in the investigation and conviction of the defendant and determined that the Bill of Rights had been violated. They then provided their reasoning and instructions for future interrogations. The Supreme Court's decisions are published in written documents referred to as opinions.

While states may enact their own constitutions and rules of criminal procedure, they cannot provide their citizens with less protection than required by the U.S. Constitution and the Supreme Court. On occasion an individual state will provide additional criminal procedure protections for their state criminal proceedings. For example, the U.S. Supreme Court has identified the criteria for determining if the right to speedy trial has been violated. Some states have developed rules that are more restrictive than those required by the U.S. Supreme Court. That is permissible so long as the state rule also meets the Supreme Court criteria.

The Decision Process

If the U.S. Supreme Court agrees to review a case, the attorney for the prosecution and defense must submit written briefs. These legal briefs provide details of the case including the identification of the alleged errors of the trial and lower appellate courts. The briefs also include the arguments for the respective positions. The attorneys may then be allowed to appear before the court and present oral arguments. During the oral arguments, the individual justices may ask the attorney questions concerning their positions. There are no witnesses or evidence offered during the hearing. The justices will then confer and deliberate. The deliberation often takes several months but once they reach a decision, the justices will announce their decision in open court and provide the written opinion that details their reasoning.

How to Read a Case Opinion

The official publication of the U.S. Supreme Court is called the U.S Reports. They are published in hardbound books and are available in law libraries. However, they are now available online from a variety of sources. The official Web site of the U.S. Supreme Court is: www.supremecourt.gov. You may also find most opinions by conducting an Internet search by case name. Beware, however, that some nonofficial Web sites may only be providing analysis and not the actual opinion. It is beneficial to read the accurate opinion.

All appellate court decisions are identified by a citation that includes the case name and identifying numbers. Consider the following case example.

MIRANDA v. ARIZONA

384 U.S. 436 (1966)

The title of this case is, of course, *Miranda v. Arizona*. The title will provide some, but not all, information about the origin of the case. In this case, the criminal defendant was Ernesto Miranda and the original charge was prosecuted in Arizona. The name of a state in a criminal case title indicates the state from which it originated. However, some state cases might use the term "State" or "People." For example, a title such as *State v. Johnson* would not identify the originating state. Occasionally, a state case will use the name of an attorney general or another government official. In the famous case of *Gideon v. Wainwright*, Gideon was the criminal defendant and the other party was Lewis Wainwright, the Secretary to the Florida Department of Corrections. If one of the parties in the title is the United States, then it is a federal case. In those cases, you must read the opinion in order to discover additional information. The "U.S." in the citation identifies the case as an official opinion of the U.S. Supreme Court. The official reporter of the U.S. Supreme Court is the U.S. Reports. The first set of numbers indicates the volume of the U.S. Reports in which the opinion may be found. The second set is simply the page number. The number in parentheses indicates the year in which the decision was made. It is not when the case occurred. The Miranda case was a kidnapping and rape case that occurred in 1963 but the Court's decision was presented in 1966.

The Facts: Each case will include its unique set of facts. The facts describe the crime, the actions taken by the police and courts, and any other pertinent events. The facts will often also identify the issues that are being addressed by the court.

The Decision: The case opinion will provide a discussion of the court's reasoning and their ultimate ruling. The decision explains the interpretation of the law and its application to the facts of the case. The reasoning is instructive to the police, lower courts, and attorneys in understanding how the court expects the decision to be applied in future cases.

Decisions of the U.S. Supreme Court are seldom unanimous. The justices make their decisions after discussion and deliberation and ultimately rely on majority rule. If at least five of the nine justices agree, then they have reached a majority opinion. They will select one justice to be the primary writer of the opinion. Justices who disagree may write dissenting opinions indicating why they disagree with the majority. While the dissenting opinions are not law, they are sometimes very helpful in interpreting the actions of the court. If a justice agrees with the court's decision but does not agree with the reason for the decision, the justice may write a concurring opinion. Though rarer, the Court will occasionally extend a **plurality opinion**. In that case, a majority of the justices are unable to agree on the holding and reasoning. The plurality is that of the most justices who agree on a particular outcome and point of law.

Plurality opinion
In a case in which a majority of the justices are unable to agree on the holding or reasoning, a plurality opinion represents the reasoning of the highest number of judges.

Summary

The nation's appellate court systems are charged with interpreting and applying both their state constitutions as well as the U.S. Constitution. The rules impacting criminal procedure have primarily been developed as a result of the U.S. Supreme Court acting in its role as the highest appellate court in the nation. This chapter has also outlined how a criminal case travels through both state and federal appellate systems. The student of criminal justice has had the opportunity to examine the distinctions between discretionary and mandatory appeals, the differences between majority, concurring, plurality, and dissenting opinions. The executive branches of state and federal government also have a related role to the ultimate outcome of criminal cases in the exercise of pardons and commutations.

Review Questions

1. What is an interlocutory appeal?
2. An appellate court does not hear evidence or determine guilt or innocence. Why?
3. Explain the distinction between a commutation of sentence and a pardon.
4. What is the role of an appellate court?
5. Explain the difference between first right of appeal and a discretionary appeal.

Legal Terminology

Commutation
Courts of record
En banc
Habeas corpus
Interlocutory appeal

Pardon
Plurality opinion
Remand
Writ of certiorari

References

28 U.S. Code §2254. State custody; remedies in Federal courts.

Chapter 3
The History and Development of Due Process

The U.S. Constitution originally provided that individual states were free to enact their own laws so long as they did not conflict with the federal constitution. As a result, state and local jurisdictions make their own decisions regarding criminal law. States and local legislatures determine the crimes in their respective jurisdictions. Decisions as to punishment also lie with the individual states. Initially, states were allowed freedom to determine how to enforce their criminal laws as well. In modern law, however, all states must comply with the requirements set forth in the Bill of Rights that affect the enforcement of criminal laws. As strange as it may seem today, those rights guaranteed by the Bill of Rights, such as the right to counsel and the protections against unreasonable search and seizure, did not always apply to state criminal proceedings. Those rights were ultimately applied to the states as a result of a series of cases over the course of time. The U.S. Supreme Court addressed many of those rights during the 1960s. The impetus for the application of the individual rights to the states comes primarily from the Fourteenth Amendment which was enacted at the end of the American Civil War. That amendment, ratified in 1968, guaranteed due process of law.

> **The Fourteenth Amendment Section I**
>
> All persons born or naturalized in the United States, and subject to the jurisdiction thereof, are citizens of the United States and of the state wherein they reside. No state shall make or enforce any law which shall abridge the privileges or immunities of citizens of the United States; nor shall any state deprive any person of life, liberty, or property, without due process of law; nor deny to any person within its jurisdiction the equal protection of the laws.

Historically, the individual rights were not applied to the states at a single identifiable moment. There was a gradual examination and application of due process via a series of cases which were appealed to the U.S. Supreme Court. One of the early landmark cases that considered due process was *Brown v. Mississippi* in 1936.

BROWN v. MISSISSIPPI

297 U.S. 278 (1936)

The Facts: Ed Brown, Henry Shields, and Arthur Ellington were suspected of killing Raymond Stewart who was found murdered on the afternoon of March 30, 1934. Stewart was described as a white plantation owner. Ellington was arrested that same evening by Sheriff Deputy Dial. However, instead of transporting Ellington to jail, the deputy took him to the home of the victim where a crowd was gathered. There, the deputy and the crowd accused Ellington of the murder, but he denied his involvement. They then hanged him from a tree. They did not hang him in a manner that would break his neck and kill him. They just wrapped the rope around his neck so he would swing wildly. Then they whipped him. In spite of the torture, Ellington refused to confess. At one point they cut him down only to hang him again and whip him some more. After it was clear that he would not confess, they cut him down and allowed him to crawl away. The court record stated that he suffered severe pain and agony and that the rope marks were still visible at trial. Two days later, the same deputy arrested Ellington again. However, instead of taking him directly to jail, Dial took him across the state line into Alabama. There, he severely whipped him again until he finally agreed to confess according to the deputy's specific terms.

Meanwhile, deputies also arrested Shields and Brown. In jail, they were whipped until they agreed to confess exactly as directed. The Supreme Court described the torture as follows:

> On Sunday night, April 1, 1934, the same deputy, accompanied by a number of white men, one of whom was also an officer, and by the jailer, came to the jail, and the two last named defendants were made to strip and they were laid over chairs and their backs were cut to pieces with a leather strap with buckles on it, and they were likewise made by the said deputy definitely to understand that the whipping would be continued unless and until they confessed, and not only confessed, but confessed in every matter of detail as demanded by those present; and in this manner the defendants confessed to the crime, and, as the whippings progressed and were repeated, they changed or adjusted their confession in all particulars of detail so as to conform to the demands of their torturers. When the confessions had been obtained in the exact form and contents as desired by the mob, they left with the parting admonition and warning that, if the defendants changed their story at any time in any respect from that last stated, the perpetrators of the outrage would administer the same or equally effective treatment.

The grand jury indicted Shield, Ellington, and Brown on April 4, and the trial began the following day. Counsel was appointed even though the defendants did not believe they could be helped at that juncture. Remarkably, the law enforcement officers did not deny that they tortured the defendants. During the trial, Deputy Dial was asked if he whipped Ellington. He responded, "Not too much for a negro; not as much as I would have done if it were left to me." The fact that the defendants were tortured did not matter to the trial judge. He admitted the confessions into evidence and all three defendants were convicted and sentenced to death.

Upon appeal, both the Mississippi Court of Appeals and the Mississippi Supreme Court upheld the convictions. In 1934, the State of Mississippi did not exclude evidence that was obtained in an unlawful manner. State courts were not bound by federal rules. At that point in time, the Fifth Amendment to the U.S. Constitution which forbade compelling defendants to incriminate themselves did not apply to state criminal proceedings. In *Brown*, the U.S. Supreme Court changed that premise.

The Decision: The U.S. Supreme Court overturned the decision of the Mississippi courts. They determined that even in a state criminal case, all citizens of the United States are entitled to due process. They did not go so far as to require states to exclude all illegally obtained evidence, but they ruled that using torture to compel a defendant to confess was a violation of due process of law. The Court offered a strong signal that they were willing to regulate state criminal procedure in situations that denied a defendant's right to due process. The Court stated:

> But the freedom of the state in establishing its policy is the freedom of constitutional government and is limited by the requirement of due process of law.

> The **due process clause** requires "that state action, whether through one agency or another, shall be consistent with the fundamental principles of liberty and justice which lie at the base of all our civil and political institutions." *Hebert v. Louisiana*, 272 U.S. 312, 316 , 47 S. Ct. 103, 104, 48 A.L.R. 1102. It would be difficult to conceive of methods more revolting to the sense of justice than those taken to procure the confessions of these petitioners, and the use of the confessions thus obtained as the basis for conviction and sentence was a clear denial of due process.

> In the instant case, the trial court was fully advised by the undisputed evidence of the way in which the confessions had been procured. The trial court knew that there was no other evidence upon which conviction and sentence could be based. Yet it proceeded to permit conviction and to pronounce sentence. The conviction and sentence were void for want of the essential elements of due process, and the proceeding thus vitiated could be challenged in any appropriate manner. *Mooney v. Holohan*, supra. It was challenged before the Supreme Court of the State by the express invocation of the Fourteenth Amendment. That court entertained the challenge, considered the federal question thus presented, but declined to enforce petitioners' constitutional right. The court thus denied a federal right fully established and specially set up and claimed, and the judgment must be reversed.

As a result of their decision, the case was remanded to the Mississippi trial court with instructions that the confessions could not be used in evidence at a new trial. However, as a result of a plea bargain, all three defendants agreed to less serious manslaughter charges in order to avoid a new trial.

Due process clause
The Fourteenth Amendment guarantees that all citizens of the United States cannot be denied life or liberty without due process of law.

What Is Due Process?

Defining due process is difficult. Neither the Fifth nor Fourteenth Amendment provides a textbook-style definition. Though continually debated by jurists and legal scholars, specific descriptions are elusive. However, the U.S. Supreme Court has provided guidance in determining if an individual's right to due process has been violated. Their defining instructions have evolved over many cases and a considerable period of time. In particular, they have clarified the role of due process by identifying when violations occur. The denial of certain rights constitutes a denial of due process. For example, if the court denied a criminal defendant his or her right to an attorney, that would be a violation of due process. The denial of a fair trial would violate due process. Criminal defendants must be afforded protection from double jeopardy and cruel and unusual punishment. Again, the denial of those rights would also be a denial of due process of law. If the right is fundamentally necessary to ensure fairness, then it is a requirement to ensure due process.

On the Street

Right to Counsel and Due Process

Peyton has a part-time job at a video store making minimum wage. She has no savings and is barely making ends meet. Her store manager claims that she took $600 from a hidden cash box he kept in the freezer. The police search her car and question her extensively. She is then arrested for felony theft. At her arraignment, she tells the judge that she does not have any money and that she needs an attorney. She claims she is not guilty and just cannot face going to prison. The judge refuses to appoint counsel claiming he is sick and tired of the county spending money on thieves. He tells her that the county just cannot afford to provide every fool with a free attorney. Has Peyton been denied due process of law? Why or why not? ■

In *Powell v. Alabama*, 287 U.S. 45 (1932), the U.S. Supreme Court used due process to overturn a highly publicized state conviction. Infamously known as the Scottsboro Boys case, nine young black men were accused of raping two white women on a train. The defendants, described by the court as "ignorant and illiterate," were taken off of the train in Scottsboro, Alabama, and arrested by an angry mob on March 25, 1931. Because of the tense and hostile atmosphere, the defendants were then detained in a military facility in nearby Gadsen under guard by the local militia. All of the defendants were from out of state and knew no one else in Alabama. They were indicted March 31 and forced to trial a few days later. Though the trial judge appointed all of the attorneys of the Alabama bar as counsel, the only person who came forward to represent the defendants was a lawyer who provided little or no help. They were convicted in a one-day trial and sentenced to death. Rape was a **capital offense** in 1932 so the convicted defendants were facing death. The U.S. Supreme Court, citing due process of law, overturned their convictions. The Court stated:

Capital offense
A crime that carries the possible punishment of death.

In the light of the facts outlined in the forepart of this opinion—the ignorance and illiteracy of the defendants, their youth, the circumstances of public hostility, the imprisonment and the close surveillance of the defendants by the military forces, the fact that their friends and families were all in other states and communication with them necessarily difficult, and above all that they stood in deadly peril of their lives—we think the failure of the trial court to give them reasonable time and opportunity to secure counsel was a clear denial of due process.

The Court did not go so far as to require appointed counsel in all cases. However, they did say in this particular case that the overall oppressive situation denied the defendants their constitutional right to due process of law. They also inferred that the right to counsel was necessary in a death penalty case.

On a historical note, the Scottsboro Boys were originally sentenced to death for rape. Today, that is no longer allowed. The death penalty is only appropriate punishment for murder now. In 2009, the Supreme Court ruled that state laws calling for the death penalty in the rape of a child were unconstitutional and a violation of the Eighth Amendment prohibition against cruel and unusual punishment.

Due Process and Illegal Search

Exclusionary rule
Evidence that is illegally obtained is inadmissible in court.

The next chapter begins a discussion of the **exclusionary rule**, which prohibits the use of illegally seized evidence in most court settings. The U.S. Supreme Court did not require a blanket exclusion of illegally seized evidence in state cases until 1961. They did, however, disallow evidence if the conduct of law enforcement was so egregious that it resulted in a denial of due process.

ROCHIN v. CALIFORNIA

342 U.S. 165 (1952)

The Facts: On the morning of July 1, 1949, three Los Angeles County deputy sheriffs entered the home of Antonio Rochin. They did not have a search warrant but they had some information that Rochin was selling narcotics. After finding the outside door open, they entered the dwelling and climbed the stairs to the second floor. The deputies then forced open the door to Rochin's bedroom. Rochin, partially dressed, was sitting on the side of the bed with his wife lying next to him. On the nightstand were two capsules. A deputy asked, "Whose stuff is this?" Rochin grabbed the capsules and put them in his mouth. The three deputies then wrestled with Rochin and tried unsuccessfully to force open his mouth so they could extract the pills. He managed to swallow them. They then handcuffed Rochin and took him to a hospital where they directed a doctor to pump Rochin's stomach. The doctor induced vomiting by forcing an emetic solution through a tube into his stomach. In the vomited matter the deputies found two partially dissolved morphine capsules.

California did not recognize the exclusionary rule in 1949 so even though the deputies conducted an illegal search, the trial judge allowed the evidence. The officers broke into Rochin's house without a warrant, tried to physically force open his mouth, arrested him, and had his stomach pumped against his will. Even though it was clear that the morphine was illegally seized, Rochin was convicted. The California Supreme Court as well as the California Court of Appeals affirmed his conviction. The U.S. Supreme Court agreed to hear the case.

The Decision: The U.S. Supreme Court ruled that the police misconduct in this case deprived Rochin of his right to due process of law. Using strong language, the Court indicated that they would not hesitate to exclude evidence in a state case in which police violate a suspect's due process of law. As in *Brown*, they did not go so far as to say that all evidence obtained illegally must be excluded, but they did say that the combination of police abuses in this case constituted a violation of due process.

> Applying these general considerations to the circumstances of the present case, we are compelled to conclude that the proceedings by which this conviction was obtained do more than offend some fastidious squeamishness or private sentimentalism about combatting crime too energetically. This is conduct that shocks the conscience. Illegally breaking into the privacy of the petitioner, the struggle to open his mouth and remove what was there, the forcible extraction of his stomach's contents—this course of proceeding by agents of government to obtain evidence is bound to offend even hardened sensibilities. They are methods too close to the rack and the screw to permit of constitutional differentiation.

While the Court did not go so far as to require that states exclude all illegally obtained evidence, their opinion served a strong message that horrific police misconduct would not be allowed. By linking the misconduct to the due process clause, they also provided a preview of their future decisions.

The Application of the Individual Rights to the States

As indicated in the chapter's introduction and the preceding cases, the individual rights set forth in the Bill of Rights to the U.S. Constitution were not initially applied to state criminal proceedings. In a sense, many were applied on a right-by-right, case-by-case basis over a long period of time. The U.S. Supreme Court has considered several theories in their journey to determine which rights and procedures should ultimately be mandated to the states. The commonly discussed doctrines include selective incorporation, total incorporation, and fundamental fairness.

The proponents of total incorporation suggested that the Fourteenth Amendment automatically incorporated all of the rights in the first eight amendments to the states. This doctrine was never accepted by the Court. Instead, the Court has used the process of selective incorporation to identify which specific rights and procedures to mandate to the states. The advocates of the concept of fundamental fairness took a more general approach to incorporation by proposing incorporation of the general rights while allowing the states to determine their own specific procedures in order to protect those rights.

Today, most of the individual protections in the original Bill of Rights have been applied to the states, but not all. And in many cases, the U.S. Supreme Court has identified specific procedures that all states must follow.

Summary

The cases of *Brown, Powell,* and *Rochin* provide a historical perspective of how the U.S. Supreme Court used the Fourteenth Amendment due process clause to ensure that all citizens receive fundamental fairness in state cases. They also helped define due process of law. Today, criminal defendants are entitled to those fundamental rights regardless of whether it is a state or federal prosecution.

The Fourteenth Amendment to the U.S. Constitution guaranteed that every citizen could be denied life or liberty without due process of law. This guarantee ultimately became the vehicle to provide the individual rights such as right to counsel, protection from unreasonable search and seizure, and protection from compelled self-incrimination to everyone. The original protections of the Bill of Rights did not apply to state criminal proceedings. However, through a series of cases, the U.S. Supreme Court determined that without those protections, citizens were denied due process of law.

Review Questions

1. Why is the denial of counsel a denial of due process of law?
2. What is the relationship between due process and state criminal law?
3. In *Rochin v. California*, why did the trial judge allow the morphine evidence in court?
4. Without using the examples in *Rochin, Powell,* and *Brown*, describe a situation that would involve the denial of due process.

Legal Terminology

Capital offense   Exclusionary rule
Due process clause

References

Brown v. Mississippi, 297 U.S. 278 (1936)
Powell v. Alabama, 287 U.S. 45 (1932)
Rochin v. California, 342 U.S. 165 (1952)

Chapter 4
The Exclusionary Rule

Exclusionary rule
Evidence that is illegally obtained is inadmissible in court.

The **exclusionary rule** was developed as a remedy to a problem. The problem was that law enforcement officers, on occasion, violated the rules regarding the collection of evidence. They might conduct illegal searches or engage in unlawful interrogations in violation of a suspect's constitutional rights. In order to deter these unlawful practices by law enforcement, the U.S. Supreme Court decided that the punishment for such police misconduct would be the exclusion of the illegally obtained evidence. The rule was first applied to federal criminal prosecutions and ultimately expanded to include all state criminal cases. Like many rules, there are a number of exceptions. In order to understand the purpose and application of the rule and its exceptions, one must first consider its history and development.

The Origin of the Exclusionary Rule

The concept of excluding illegally obtained evidence was not expressly included in the U.S. Constitution or the Bill of Rights. It was also not enacted by Congress or any other legislative body. While the Bill of Rights provided citizens with protections from violations of illegal searches and guaranteed due process, it did not expressly indicate the consequences of a violation of its rights. The Fourth Amendment stated that the government could not conduct unreasonable searches, but it did not identify the penalty for a violation. Likewise, the Fifth Amendment did not offer a remedy for law enforcement conducting an unlawful interrogation.

Consider the following: It is common for a parent to require a young child to hold his or her hand while crossing the street. If the child refuses or breaks free, then the parent must determine how to enforce the rule. There might be some type of punishment. It is important to find a way to ensure that the child holds the parent's hand because failure to comply with the parent's rule could result in injury to the child. In a sense, the Bill of Rights created rules but did not identify the consequences for breaking the rules. A parent might tell the child that the child will be grounded or spanked in order to enforce the hand holding rule. However, the constitutional forefathers did not identify the consequences. Ultimately, the U.S. Supreme Court recognized the necessity of an enforcement mechanism. They decided that the exclusionary rule was the remedy to the problem. Its purpose was to deter police misconduct.

The History of the Exclusionary Rule

In 1914, the U.S. Supreme Court initially established the rule in the case of *United States v. Weeks* 232 U.S. 383. In *Weeks*, police were investigating Fremont Weeks for using the mail to sell illegal gambling lottery tickets. On two occasions they searched his Kansas City, Missouri, home without a warrant. The U.S. Supreme Court threw out the seized evidence and ruled that evidence illegally seized by law enforcement would be inadmissible in criminal prosecutions of violations of the U.S. Code. This was a federal case, however. The decision did not require the exclusion of evidence in state cases—at least, not yet.

In the meantime, the concern over illegal searches and interrogations continued in state cases. Individual states were reluctant to create a rule that could result in the exclusion of valuable evidence.

Why was the problem continuing? One of the primary reasons was ignorance of the rules of search and seizure. Law enforcement was not professionalized until the early 1970s. Most law enforcement agencies required minimal education. Some agencies hired individuals at 18 years of age with minimal qualifications. Aside from the larger city and state agencies, training was fairly unsophisticated and focused primarily on tactics as opposed to law. States seldom had standardized training requirements, and in some areas, there were no requirements at all. It was not unusual in many rural agencies for newly hired officers to be given a badge and a gun and sent on patrol. The dearth of education and training certainly impacted the application of rights. While ignorance of the law was one of the primary reasons for violations of search and seizure rules, poor hiring practices and low pay attracted applicants with character and ethical deficiencies as well. Some rights violations such as those depicted in *Brown v. Mississippi* were intentional.

After the *Weeks* case was decided, a few states enacted their own exclusionary rules but most did not. The problems continued. In 1949, the U.S. Supreme Court heard *Wolf v. Colorado*, 338 U.S. 25. In *Wolf*, police in Colorado conducted an illegal search and obtained evidence. If it had been a federal case, the evidence would have been excluded. The defendant/appellant in *Wolf* asked the U.S. Supreme Court to apply the exclusionary rule to the states. They refused, suggesting that while they were aware of the problems, they were going to allow the individual states decide how to solve them. There was an inference that civil and administrative remedies might be used if the states did not want to adopt the exclusionary rule. Their decision served as a warning to the states that they needed to find effective solutions. In 1961, the U.S. Supreme Court solved the problem for them and applied the exclusionary rule to the states.

MAPP v. OHIO

367 U.S. 643 (1961)

The Facts: Dollree Mapp and her daughter lived on the top floor of a two-family dwelling in Cleveland, Ohio. On May 23, 1957, three police officers knocked on her door. They believed a person who was responsible for a domestic bombing might be hiding out in her apartment, and there was also some physical evidence in her home. After calling her attorney, she refused to let them in since they did not have a search warrant. They did not come in but stayed on the street outside of her home. Three hours later, after conferring with their headquarters, they again knocked on her door. Four additional police officers had joined them. Ms. Mapp refused again. However, this time they forced their way inside. About the same time, Ms. Mapp's attorney arrived but the officers refused to let him see her or enter the house. When she demanded to see a warrant, the officers presented a sheet of paper that they claimed to be a warrant. She grabbed it and stuffed it down her bosom. After a physical struggle, the officers then forcibly retrieved the paper and handcuffed her. Evidence of the existence of the warrant was never produced at trial. The officers then searched her home. Their search included photo albums, personal papers, her bedroom dresser and chest of drawers, and even her child's room. After finding nothing in the upper floors of her home, the police searched a trunk in the basement and discovered what they identified as lewd and lascivious books and photographs. Ms. Mapp was charged with the illegal possession of obscene material, prosecuted, and convicted in an Ohio trial court. Though the trial judge determined that the evidence was illegally obtained, the evidence was allowed. The Ohio Court of Appeals and the Ohio Supreme Court agreed, citing the aforementioned *Wolf* case, that a state court was not required to exclude evidence simply because it was illegally obtained. Ms. Mapp appealed her case to the U.S. Supreme Court.

The Decision: The U.S. Supreme Court decided that the remedy of the exclusionary rule must now apply to state criminal proceedings. In a sense, they had had enough. In the wake of their warnings in *Wolf*, the states had failed to identify or enforce solutions to the problem of police misconduct. The court ruled that in order to deter police from illegally obtaining evidence, evidence that was illegally obtained must be excluded.

By applying the exclusionary rule to the states, *Mapp* became one of the most significant criminal procedure cases in our history. Police agencies were compelled to improve their hiring and retention practices and to update their training regarding constitutional criminal procedure. In the early 1970s a trend toward professionalism in law enforcement began. Federal funding allowed agencies to improve training and raise requirements. As salaries and benefits rose, the job became attractive to more qualified applicants. Colleges and universities began to develop criminal justice programs. By the late 1980s, many states had enacted mandated training requirements for law enforcement officers, and some agencies instituted college educational requirements. Criminal procedure and the constitutional rules are now addressed in law enforcement academies and college criminal justice programs nationwide.

The Fruit of the Poisonous Tree Doctrine

Fruit of the poisonous tree doctrine
An extension of the exclusionary rule, the doctrine also excludes any evidence that was discovered as a result of a previous original illegality.

Herbicide
A chemical compound that poisons and kills plants.

An extension of the exclusionary rule, the **fruit of the poisonous tree doctrine** excludes any evidence that is discovered as a result of some previous illegality. The name is a metaphor. If the tree is poisoned, then the fruit is also poisoned. If someone dumped a poisonous **herbicide** on the roots of a beautiful pear tree, all of the pears and the leaves would be destroyed. By poisoning the root, you also poison the fruit. For example, a police officer has a right to search a suspect who has been legally arrested. However, if the arrest was unlawful, then any evidence discovered during a search of the suspect would also be inadmissible because it was only obtained as a result of the previous illegality. The unlawful arrest would be the poison. The subsequent evidence would be considered the fruits.

On the Street

Should the evidence be excluded?

The police are called to a bar fight. Upon their arrival, they discover that Jillian has been stabbed to death. Her body is draped over a pool table. The police could not locate any witnesses who saw the incident. However, one witness said that Jillian and her boyfriend Morgan had been in a very dramatic argument the previous evening. The police put a broadcast out for Morgan over the police radio. Officer Fletcher went to Morgan's house and knocked on the door. When Morgan answered, the officer pushed his way inside and told Morgan to sit down and shut up. The officer then searched Morgan's house without a warrant. Underneath a blanket in the bedroom, the officer found a storage unit key. Imprinted on the key was the facility name and unit number. The police then sought a warrant from a judge indicating that they had found the storage key during a search of Morgan's house. They lied to the judge by claiming Morgan consented to the search. The judge issued a search warrant. The officer then went to the storage unit, opened it, and discovered the bloody knife that had been used in the stabbing. The original search of Morgan's house was illegal as it was conducted without a warrant or valid consent. What about the knife? Is it admissible? Or is it the fruit of a poisonous tree? ■

The exclusionary rule has proven to be controversial. It has the unfortunate result of occasionally excluding valuable and true evidence in criminal cases, thus allowing guilty offenders to avoid prosecution. Proponents of the rule contend that the process by which justice is obtained is more important than the result. Like the cliché, the end does not justify the means. In addition to the complaint that the guilty go unpunished, critics point out that it was a court-developed remedy and is not part of the constitution.

The Exceptions to the Exclusionary Rule

Like many rules, there are exceptions. Since the 1961 decision of *Mapp v. Ohio*, the U.S. Supreme Court has identified several exceptions in which the purpose of deterring police misconduct would not be served by excluding the evidence.

The Exceptions:
   Attenuation
   Good Faith
   Independent Source
   Ultimate and Inevitable Discovery
   Collateral Source
   Civil Litigation
   Search by Private Persons

Attenuation Doctrine

Evidence, though initially obtained illegally, may be admissible if the evidence is obtained later in a legal manner and the connection between the initial illegality and the evidence is sufficiently remote. This concept is also referred to as the "purged taint" exception because the taint has become so attenuated or weakened that it has been purged.

The U.S. Supreme Court established the exception in the case of *Wong Sun v. United States*, 371 U.S. 471 (1963). While conducting a narcotics investigation, police obtained evidence that led them to arrest Wong Sun. After his arraignment, he was **released on his own recognizance**. However, a few days later, Wong Sun voluntarily went back to the police station and made incriminating statements. He was ultimately convicted in federal court of **trafficking** in heroin. Upon appeal, it was determined that the evidence that led police to Wong Sun in the first place was obtained illegally and that he was unlawfully arrested. As a result, Wong Sun argued that it should have been excluded because it was a fruit of the poisonous tree. While the Supreme Court agreed that the initial arrest was unlawful, they also determined that Wong Sun had voluntarily returned for police questioning thus indicating a break in the connection between the original illegality and his statement. They determined that the taint had been attenuated, or purged. Metaphorically, the poison of the root had not reached the fruit of the tree.

Release on own recognizance
A criminal defendant is released from jail while awaiting trial without the requirement of posting bail.

Trafficking
Sale or distribution of a product usually in reference to illegal drugs or other contraband. In some jurisdictions, trafficking also includes possession with intent to sell and manufacture of contraband.

Good Faith Exception

Evidence obtained as a result of the execution of a defective search warrant will not be excluded if the officers conducting the search were acting in good faith reliance on a judicially issued warrant based on an accurate and truthful affidavit.

Affidavit
A legal sworn document used in warrant requests stating the facts establishing probable cause.

The Good Faith Exception, created in *United States v. Leon*, 468 U.S. 897 (1984), is the result of a very narrow and restrictive ruling. After a lengthy and complicated drug investigation, a detective asked a state court magistrate for a search warrant of some property owned by Leon. The officer honestly provided accurate information in the **affidavit** for the warrant. The information was neither misleading nor untruthful. The magistrate issued a search warrant after determining that the facts contained in the affidavit constituted probable cause. Police, acting on that search warrant, searched Leon's property and discovered incriminating evidence. At trial, the defendant filed a motion to suppress requesting that the evidence be excluded. The trial court, a U.S. District Court, ruled that the magistrate had erred in determining that probable cause existed for the warrant. However, the U.S. Supreme Court allowed the evidence by creating the "Good Faith" exception. They stated that the exclusionary rule was designed to deter police misconduct, not judicial error. In this case, the police did nothing wrong. They were acting in a reasonable and objective manner by relying on a judicially issued search warrant. They did not lie or in any way misstate the facts in the affidavit. Since the police acted in good-faith reliance on a judicially issued search warrant, the evidence was allowed.

Note that the good faith exception does not mean that evidence is admissible if a police officer, though mistaken, was acting in good faith. The exclusionary rule does not allow the admission of evidence obtained as a result of an officer's unintentional mistake. If that were the case, police officers would not have to understand the law. They could just argue that they honestly thought they were legally obtaining evidence. Ignorance of the rules of criminal procedure is not an excuse.

On the Street

Good faith exception?

Deputy Kensington had been interested in Kurt for a long time. He knew that Kurt just graduated from high school six months earlier and was now driving an expensive sports utility vehicle with tricked-out wheels. Yet as far as Officer Kensington knew, Kurt only worked part-time at the local video store. Kurt also seemed to have a new set of tattoos every week. Kensington observed him hanging out in his SUV at the local basketball court every Sunday afternoon but never saw him play. He just sat on the hood of his car and talked to the other guys. The deputy had had enough. He pulled up behind Kurt and told him to keep his hands on top of his car. Without any legal justification, Kensington searched Kurt's car and discovered marijuana under the spare tire rack. He then arrested Kurt. In court, the judge indicated that she was going to throw out the marijuana evidence because the deputy did not have probable cause.

The deputy told the judge that he was acting in good faith that he had probable cause and that it was an honest mistake. He just didn't understand the law clearly. Would the good faith exception apply? ▨

No. The officer made the mistake. He was relying on his own poor judgment and misunderstanding of the law. The evidence would be excluded.

Independent Source Exception

Evidence obtained as a result of an illegal search is admissible if the evidence would also be discoverable based on an independent reason untainted by the initial illegality.

The exclusionary rule prohibits the use of evidence obtained by the police as a result of an illegal search. However, if the police have another legal justification for obtaining the same evidence wholly independent of the constitutional violation, then the evidence may be admissible. Again, the purpose of the exclusionary rule is to deter police misconduct. The exclusion of evidence obtained in an independent legal manner would not serve the purpose of deterring misconduct.

SEGURA v. UNITED STATES

468 U.S. 796 (1984)

The Facts: As a result of a New York Drug Enforcement Task Force investigation, agents established probable cause that Andres Segura and others were involved in drug trafficking. During a stakeout, they arrested Segura in the lobby of his apartment building and walked him back up to his apartment. The agents then knocked on Segura's door. When another suspect, Luz Marina Colon, opened the door, the agents pushed their way inside without permission. They immediately conducted a limited security check of the apartment and discovered **drug paraphernalia**. Colon was arrested. They had sufficient probable cause for the legal arrests of Colon and Segura. They also had probable cause that would allow them to obtain a search warrant for Segura's apartment prior to their entry. Because of an administrative delay, however, they could not immediately obtain a search warrant and would have to wait until morning. They would have certainly had a right to secure the apartment to ensure that no one else entered to destroy or remove evidence. Instead, two agents entered the apartment unlawfully and stayed until the search warrant was obtained 19 hours later. Upon obtaining the search warrant they continued the search and discovered drugs and other evidence.

The Decision: Segura, the defendant, contended that all evidence from the search should be excluded. The Supreme Court agreed that the warrantless entry into Segura's apartment and the subsequent all-night occupation were illegal. However, the Court allowed the evidence anyway. They said that the search warrant was an

Drug paraphernalia
Tools and items used to manufacture or use illegal drugs. Examples would include bongs, pipes, scales, and hypodermic needles.

independent source, legal and wholly independent from the illegal entry. The court did not allow the drug paraphernalia discovered during the initial security sweep, but the evidence obtained during the subsequent search pursuant to the warrant was allowed. The Court indicated that the police gained no advantage from the illegal entry.

Ultimate and Inevitable Discovery

If illegally obtained evidence would have ultimately and inevitably been discovered without the constitutional violation, then the evidence is admissible.

This exception arose from an extraordinary homicide case that was reviewed twice by the U.S. Supreme Court. The first appeal, *Brewer v. Williams*, 430 U.S. 387 (1977), resulted in the exclusion of the defendant's incriminating statements and the granting of a new trial. During the second trial, the prosecution presented physical evidence obtained from the victim's body and obtained a conviction. In the second appeal, the Supreme Court addressed the issue of whether the physical evidence had to be excluded under the fruit of a poisonous tree doctrine.

NIX v. WILLIAMS

467 U.S. 431 (1984)

The Facts: The family of ten-year-old Pamela Powers attended an athletic event at the YMCA in Des Moines, Iowa, on Christmas Eve, 1968. Sometime during the event they realized that Pamela was missing. As they started looking for her, a young boy told them that he had opened a car door for a man carrying a blanketed bundle and that "there were two legs in it and they were skinny and white." Police quickly determined that the child had been abducted and that the suspect was Robert Williams.

The next day, William's car was found at an I-80 rest stop approximately 160 miles east of Des Moines near the town of Davenport. In the car, police discovered an army blanket matching the description of the one used to carry the victim out of the YMCA. Investigators surmised that Pamela or her body would likely be in an area between the Grinell rest stop and Davenport. The Iowa Bureau of Criminal Investigation organized a massive search with over 200 volunteers. The searchers were instructed to search all roads, abandoned farm buildings, ditches, culverts, and any other place in which the body of a small child could be hidden. A warrant was issued for the arrest of Robert Williams.

On December 26, Henry McKnight, a lawyer from Des Moines, contacted the police and said that he had spoken with Robert Williams who wished to turn himself in. However, Williams was now near Davenport. McKnight and the Des Moines police made arrangements for Williams to turn himself in at the Davenport Police Department, and Williams was assured that he would not be mistreated or interrogated. They also agreed that he would be transported back to Des Moines. Upon his arrival at the Davenport police station, he was arrested and advised of his *Miranda* rights. Williams indicated that he was invoking his rights and was unwilling to answer any questions. He was arraigned on the warrant in a Davenport courtroom, and the judge also advised him of his *Miranda* rights.

Des Moines Detective Cleatus Leaming was dispatched to transport Williams back to Des Moines. It was clear to Detective Leaming that Williams was not to be interrogated. However, as they were traveling back to Des Moines, the detective started talking to Williams. Leaming was aware that Williams had been a former mental patient and was deeply religious. Leaming, while calling the suspect, Reverend Williams, then gave what is now infamously known as the "Christian burial speech." The detective conveyed an emotional plea in which he suggested that the family of Pamela Powers would not be able to even give their child a proper Christian burial. Ultimately, Williams directed Leaming to a gas station where he had left the victim's shoes though none were found. Robert Williams then started telling him where some of the evidence was and ultimately directed him to the girl's body.

The Legal Issue: Williams' statements directing the police to Pamela's body were introduced into evidence at his initial trial. However, if the suspect has invoked the *Miranda* rights by either requesting an attorney or refusing to talk, the police could not conduct an interrogation. If they continued to interrogate the suspect, any statements would be inadmissible in court. In *Brewer*, the U.S. Supreme Court had to determine if Leaming's "Christian burial" speech was an interrogation. Deciding that Leaming had intended to elicit incriminating information from Williams, they agreed it was an interrogation. They overturned the conviction and remanded the case back to Iowa for a new trial. The *Brewer* case is also discussed in Chapter 12.

As a result of the *Brewer* decision, the prosecution could not use William's statements at the second trial. However, they presented the physical evidence obtained from Pamela Power's body. The trial court admitted into evidence the condition of her body, photographs, articles of her clothing, and the results of post-mortem medical and chemical tests. Williams was again convicted and appealed his case. In *Nix v. Williams*, the U.S. Supreme Court had to determine if the physical evidence found on Pamela's body should have been excluded. The defense claimed that the evidence was fruit of the poisonous tree because it would not have been discovered without the illegal interrogation conducted by Detective Leaming.

The Decision: The court allowed the evidence. They determined that because of the location of the evidence and the extensive search, the girl's body would have ultimately and inevitably been discovered. Upon the discovery of the suspect's vehicle and the blanket, the police had narrowed the search area before they arrested Williams. As a result, they found Pamela's body in a concrete culvert which was in the planned search grid. With over 200 volunteers and a defined and logical search pattern, it was reasonable to believe that they would have discovered the evidence without the information given by Robert Williams. The ultimate and inevitable discovery exception may be applied in those situations in which it is reasonable to believe that the evidence would have been found without the illegal conduct of the police.

Collateral Use Exceptions

The exclusionary rule does not apply to criminal court proceedings other than the prosecution's case at trial.

Illegally obtained evidence is admissible in nontrial settings such as preliminary hearings, grand jury, habeas corpus hearings, bail determinations, and sentencing. The use of such evidence in these nontrial settings is referred to as a **collateral use exception**. The exception applies because these are not hearings in which guilt or innocence is being determined. There are also some practical considerations. Bail determinations and preliminary hearings are often held before any **discovery** has occurred. There may be ongoing investigations and analysis which will ultimately affect the evidence decision. The exception also applies to the grand jury. Only the prosecuting attorney and jurors are present during grand jury deliberations. There is no judge to rule on the admission of evidence or defense attorney to confront and object to its inclusion. (Caution: Some states do not apply this exception.)

Under the collateral use exception, a prosecutor may also use illegally obtained evidence to **impeach** a witness so long as it is not a part of his case in chief. In the event that the defense presented testimony that was contradictory to some illegally obtained evidence, the prosecution could then offer that evidence in order to discredit the witness's statement. Consider the following.

Collateral use exception
Allows the use of illegally seized evidence in court settings which do not result in the determination of guilt or innocence.

Discovery
The process in which the prosecutor and defense attorney disclose evidence impacting the case.

Impeachment
The discrediting of a witness.

On the Street

Too Many Lies

Arnold was arrested for selling marijuana. The police questioned him but failed to advise him of his *Miranda* rights. During the interrogation, Arnold admitted selling marijuana to Candace. At trial, the prosecutor could not present Arnold's confession into evidence since it had been illegally obtained. However, the defense attorney called Arnold to testify. Under oath, Arnold testified that he had not sold marijuana to anyone. Because Arnold lied, the prosecutor was then allowed to present evidence of Arnold's illegally obtained confession in order to impeach him. ■

Civil Cases

The exclusionary rule does not apply to evidence used in civil cases.

As previously discussed the rule was developed as a deterrent to police misconduct in obtaining evidence. Therefore, it does not apply to civil cases such as contract disputes, divorce, and personal injury. The rules of civil procedure govern the use of evidence in civil proceedings. As a result, there are often situations in which evidence is excluded in a criminal case but allowed in a subsequent civil case.

On the Street

Does the exclusionary rule apply at a divorce hearing?

The police suspect that Delrae is selling drugs. They break into his house without a warrant. They search his toolbox which is in his garage. Inside a tray of his toolbox, they find a large amount of cocaine. Before his trial for possession of the controlled substance, the criminal trial judge throws out the evidence because the police illegally searched his house without a warrant. However, his wife Vanessa is outraged by the fact that Delrae had drugs in the garage. She files for divorce and demands custody of the children. She claims that he is an unfit father because he uses cocaine. He denies it. At their custody hearing, the police officers who illegally broke into his house testify about the cocaine in Delrae's toolbox, and they present the cocaine into evidence. May they testify? Is the cocaine admissible? Yes. This is a civil hearing not a criminal trial. The exclusionary rule does not apply. ■

Evidence Obtained by Private Citizens

The exclusionary rule does not apply to evidence obtained by civilians.

The reason for this exception is straightforward. The purpose of the exclusionary rule is to deter police misconduct. It is not intended to impact the conduct of private persons. If a person who is not acting on behalf of the government discovers evidence and delivers it to the police or advises the police of its whereabouts, the evidence would be admissible even if the civilian violated the law. The civilian could, of course, also be prosecuted if his conduct violated a criminal law in order to obtain the evidence. This exception does not allow the police to ask a private citizen to conduct an illegal search on their behalf. In that circumstance, the exclusionary rule would still apply.

On the Street

Is the evidence admissible?

Alonzo's girlfriend, Kylie, suspects that he is cheating on her. Late one night, Kylie breaks into Alonzo's house hoping to catch him with another woman. After she pried opened the patio door, she searched the entire house but Alonzo was nowhere to be found. She decided maybe he was hiding in a closet somewhere. She forced open a locked closet door in the basement and found a box containing child pornography.

Livid, she called the local police. She then went outside and waited on Alonzo's porch. When the police arrived she handed them the box and told them the whole story. Is the child pornography admissible as evidence in a criminal prosecution against Kylie's soon to be ex-boyfriend? Can Kylie be prosecuted for burglary? ▪

Summary

The application of the exclusionary rule has been an evolving process. Critics have contended that the exclusion of otherwise truthful evidence had the unintended result of allowing criminals to go unpunished. Yet, it has also been lauded as a method of ensuring that the protections provided in the Bill of Rights would be enforced. The development of the exceptions evolved in an effort to allow valuable evidence while still deterring police misconduct. Recent concerns about terrorism and the safety of the American public have increased the focus on law enforcement's need to discover and obtain evidence. And, of course, the application of the exclusionary rule and its exceptions are directly linked to the determination of whether evidence was obtained illegally in the first place. The subsequent chapters will address the procedures affecting arrest, search, and seizure.

Review Questions

1. Why didn't the Supreme Court apply the exclusionary rule to the states in *United States v. Weeks*?
2. Why didn't the Supreme Court apply the exclusionary rule to the states in *Wolf v. Colorado*?
3. Define the exclusionary rule.
4. Explain the fruit of the poisonous tree doctrine.
5. Discuss the advantages and disadvantages of the exclusionary rule.
6. What is the purpose of the exclusionary rule?
7. Define *impeachment* as it relates to testimonial evidence.
8. Describe a situation in which the ultimate and inevitable exception might be applied.
9. Why doesn't the exclusionary rule apply to the illegal seizure of evidence by civilians?
10. In *Segura v. United States*, what should the officers have done?

Legal Terminology

Affidavit
Collateral use exception
Discovery
Drug paraphernalia
Exclusionary rule

Fruit of poisonous tree doctrine
Herbicide
Impeachment
Release on own recognizance
Trafficking

References

Mapp v. Ohio, 367 U.S. 643 (1961)
Nix v. Williams, 467 U.S. 431 (1984)
Segura v. United States, 468 U.S. 796 (1984)
United States v. Leon, 468 U.S. 897 (1984)
United States v. Weeks, 232 U.S. 383 (1914)
Wolf v. Colorado, 338 U.S. 25 (1949)
Wong Sun v. United States, 371 U.S. 471 (1963)

Section II
Search and Seizure

The Fourth Amendment to the U.S. Constitution states:

The right of the people to be secure in their persons, houses, papers, and effects, against unreasonable searches and seizures, shall not be violated, and no warrants shall issue, but upon probable cause, supported by oath or affirmation, and particularly describing the place to be searched, and the persons or things to be seized.

As indicated in Chapter 1, the initial stages of a criminal case involve investigation and arrest. An arrest, the physical seizure of a person with the intention of accusing them of a criminal offense, first requires the identification and location of the suspect. The police must often search not only for evidence but also for the person suspected of committing the offense. Arrests must also be based on probable cause. The previous chapters have also examined the consequences of illegal arrests as they relate to the admissibility of evidence. However, not all seizures of persons are considered arrests, nor do they require the same level of proof as an arrest. Temporary detentions such as traffic stops, stop and frisks, and some checkpoint stops may require less supporting proof than probable cause.

The Fourth Amendment also provides protection from the unlawful and unreasonable search and seizure of a person's property. The amendment also outlines the foundational requirements for the issuance of search and arrest warrants. In the years after the ratification of the Bill of Rights, the U.S. Supreme Court has decided numerous cases in which they interpreted and applied the Fourth Amendment to police and government actions. The following chapters examine the laws of arrest, probable cause, investigative detentions, and many complex rules impacting the search and seizure of evidence in criminal cases.

Chapter 5
Search and Seizure of Persons

Arrest
The physical seizure of a person with the intention of accusing them of a criminal offense.

Probable cause
standard of proof required for an arrest and to issue an arrest or search warrant. Also legal justification for search under specific circumstances.

An **arrest** is the physical seizure of a person with the intention of accusing them of a criminal offense. The police may not arrest an individual without legal justification. The standard of proof required for an arrest is **probable cause**. However, probable cause alone may not be sufficient for some misdemeanor arrests. This chapter will examine the concept of **probable cause as it applies to an arrest**, the additional requirements for misdemeanor arrests, and the role of arrest warrants. Police also possess some search powers when attempting to find a suspect they are intending to arrest.

Not all detentions of persons are considered arrests. The discussions in this and subsequent chapters will address a variety of situations in which the police may temporarily detain citizens. Those detentions do not require probable cause. However, if the detention reaches the level of an arrest, then probable cause is required.

> **The Elements of Arrest**
> Authority to arrest
> Intent to investigate or accuse of crime
> Substantial custody through compliance or physical restraint
> Reasonable understanding that arrest has occurred

If a suspect is involuntarily taken to the police station or a detention facility, then it is an arrest. The concept of being taken in for investigation constitutes an arrest unless the individual has voluntarily agreed to come to the police station. Generally the application of handcuffs would reasonably indicate an arrest unless the subject was expressly told that it was a temporary security measure and not an arrest. The person who is making the arrest must be legally authorized to do so or the arrest is considered illegal. Law enforcement officers have arrest powers within their jurisdiction, and most jurisdictions allow some form of citizen's arrest. Also, if a person has not been successfully apprehended, then the arrest has not occurred. A police chase does not constitute an arrest until the suspect is actually taken into physical custody. It is not necessary for an officer to verbally indicate that a person is under arrest. It would be reasonable for an individual to believe he or she was under arrest if that individual was subjected to certain actions such as being involuntarily placed in the back of a police car, handcuffed, or otherwise restrained in a manner in which that person could not leave. A situation in which a person would reasonably believe he or she was under arrest is considered a **de facto arrest** regardless of the intent of the officer.

Probable Cause

Probable Cause as It Applies to an Arrest

Probable cause is the standard of proof required for the issuance of arrest and search warrants, indictments, and in some cases, conducting warrantless arrests or searches. In jurisdictions that require preliminary hearings, it is the standard that must be met in order to bind a case over to a grand jury. The application of the probable cause standard to an arrest differs from its role in a search.

Probable cause is the amount of proof required for the issuance of an arrest warrant. The judge or magistrate must consider the facts presented in an affidavit and determine if probable cause exists. Police officers may also arrest a felony suspect without a warrant if probable cause exists. Generally, police may not make a misdemeanor arrest without a warrant unless the crime was committed in the officer's presence. However, most jurisdictions have enacted statutory exceptions for specific misdemeanors such as domestic violence. Many states allow police to make an arrest in domestic violence cases without a warrant so long as they have probable cause to believe that the suspect has committed the offense.

Not all detentions of persons are considered arrests. The discussions in Chapters 6 and 7 address a variety of situations in which the police may temporarily detain citizens. Those detentions do not require probable cause. However, if the detention reaches the level of an arrest, then probable cause is required. If a suspect is involuntarily taken to the police station or a detention facility, then it is an arrest.

Sources of Probable Cause

Probable cause may be developed from a variety of sources. The facts and circumstances necessary may be a culmination of an extensive police investigation or, in some cases, simply the word of one witness. Sources may include statements from victims, witnesses, or confidential informants; evidence from forensic analysis, officer observations, and technology such as video; or even information provided from other law enforcement agencies.

Information provided by a victim alone may be sufficient to establish probable cause to arrest. For example, the identification of a rape suspect by his or her victim may be sufficient to arrest. In other cases, it may require the combination of many bits of information and evidence to reach the level of probable cause. In any event,

De facto arrest
An individual would reasonably believe he or she was under arrest even though it was not the intention of the officer to arrest.

Probable cause as it applies to an arrest
Facts and circumstances that would lead a reasonable person to believe that a crime has occurred and a particular person has committed it.

there must be a reasonable commonsense conclusion that the suspect committed a criminal act. Who makes the probable cause decision? As previously discussed, judges and grand juries have the opportunity to examine and consider evidence presented to them in a court environment. However, law enforcement officers often must make probable cause decisions during dynamic and volatile events. The decision to make a warrantless arrest is usually made on the street by a single individual officer. An incorrect decision could result in a lawsuit for a false arrest or in the exclusion of critical evidence. Consider the following decisions.

On the Street

Is there probable cause to arrest?

Bennie's Bagel Bistro is robbed a few minutes after it opened. When the police arrived seven minutes later, the clerk excitedly told them that a white man had just pulled a rifle on her and demanded all of the money from the cash register. She described the robber as approximately 25 years of age, shorter than the average man with a bad complexion. She also stated he had bright red, curly hair and was a little on the pudgy side. She thought he was wearing a white T-shirt with some writing on the front, jeans, and Michael Jordan basketball shoes. She said she knew they were Jordans because she recently bought some for her boyfriend. The suspect put the cash in a Bennie's paper sack. The police put out a broadcast with the description.

Fifteen minutes later an officer spotted a man hiding under a railroad car about a mile from the bagel shop. When the man came out from under the car, the officer realized that he was a white man in his early twenties. He was 5 feet 6 inches tall and weighed 185 pounds. He was wearing a white t-shirt emblazoned with the word "Heat" in bold black letters. He was also wearing jeans and Nike basketball shoes though they were Lebron James versions, not Air Jordans. The officer found a Bennie's Bagel bag nearby on the ground with a wad of cash inside. Does the officer have probable cause to arrest this suspect for the armed robbery? ▪

On the Street

Another Probable Cause Decision

A woman was sexually assaulted in a mall parking lot. She was unable to give an accurate description of the man because it was dark, but she told the police that she knew exactly who had assaulted her. She said it was Brian who worked as a cashier at the computer store in the mall. She had visited the store an hour earlier and Brian had waited on her. He was very pushy and asked her some inappropriate questions concerning whether she viewed porn on her computer. She also recognized the "horrid" cologne that he had been wearing. The police, upon checking with the store's management, determined that Brian had left the store without permission shortly after the victim had visited the store. Their security video confirmed this. Do the police have probable cause to arrest Brian? ▨

The Role of Statutory Law in the Probable Cause Arrest Decision

The probable cause standard for arrest requires a reasonable belief that a crime has been committed. Therefore, the decision maker, whether it is the arresting officer or an official issuing a warrant, must have a basic understanding of criminal statutes. In addition to a reasonable belief that a particular person is the perpetrator, the actions of the suspect must constitute a violation of law. For example, in the first On the Street scenario on page 55, it would be reasonable to believe that a person who pulled a rifle on the clerk and demanded money had committed a serious offense. It is not, however, necessary to know the exact elements of each specific criminal offense. The knowledge of whether the action constitutes a specific degree of robbery is not a requisite for a probable cause arrest.

Arrest by Private Citizens

The right of a private citizen to make an arrest is determined by the state law in which the arrest occurs. The authority varies a great deal from state to state. Some jurisdictions allow private citizens to make arrests only in circumstances where they actually witness the offender committing the crime in their presence. For example, if a citizen observed a suspect breaking into a car, the citizen would have the right to use reasonable force to arrest the individual. A few states allow citizens to make arrests based on probable cause in felony cases giving them essentially the same arrest authority as law enforcement. Many states also provide statutes specifically allowing arrests by private merchants for theft-related offenses. Law enforcement generally discourages private citizens from making arrests due to the danger involved.

Arrest Warrants

Arrest warrants provide the authority to arrest. They do not expire until the person has been arrested or the warrant has been rescinded. Officers are not required to have the warrant in their possession in order to effect an arrest. They may rely on radio transmission, electronic data, or even the word of another officer. The arresting officer does not need to be aware of the probable cause justification, only the existence of the arrest warrant. Arrest warrants are also valid across state lines, thus allowing a law enforcement officer in one state to make an arrest based on a warrant issued in another. If an officer from one state arrests a person relying on a warrant issued in another state, the suspect will be held in the state of the arrest until **extradition** proceedings are held.

Extradition
The legal procedure in the state where the arrest is made which determines the validity of the warrant and whether to transfer the arrestee back to the originating state.

Extradition is a legal procedure in which the state where the arrest is made determines the validity of the warrant and determines if the arrestee should be transferred back to the originating state. For example, if a suspect was arrested in Kentucky for a murder in Colorado, Kentucky could order the suspect be extradited back to Colorado. States seldom extradite in misdemeanor cases.

The Search Authority of an Arrest Warrant

Arrest warrants also provide limited search authority. With an arrest warrant, the police may enter a suspect's home if they have reasonable belief that he or she is present. They are only allowed to search for the suspect. While they may discover evidence in plain view while looking for the suspect, the arrest warrant does not give them the authority to conduct a more extensive evidence search. In *Maryland v. Buie*, the Supreme Court also authorized a **protective sweep** search of the premises for suspects.

Protective sweep
A quick search of the premises to determine the presence of individuals who might cause harm to officers.

MARYLAND v. BUIE

494 U.S. 325 (1990)

The Facts: On February 3, 1986, a Godfather's Pizza in Prince George County, Maryland, was robbed by two men. One of the men was described as wearing a red running suit. After a brief investigation, police obtained arrest warrants for Jerome Edward Buie and his accomplice, Lloyd Allen. On February 5, the police went to Buie's home in an effort to arrest him. They first called his home and talked to him so they knew that he was present. Several officers entered the house and fanned out through the first and second floors. Corporal James Rozar shouted into the basement ordering anyone present to come out. He announced three times, "this is the police, show me your hands." Jerome Buie came up the stairs and was arrested. Detective Joseph Frolich then went down into the basement to determine if anyone else was present. As he searched the basement, he discovered a red running suit lying on a stack of clothing and seized it as evidence.

The Decision: The Court allowed the evidence. They ruled that the police could conduct a protective sweep of a home in conjunction with an in-home arrest when the searching officer possesses a reasonable belief based on specific and articulable facts that the area to be swept harbors an individual posing a danger to those on the arrest scene.

This limited search pursuant to an arrest warrant does not give the police the right to search a third-party's property, however. In *Steagald v. United States*, 425 U.S. 204, (1981), police searched the home of Steagald in an effort to arrest Ricky Lyons. Armed with an arrest warrant and information that Lyons was in Steagald's home, they conducted a search and discovered drugs. The U.S. Supreme Court ruled that the drugs were inadmissible because the homeowner, Steagald, had Fourth Amendment protection against unreasonable search and seizure.

On the Street

May the police search?

A felony arrest warrant has been issued for Candice Menutia. When the police knock on her door in late afternoon, there is no answer. They hear a dog barking. They cannot see inside any of the windows. Can they enter? Why or why not?

Exigent Circumstances Relating to Arrests

Exigent circumstances
Extraordinary and emergency circumstances that allow the police to conduct a search for persons or evidence without first obtaining a warrant.

Police officers often encounter extraordinary or emergency situations in which quick action is necessary to prevent harm to another, apprehend a suspect, or prevent the destruction of evidence. The situations are considered **exigent circumstances** that allow the police to conduct warrantless intrusions or searches.

Exigent Circumstances
1. Hot pursuit
2. Danger to persons
3. Imminent escape of suspect
4. Immediate destruction of evidence

Hot Pursuit

When the police have legal justification to arrest an individual, they may pursue that person in order to make the arrest. If the suspect flees the police, they may pursue the suspect wherever he or she goes even if the chase leads them onto private property. If a suspect runs into a home or other private building, the police may enter without a warrant. They are limited to searching only for the suspect or any evidence that the suspect might destroy during the pursuit. This type of pursuit often leads to other evidence that the police observe in plain view during their search for the suspect. In 1976, the U.S. Supreme Court considered whether a pursuit could begin in the door of a house.

UNITED STATES v. SANTANA

427 U.S. 38 (1976)

The Facts: As a result of an undercover drug investigation, the Philadelphia Narcotics Squad had probable cause to arrest "Mom" Santana who had just been involved in a narcotics transaction. They had reason to believe that she had just provided heroin to another suspect whom the police had arrested and that she now held the "bait" money that had been provided by the police. The police spotted Santana standing in the doorway of her Philadelphia house. They shouted,

"Police," and Santana ran back into her home. The police followed her into her home without a warrant. As she was running away she dropped the bag that contained "two bundles of glazed paper packets with a white powder." They arrested her and discovered cash that included the bait money in her pockets.

The Decision: The court allowed the search concluding that a hot pursuit that began in a public place could be continued even though the suspect ran to a private area. Even though the threshold of Santana's home was private property, she had exposed herself to the police officers.

> While it may be true that under the common law of property the threshold of one's dwelling is "private," as is the yard surrounding the house, it is nonetheless clear that under the cases interpreting the Fourth Amendment Santana was in a "public" place. She was not in an area where she had any expectation of privacy. "What a person knowingly exposes to the public, even in his own house or office, is not a subject of Fourth Amendment protection." *Katz v. United States*, 389 U.S. 347, 351 (1967). She was not merely visible to the public but was as exposed to public view, speech, hearing, and touch as if she had been standing completely outside her house. *Hester v. United States*, 265 U.S. 57, 59 (1924).

Danger to Persons

If the police have reason to believe that someone is in danger, the police may enter a premises without a warrant in order to prevent the harm. Their action to rescue the individual may also result in an arrest of a person causing the harm. This exception to the warrant requirement of the Fourth Amendment often occurs when the police respond to a crime in progress. They may discover circumstances that require their immediate entry and response. These types of entries may result from an assault or robbery in progress, or they may encounter a house on fire. In addition to arrests, these exigent circumstance entries often result in the discovery of evidence as well.

On the Street

Police to the Rescue

Candace, while taking her precious poodle for a walk, hears yelling and screaming from inside one of her neighbor's homes. She has heard rumors that the couple that lives at the house has had some domestic violence incidents in the past. Candace calls the police. When the police arrive, they do not hear anything at first. As they walk toward the front door, they hear glass breaking and a woman screaming. Upon finding the front door unlocked, they immediately enter to assess the situation. They run through the house and find a woman bleeding on the bathroom floor. The shower door has been shattered and a man is standing over her threatening to hit her again. The police arrest the man for felonious assault. Were the police allowed to enter the house without first obtaining a warrant?

MICHIGAN v. FISHER

130 S.Ct. 546 (2009)

The Facts: Police officers responded to a disturbance complaint in Brownstown, Michigan. Upon their arrival, they were met by a couple who directed them to a house where a man was "going crazy." The officers found a number of indicators of disarray. They found a pickup truck in the driveway with the front end smashed, damaged fence posts, and three broken windows in the house with the glass still on the ground. They also discovered blood on the hood of the truck, on some clothes inside the cab, and on one of the doors of the house. Through a window, they saw Jeremy Fisher screaming and throwing things. A sofa blocked the front door and the rear door was locked. Fisher refused to answer the door. The officers, who could see that Fisher had a cut on his hand, asked him if he needed medical attention, but he refused to answer. He then cursed the officers and told them to get a search warrant. At that point, officers forced the front door partially open and entered the house. Fisher then pointed a long gun at the officers. They withdrew under the threat. Fisher was ultimately arrested and charged with assault with a dangerous weapon and possession of a firearm during the commission of a felony under Michigan law.

The Decision: The U.S. Supreme Court allowed the warrantless entry. They reiterated their previous view that officers may enter a premise without a warrant if there is a "need to assist persons who are seriously injured or threatened with such injury." They stated that a law enforcement officer "may enter a home without a warrant to render emergency assistance to an injured occupant or to protect an occupant from imminent injury." They further indicated that the officer's decision to enter required only "an objectively reasonable basis for believing" that the occupant needed emergency aid.

Escape of Suspect

In most circumstances, law enforcement officers may not enter a premise without a warrant or consent in order to make an arrest. However, they may enter without a warrant if it is necessary to prevent the escape of an offender who has committed a serious offense. This exception to the Fourth Amendment warrant requirement does not apply to minor offenses. Some state jurisdictions impose a more restrictive view, requiring that the offender has committed a violent serious crime such as robbery or murder.

Immediate Destruction of Evidence

The police may also conduct warrantless entries in order to prevent the immediate destruction of physical evidence. This exigency is addressed in a detailed discussion of warrantless searches later in this chapter.

Search Incidental to Arrest

Search incidental to arrest
A search conducted pursuant to a lawful arrest.

Law enforcement officers may search a suspect upon physical arrest. This is considered a **search incidental to arrest**. According to the Federal Bureau of Investigation over 12 million arrests were made in the United States in 2011. Every time a police officer makes an arrest the officer is exposed to a potentially dangerous situation. Suspects may be carrying weapons that could be used to harm the officer or others. They also may be in possession of evidence or contraband that they could easily discard or destroy if not discovered at the time of the arrest. The moment of arrest is particularly dangerous because the suspect knows that he or she is going to be physically restrained and transported to jail. Some suspects realize it is the last best opportunity to escape or dispose of evidence. They may also attempt to discard or destroy evidence during the transport to the correctional facility. Due to these considerations, a search incidental to arrest is justified regardless of the gravity of the charge. The rule is applied to felonies and misdemeanors alike as the search is legally justified by the arrest, and the officer may search for weapons and other evidence. The U.S. Supreme Court addressed the issue in the 1973 landmark case of *United States v. Robinson* in 1973.

UNITED STATES v. ROBINSON

414 U.S. 218 (1973)

The Facts: As stated by the Court:

> On April 23, 1968, at approximately 11 P.M., Officer Richard Jenks, a 15-year veteran of the District of Columbia Metropolitan Police Department, observed the respondent driving a 1965 Cadillac near the intersection of 8th and C Streets, N. E., in the District of Columbia. Jenks, as a result of a previous investigation following a check of **respondent**'s operator's permit four days earlier, determined there was reason to believe that respondent was operating a motor vehicle after the revocation of his operator's permit. This is an offense defined by statute in the District of Columbia which carries a **mandatory minimum** jail term, a mandatory minimum fine, or both. D.C. Code Ann. 40-302 (d) (1967).
>
> Jenks signaled respondent to stop the automobile, which respondent did, and all three of the occupants emerged from the car. At that point Jenks informed respondent that he was under arrest for "**operating after revocation** and obtaining a permit by misrepresentation." It was assumed by the Court of Appeals, and is conceded by the respondent here, that Jenks had [414 U.S. 218, 221] probable cause to arrest respondent, and that he affected a full-custody arrest.
>
> In accordance with procedures prescribed in police department instructions, Jenks then began to search [414 U.S. 218, 222] respondent. He explained at a subsequent hearing that he was "face-to-face" with the respondent, and "placed [his] hands on [the respondent], my right-hand to his [414 U.S. 218, 223] left breast like this (demonstrating) and proceeded to pat him down thus [with the right hand]." During this pat down, Jenks felt an object in the left breast pocket of the heavy coat respondent was wearing, but testified that he "couldn't tell what it was" and also that

Respondent
The party responding to an appeal.

Mandatory minimum
Criminal statutes that require mandatory sentences thus taking discretion on sentencing away from the judge.

Operating after revocation
Driving with a revoked driver's license.

he "couldn't actually tell the size of it." Jenks then reached into the pocket and pulled out the object, which turned out to be a "crumpled up cigarette package." Jenks testified that at this point he still did not know what was in the package: "As I felt the package I could feel objects in the package but I couldn't tell what they were. . . . I knew they weren't cigarettes."

The officer then opened the cigarette pack and found 14 gelatin capsules of white powder that he thought to be, and which later analysis proved to be, heroin. Jenks then continued his search of respondent, feeling around his waist and trouser legs, and examining his remaining pockets. The heroin seized from the respondent was admitted into evidence at the trial which resulted in his conviction in the District Court.

The Decision: The Court determined that the search was reasonable and upheld Mr. Robinson's conviction for possession of drugs. The U.S. Supreme Court stated: "It is well settled that a search incident to a lawful arrest is a traditional exception to the warrant requirement of the Fourth Amendment. This general exception has historically been formulated into two distinct propositions. The first is that a search may be made of the person of the **arrestee** by virtue of the lawful arrest. The second is that a search may be made of the area within the control of the arrestee." The 14 gelatin capsules of heroin were admissible.

Arrestee
A person who has been placed under arrest.

The justification of a search incidental to arrest is fairly straightforward. The search is valid so long as the arrest is legal. It is not unusual that the discovered evidence involves a crime unrelated to the initial arrest. Robinson was initially arrested for driving on a revoked license yet the contraband discovered in the search led to federal drug charges. If a police officer arrested a person for theft but discovered a weapon in that person's pants during the search incidental to arrest, the gun would be admissible toward a weapons charge. Simple arrests may result in more complicated and serious criminal charges when evidence of additional crimes is discovered.

An officer searching incidental to arrest is not limited to a pat down of the clothing. The officer may intrude into a suspect's pockets, shoes, under the hat, under the waistband, and other areas in which evidence or weapons could be hidden. However, most individual states have specific guidelines regulating strip and body cavity searches. Those searches are usually conducted within the confines of a correctional facility under supervision and, in some instances, with a court order. States always have the right to impose more privacy protection but never less than those provided by the U.S. Supreme Court.

Constitutional law does not consider gender when applying the rules of search incidental to arrest. An officer may conduct a search of a suspect of the opposite sex so long as they are complying with the rules of arrest and search. However, many law enforcement agencies adopt internal policies regulating such searches. Many police departments require a search to be conducted by a same-sex officer unless an emergency exists or if a same-sex officer is not available. Again, these are internal administrative regulations and are not required by law. If an officer exceeded the bounds of a reasonable search, they could also be sued in a civil action for damages.

On the Street

Is the cocaine admissible?

Officer Karam responds to a silent burglar alarm at Walt's Fried Fish Emporium, a popular local restaurant. As he approaches the business, he realizes that the front door glass is broken out and there is a man standing behind the cash register attempting to pry it open. Officer Karam points his service weapon at the intruder and demands that he slowly exit the building. The burglar does. Once outside, Karam orders him to lie down on the ground. Karam then places handcuffs on the suspect and searches his clothing. In the right front pocket of his cargo pants, the officer finds what appears to be crack cocaine. Further chemical analysis confirms his suspicions. In addition to the breaking and entering, the suspect is prosecuted for possession of crack cocaine. Is the cocaine admissible? Why or why not? ▪

Search Within the Immediate Reach and Control

The Court in *Robinson* stated that a search may be made of the area within the control of the arrestee. As a result of that language, the police are not limited to searching the person only. They are also permitted to search the area in which the arrested person could reasonably reach for a weapon or destroy evidence. If they legally arrest a person sitting on a sofa, they could certainly reach underneath the cushions to check for accessible weapons or to ensure that the suspect had not hid evidence during the arrest. On the other hand, an arrest of a suspect in the living room of his or her home would not justify the search of the garage. It would be unreasonable to believe that the arrestee could reasonably obtain a weapon from the garage. The difficulty with this legal standard is determining the reasonable scope of the search. The courts have not drawn a bright line rule indicating exactly how many feet or describing a specific circumference though they have rendered a number of decisions that provide parameters.

   In the 1969 case of *Chimel v. California*, police went to the home of Ted Steven Chimel to arrest him pursuant to an arrest warrant for the burglary of a coin shop. Though he was not at home, his wife invited the officers inside. They sat in the living room until he arrived home from work at which time they placed him under arrest. They asked Chimel if they could look around the house and he refused. They falsely told him that the warrant gave them the right to search, and they conducted a full search of the premises. They had his wife open drawers in the master bedroom and a sewing room. As a result they found coins and other items taken from the burglaries. The Supreme Court ruled that the search was unconstitutional in that it went beyond the area within Chimel's immediate reach and control. The case addressed the issue that is raised by many arrests. Where could the suspect reasonably reach to either grab a weapon or destroy evidence? In this case it would be unreasonable to think that Chimel could reach into his bedroom or sewing room from the point of arrest in the living room. *Chimel v. California*, 395 U.S. 752 (1969).

VALE v. LOUISIANA

399 U.S. 30 (1970)

The Facts: On April 24, 1967, police set up a surveillance of the home of Donald Vale for whom they had two warrants for his arrest on narcotics charges. They observed a green Chevy stop in front of Vale's house. Vale came out of the house, walked to the car, and spoke briefly with the occupants. The driver of the car was known to the police as a local narcotics addict. Vale briefly went back into his house and then returned to the car. He then engaged in what officers believed to be a drug deal. When the officer approached them, the car attempted to pull away but was blocked in by police. The officers observed the driver swallowing something. Vale turned and started walking back toward his house but the police arrested him just as he reached his front porch. At this point an officer went inside Vale's house and made a quick sweep to determine if anyone else was inside. No one was inside, but Vale's sister and mother came in from shopping a few minutes later. The officers then conducted a full search of Vale's house and found illegal narcotics in a rear bedroom. The drugs were used against him in his subsequent trial for possession of heroin. Vale was convicted and sentenced to 15 years in prison.

The Decision: The attorney general of Louisiana argued that the police lawfully searched the house incident to arrest. However the Supreme Court disagreed. They explained that the police could search only those areas that would have been in the immediate reach and control of the suspect at the time of arrest. The police were not permitted to move Vale to another location and then claim that the area was then within his reach and control. It would have been unreasonable to believe that Vale could reach the rear bedroom of his house from his front porch steps. The U.S. Supreme Court overturned Vale's conviction and ruled that the search of his home was illegal. The arrest warrants for Vale certainly justified his arrest. The warrants did not, however, allow the search of the house, and the search was not within Vale's immediate reach and control. The police should have obtained a separate search warrant.

On the Street

What if the suspect voluntarily changes locations?

It is a scorching hot summer day. Renee is sunbathing in a skimpy bikini beside her apartment pool when she is confronted by two uniform police officers. They inform her that they have a warrant for her arrest and ask her for some identification. She confirms that she is the Renee they are looking for, and she reaches for her purse that is underneath her lawn chair. One of the officers grabs the purse and tells her he will have to look through it first. She says fine. He looks in her purse and discovers a small-caliber handgun. Renee does not have a permit. When the officers inform her that she must go with them to the downtown jail she asks if she can go to her apartment and change clothes. She says she wants to be cooperative but she does not want to go to jail in her swimsuit. They agree. However, they inform her that if she is going to get clothes out of her closet or her drawers, they must search them first. Do they have the right to search? Did they have the right to search her purse? Why or why not? ▣

On the Street

The porch beer cooler?

Deputy Diamond has an arrest warrant for Leon for failing to pay child support. The warrant states that Leon resides at 944 Rose Avenue. When the deputy arrives at the residence, he sees Leon sitting in the front porch swing. Next to him is a large red ice chest. Leon has a beer in his hand. After confirming Leon's identity, the officer informs him of the warrant and tells him he is under arrest. The officer then opens the lid of the cooler. In addition to the ice cold beer, Leon has a large plastic freezer bag full of marijuana in the cooler. Is it admissible? Why or why not? ▣

Search of Contents of Cell Phones

"These cases require us to decide how the search incident to arrest doctrine applies to modern cell phones, which are now such a pervasive and insistent part of daily life that the proverbial visitor from Mars might conclude they were an important feature of human anatomy." Chief Justice Roberts in Riley v. California.

On June 25, 2014, the U.S. Supreme Court addressed the first significant cases regarding the warrantless examination of a cell phone seized incidental to arrest. In companion cases, the Court, without dissent, ruled that law enforcement may not examine the data contents of a cell phone or smartphone even though the device itself was legally seized congruent to a lawful arrest.

DAVID LEON RILEY v. CALIFORNIA/UNITED STATES v. BRIMA WURIE

573 U.S. ____ (2014)

The Facts: Police in San Diego, California, pulled over David Leon Riley for driving with an expired license tag. During the traffic stop they also discovered that his operator's license had been suspended. Pursuant to departmental policy his car was impounded. An inventory search of his vehicle revealed two handguns. Riley was subsequently physically arrested for carrying concealed and loaded firearms. While searching Riley incident to arrest, the police retrieved a "smart phone" from his pants pocket. The phone was a "smart phone" which had a broad range of functions including advanced computing, Internet connectivity, and mass storage capacity.

The arresting officer examined the phone's information and discovered a number of references to the letters "CK" which was believed to represent "Crip Killers," a slang term associated with the Bloods gang. A couple of hours after the initial arrest, another detective conducted a more intensive examination of the phone in an effort to find evidence of gang activity. In addition to a variety of gang-related videos, the examination revealed a photograph of Riley standing in front of a car that had been involved in a recent gang shooting. Riley was ultimately charged with attempted murder in relation to that shooting. The charges also included enhanced sentencing due to the involvement of gang activity.

At trial, the officers' testimony concerning the contents of the cell phone was allowed over the defense objections. Riley was convicted and received a sentence of 15 years to life.

In the companion case, Brima Wurie was arrested after making an apparent drug sale. The search incident to arrest revealed two cell phones including a "flip phone" which did not have the same broad range of computing features as in the Riley case. When Wurie was taken to the station, the police noticed that the phone was receiving repeated calls from a phone number labeled "my house." Police linked the number with a specific apartment by tracing it via an online phone directory. They then visited the building, saw Wurie's name on a mailbox, and observed a woman through a window that resembled the wallpaper photograph on Wurie's phone. They secured the apartment and obtained a search warrant for Wurie's residence. The search revealed a firearm, ammunition, cash, marijuana, drug paraphernalia, and 215 grams of crack cocaine.

Wurie was charged with distribution of crack cocaine, possession with intent to distribute, and possession of a firearm by a felon. The trial judge denied his efforts to exclude from trial the evidence from his phone and his apartment. He was convicted of all counts and sentenced to 262 months in prison. A divided panel of the First Circuit of the U.S. Court of Appeals overturned his conviction based on the District Court's evidentiary ruling. The U.S. prosecutor appealed.

The Decision: The Court unanimously agreed that the digital evidence gathered from the phones in both cases was obtained in violation of the Fourth Amendment. Justice Roberts wrote the majority opinion that discussed the role of the cell phone in modern society. In addition to the previous reference to the "martian" viewpoint of our world, Justice Roberts wrote; "Even the word cellphone is a misnomer. They could just as easily be called cameras, video players, Rolodexes, calendars, tape recorders, libraries, diaries, albums, televisions, maps or newspapers."

The court concluded that the touchstone for a decision of a warrantless search was whether the search was reasonable. As part of their discussion, they compared the current case to *United States v. Robinson*, the landmark case on search incidental to arrest. In Robinson, there was a concern about officer safety as well as the immediate destruction of evidence. Since then the court has identified those as exigent circumstances allowing a warrantless search. However, they said there was no comparison between the contents of the cigarette package in Robinson to the digital contents of a modern cell phone. The phone's contents posed no danger to the officer, and once the phone was secured, there was no danger that the contents could be destroyed prior to the obtaining of a warrant. The Court allowed that it was certainly permissible to seize the phone incidental to arrest and to take precautions to ensure that the data were not remotely wiped, but they would not allow the warrantless extraction of the data. At one juncture, the government argued that searching the data was not any different than searching a purse, billfold, or address book found on an arrestee. Chief Roberts stated:

> That is like saying a ride on horseback is materially indistinguishable from a flight to the moon. Both are ways of getting from point A to point B, but little else justifies lumping them together. Modern cell phones, as a category, implicate privacy concerns far beyond those implicated by the search of a cigarette pack, a wallet, or a purse. A conclusion that inspecting the contents of an arrestee's pockets works no substantial additional intrusion on privacy beyond the arrest itself may make sense as applied to physical items, but any extension of that reasoning to digital data has to rest on its own bottom.

In a comprehensive decision, the Court excluded the data retrieved from the defendant's phones in both cases and ruled that absent exigent circumstances, police may not conduct a warrantless search for digital information.

Detention Facility Search

Suspects who are placed under arrest are usually transported to a detention facility such as a local jail. While the police are allowed to search a suspect upon arrest, there may also be circumstances in which they need to conduct a more comprehensive search once the arrestee is detained inside the jail. The U.S. Supreme Court addressed that issue in *United States v. Edwards,* 415 U.S. 800 (1974). The U.S. Post Office in Lebanon, Ohio, was the target of a break-in on the night of May 31, 1970. There were loose paint chips on the windowsill and wire mesh screen as a result of an attempt to pry open the window. The defendant Edwards was arrested near the scene and transported to the Lebanon City Jail. The next morning, he was given new trousers and a shirt. The clothing he was wearing at the time of arrest was taken and examined more closely. Paint chips gathered from Edward's clothes matched those of the post office window. The Court confirmed that a search of the suspect was allowed at the detention facility even though it was not contemporaneous with the initial arrest. Corrections officers are also allowed to conduct a full search of the arrestee in order to ensure security of the facility and to protect the suspect's property.

Search of Closed Containers

While the police are allowed to search an arrestee incidental to arrest, the issue becomes more difficult when a closed container is taken by the police subsequent to the arrest. The police may certainly search a purse being carried by the individual being arrested. However, if an item is seized and is not reasonably accessible by the defendant, a search warrant or some other legal justification may be required. Closed containers within automobiles may be searched without a warrant if the police have probable cause to believe there is evidence in the container.

Blood Extraction

Intrusions into a person's body have also been scrutinized by the courts. One of the more common situations involves the extraction of blood in drunk driving investigations.

SCHMERBER v. CALIFORNIA

384 U.S. 757 (1966)

The Facts: The Defendant was injured in an automobile accident in which he was driving. He was transported to a local hospital for treatment. The investigating officer detected several factors that indicated the defendant may have been driving under the influence of alcohol and placed him under arrest at the hospital. At that point, the officer asked the defendant if he would consent to a blood test, and he refused. Against the defendant's will, the officer directed medical personnel to extract blood for analysis of alcohol content. The analysis indicated impairment due to alcohol intoxication. The defendant was convicted of driving under the influence of alcohol due, in part, to the blood alcohol evidence. He appealed his case arguing that the intrusion into his body was a violation of the Fourth Amendment protection against unreasonable search and seizures and due process of law.

The Decision: The Court affirmed his conviction. They examined the balance between the minor intrusion and the necessity for gathering evidence. They determined that the routine extraction of blood at the hospital was a minor intrusion and that it was not a violation of due process of law. It did not reach the level of intrusion that was present in the *Rochin v. California* stomach pumping. They also ruled that the taking of blood was not a violation of the Fifth Amendment protection of self-incrimination.

Most states have enacted **implied consent laws** to supplement their statutes on driving while intoxicated. Implied consent laws state that the drivers of motor vehicles grant consent to blood alcohol testing if there is probable cause to believe their ability to drive is impaired because of alcohol or drugs. That means that drivers have preconsented. If a driver refuses consent, the consequences usually include license suspensions. The suspension is not contingent upon a conviction for DUI.

Implied consent laws Statutes associated with drunk driving offenses in which by operating a motor vehicle, the driver has given an implied consent to a test to determine blood alcohol levels.

Exigent Circumstances: Immediate Destruction of Evidence

As previously mentioned in this chapter, exigent circumstances involve extraordinary situations that allow the police to enter a premise without a warrant. The discussion addressed the immediate danger to persons, hot pursuit, and the imminent escape of a suspect. Police may also conduct a search of an individual or property for evidence when it is reasonable to believe that the evidence will be destroyed if they do not act immediately. This may occur when a suspect attempts to destroy evidence by washing gunpowder residue from his or her hands, flushing drugs down the toilet, or even swallowing contraband. The Supreme Court addressed the issue involving the personal search of a murder suspect in 1973.

CUPP v. MURPHY

412 U.S. 291 (1973)

The Facts: On the morning of August 25, 1967, Doris Murphy was found murdered in her Portland, Oregon, home. The investigating detectives observed lacerations and bruising on her throat. There were no signs of any struggle or forced entry. The detectives learned from the victim's son that Daniel Murphy, his father and the victim's former husband, had a hostile relationship with Mrs. Murphy. Later that afternoon, Daniel Murphy, having learned of the murder, contacted the Portland Police and agreed to come in for questioning. Murphy arrived at the Portland Police station around 7:45 P.M. and was questioned by the detectives. He was joined by two criminal defense attorneys. During the questioning, the detectives noticed dark material underneath Murphy's fingernails. Suspecting that the victim had been strangled to death, they were concerned that the dark material might be **trace evidence** from her neck. They asked Murphy if they could take scrapings of the material. He refused. Murphy then placed his hands behind his back and attempted to rub them together. He also put his hands in his pants pockets and began rubbing his fingers on his keys and change. At that point, concerned that Murphy was destroying the evidence, the officers took the scrapings against his will. The material was later determined to be blood and skin from Mrs. Murphy's throat as well as fabric from her nightgown. The evidence was presented at trial, and Daniel Murphy was convicted of murder.

The Decision: The U.S. Supreme Court allowed the evidence. They determined that the facts known to the officers certainly provided sufficient probable cause to arrest and that the defendant's actions clearly indicated his intent and motivation to destroy the evidence. If the officers had not acted immediately to secure the evidence, it would have been destroyed.

Trace evidence
Evidence that occurs when there is contact or transfer of fluids, tissue, or other tangible items. Examples include blood, fibers, semen, tissue, paint, and lipstick.

Summary

This chapter has presented a detailed examination of the laws of arrest as well as the limited search powers that are derived from valid arrests. Probable cause provides the foundation for arrest by requiring facts and circumstances that would lead a reasonable person to believe that a person has committed a crime. Probable cause can be established from a variety of sources including investigation and, in some cases, the word of a crime victim. The legal standard must be determined by a judge issuing a warrant, a police officer making a warrantless arrest decision, and in the courts at both the preliminary hearing and grand jury steps.

Lawful arrests also give rise to a number of limited search opportunities. Those include searches incidental to arrest and in conjunction with exigent circumstances. The search authority of an arrest extends beyond the suspect and includes the area within their immediate reach and control in which they could reasonably grab a weapon or destroy evidence. Arrest warrants also offer the power to conduct a limited intrusion in a home to search for a suspect.

Police officers may also conduct warrantless searches in extraordinary circumstances in which the failure to act would result in the immediate destruction of evidence or danger to someone. These exigent circumstances would allow a search in the event of the imminent escape of an individual or if the officers were in hot pursuit of a suspect. Criminal justice professionals who are entrusted with the authority and responsibility of affecting the seizure of another person must understand the laws of arrest, warrants, and probable cause.

Review Questions

1. The police make a physical arrest of a man for domestic violence. May they legally remove his shoes and search inside for evidence or weapons? Why or why not?
2. How far away from an arrestee may the police search for evidence if they do not have an arrest warrant? Explain.
3. Under what circumstances may the police change the area within the immediate reach and control of an arrestee?
4. Why are corrections officers allowed to search suspects detained in their facility without a warrant?
5. The police are questioning a suspect concerning the sale of illegal narcotics. The suspect runs into a bathroom and closes the door. Would the police have the right to enter the bathroom to determine what the suspect was doing? Why or why not?
6. Identify the elements required for a valid arrest.
7. What is the definition of probable cause as it applies to an arrest?
8. Describe four possible sources for probable cause to arrest.
9. Describe the search powers associated with an arrest warrant.
10. Identify and describe the exigent circumstances that would allow the police to conduct a warrantless search for a suspect.

Legal Terminology

Arrest
Arrestee
De facto arrest
Exigent circumstances
Extradition
Implied consent laws
Mandatory minimum

Operating after revocation
Probable cause
Probable cause as it applies to an arrest
Protective sweep
Respondent
Search incidental to arrest
Trace evidence

References

Chimel v. California, 395 U.S. 752 (1969)
Cupp v. Murphy, 412 U.S. 291 (1973)
Maryland v. Buie, 494 U.S. 325 (1990)
Michigan v. Fisher 130 S.Ct. 546 (2009)
Riley v. California, 573 U.S. ____ (2014)
Schmerber v. California, 384 U.S. 757 (1966)
Steagald v. United States, 425 U.S. 204, (1981)
United States v. Edwards, 415 U.S. 800 (1974)
United States v. Robinson, 414 U.S. 218 (1973)
United States v. Santana, 427 U.S. 38 (1976)
United States v. Brima Wurie, 573 U.S. ____ (2014)
Vale v. Louisiana, 399 U.S. 30 (1970)

Chapter 6
Stop and Frisk

In 1966, the U.S. Supreme Court provided law enforcement with an extraordinary investigative tool. Every police officer in the country now knows or should know how to both legally and tactically conduct a *Terry v. Ohio* stop and frisk. The procedure allows police to temporarily detain an individual and investigate his or her behavior without the necessity of probable cause or an arrest. In fact, these temporary detentions seldom result in an arrest. The stop and frisk procedure is not only considered to be an effective investigative technique but also a powerful crime prevention tool. The procedure is not without controversy.

There has always been concern over the fact that many stop and frisks are conducted against innocent people. Allegations have also arisen that stop and frisks are conducted in a racially disparate manner. Beginning in 2011, there were a series of protests across the United States by groups who would camp out in urban areas. While their primary targets were economic policies, they also expressed their discontent about a variety of societal concerns. The *Washington Post* reported on November 1, 2011, that the Occupy Brooklyn protesters were, in part, protesting the New York City Police Department's policies on stop and frisk. Some of the protesters shouted, *"Stop and frisk don't stop the crime; stop and frisk is the crime."* Regardless, stop and frisk has been continually used as a crime prevention and investigative procedure by police across the country.

TERRY v. OHIO

392 U.S. 1 (1968)

The Facts: It all began with Detective Martin McFadden of the Cleveland Police Department. Detective McFadden, 62 years old, had served as an officer for 39 years, 35 as a detective. For three decades, he had worked in the high-crime areas of downtown Cleveland where shoplifters, pickpockets, and other criminals were

Plainclothes
Common description of a police officer working without wearing a uniform.

prevalent. He was working a **plainclothes** detail the afternoon of October 31, 1963, when he noticed the behavior of two men, later identified as John Terry and Richard Chilton. McFadden snuggled inside the recess of a storefront near Euclid Avenue and Huron Road in order to watch them more carefully. Alternating, the men walked down Huron, peered into the window of Zucker's Store, and then returned to the corner. They each made five or six trips down the sidewalk to check out the store. A third man, Katz, momentarily joined them on the corner but then walked away. A few minutes later, all three congregated in front of Zucker's store. Suspicious that the three were casing the store for a robbery, Detective McFadden moved toward the men.

Upon carefully approaching the men, McFadden identified himself as a police officer and asked for their identification. In response to his request, the men mumbled. They did not provide him with identification nor did they say anything to clear up his concerns about their suspicious actions. At that point, McFadden grabbed Terry and spun him around. He patted down the outside of his coat and felt a gun in the left breast pocket. However, McFadden couldn't get the gun out at that moment. With Terry between him and the other two men, McFadden ordered all three inside Zucker's store. As they went in, he pulled off Terry's coat and extracted the pistol. He ordered all three to put their hands against the wall. He patted the outer clothing of both Katz and Chilton. McFadden found another gun on Chilton but nothing on Katz. He asked the store clerk to call the police for further assistance. Chilton and Terry were arrested and charged with carrying concealed weapons. Katz was released.

The weapons were introduced at trial, and both men were convicted. Upon appeal they argued that the detective had no right to stop and search them.

The case posed an interesting problem for the court. At first blush, it seemed to turn on the issue of probable cause. But this was not a probable cause case. At the moment that the detective physically stopped Terry and Chilton and put his hands on them to pat them down, he did not have probable cause to arrest. McFadden had no evidence that a crime had been committed. He was operating upon his own concerns that a crime was going to be committed. He actually stopped them because he thought they were going to commit a crime. This was an issue that the Supreme Court had not previously addressed.

The Decision: The Court was called upon to address a procedure involving real life on the street. On one hand, there was a need for law enforcement to have a workable and flexible procedure for dealing with crime as it unfolds. Do they have to wait until a crime has occurred before they can act? On the other hand, doesn't a citizen have a right to live free of government or police intrusion without some legal justification such as probable cause or a warrant? The court reached its answer by dissecting McFadden's actions. By doing so, they clearly identified the acceptable police procedure for managing these "on the street" confrontations.

The Court's words:

We merely hold today that where a police officer observes unusual conduct which leads him reasonably to conclude in light of his experience that criminal activity may be afoot and that the persons with whom he is dealing may be armed and presently dangerous, where in the course of investigating this behavior he identifies himself as a policeman and makes reasonable inquiries, and where nothing in the initial stages of the encounter serves to dispel his reasonable fear for his own or others' safety, he is entitled for the protection of himself and others in the area to conduct a carefully limited search of the outer clothing of such persons in an attempt to discover weapons which might be used to assault him. Such a search is a reasonable search under the Fourth Amendment, and any weapons seized may properly be introduced in evidence against the person from whom they were taken.

The evidence was allowed, and Terry and Chilton's convictions were upheld. The ruling also defined the circumstances in which the stop and frisk procedures could be used. The result of the U.S. Supreme Court's decision was a practical seven-step procedure.

The Steps Required in a *Terry v. Ohio* Stop and Frisk
1. **Reasonable suspicion**
2. **Identify as police officer**
3. **Stop**
4. **General inquiry**
5. **If fear is not dispelled**
6. **Frisk (pat down) for weapons**
7. **If weapon found, then search**

Step One: Reasonable Suspicion

Facts and Circumstances That Would Lead a Reasonable Police Officer to Believe That Criminal Activity Is Afoot

Reasonable suspicion
Facts and circumstances that would lead a reasonable police officer to believe that criminal activity is afoot.

The process begins with the officer acquiring **reasonable suspicion**. This standard of proof is applied by police officers and not private citizens. That is because part of the equation is based upon an officer's own training, experience, and understanding of criminal behavior. In the *Terry* case, Detective McFadden had many years of experience and was certainly knowledgeable about the area where he was working. However, one does not have to be a 39-year police veteran to reasonably believe that the three men were checking out a place to commit a crime.

Articulate
Clearly explain.

The officer must **articulate** or clearly explain the facts and circumstances that comprise the reasonable suspicion. Remember, in these situations, the actual behavior may not constitute a violation of the law. It is certainly not against the law to walk up and down the sidewalk and peer into a store window. But this is not about a violation of the law. It is about conduct that would alert the officer that a crime is either occurring or about to occur. In the *Terry* case, McFadden was able to detail the repeated trips down the street and the continuous casing of the store in question. Based on his experience, McFadden was well aware of the criminal activity in this particular downtown area and that the activities of the men were consistent with someone who may be planning a robbery.

On the Street

Reasonably Suspicious Behavior

An officer is driving his police car patrolling a residential neighborhood. At 3:00 A.M., he notices a man in the side yard of a house. The man runs and hides under a large bush as the patrol car passes. Does the officer have reasonable suspicion? He absolutely does. Based on his observations, knowledge of the neighborhood, and understanding of criminal behavior, it would be reasonable for him to suspect that the man was involved in some type of crime. Therefore, the officer can proceed to the next step.

Step Two: Identification as a Police Officer

The suspect must understand that he or she is being confronted by a law enforcement officer. A suspect's reaction to a police officer would likely be quite different than that of a private citizen. The *Terry* stop and frisk procedure is available only to police officers.

Detective McFadden was working plainclothes so Terry, Chilton, and Katz would have had no idea that he was an officer. His first action upon approaching them was to identify himself as an officer. As a result, they were aware they were responding to someone with law enforcement authority. If a uniformed officer pulled up in a police car, it would be obvious that he was a police officer. It may, however, be necessary to verbalize the identification even if the officer is in uniform if the suspect is not in a position to see and identify the officer, like the suspect in the previous scenario hiding under the bush.

On the Street

Identification as Law Enforcement

Speaking of our guy under the bush, let's check out his progress. The officer observes him run and hide under a bush outside a residence. It is three in the morning. The officer stops his patrol car and sneaks up to the side of the house. As he approaches the bush, he shouts out, "Hey you, under the bush, I'm a police officer, don't move." There is the identification.

Step Three: Stop

Once reasonable suspicion has been established and the identification made, the police officer is allowed to conduct the physical stop. In most street situations, the suspect will voluntarily comply as a result of the simple presence of the officer. The stop often occurs when the officer approaches the suspect and begins a conversation. Sometimes, the officer will specifically direct the suspect to stop.

On occasion, the suspect will attempt to run away whether on foot or in a car. Since the officer already has reasonable suspicion, he now has the right and authority to physically stop the suspect. That might mean grabbing him and spinning him around as Detective McFadden did, or it might constitute chasing him and tackling him. The officer has the right to physically restrain the individual until the rest of the steps have been completed or, of course, longer if an arrest becomes necessary.

On the Street

The Stop

Let's go back to the man hiding under the bush. The officer has now approached him and demanded that he stay still. At this point there are several possibilities. It is likely that the officer, while shining a flashlight on him, would direct him to put his hands up and come out from under the bush. But suppose the suspect took off running and a foot chase ensued. There is still no legal problem. The officer has a right to chase him and stop him. But this is still not necessarily an arrest. The officer cannot use deadly force, and any other physical force would have to be reasonably necessary.

Step Four: General Inquiry

The conducting of the general inquiry is perhaps one of the trickiest issues. In a sense, the general inquiry and the next step are one fluid action. The officer is attempting to find out what is occurring and at the same time ensure his own safety in what is often a dangerous situation. Consider Detective McFadden's actions: When he first approached the men he asked them for their names. It may seem like a simple request, but it served several purposes. By demanding their names or identification, he was hoping to gain some valuable information. In addition to determining who they are, he could ascertain how they were going to respond to him. Were they going to be cooperative and forthcoming or elusive and perhaps dangerous? Also, by learning their names, he may have been preventing further criminal activity. The suspects would have been less likely to commit a crime once an officer had their names.

The Supreme Court did not dictate that McFadden's request for identification was the only acceptable approach. They described this step as a general inquiry in order to determine if criminal activity was, in fact, occurring or if the officer was in danger. Arguably the more common question that police officers ask in this situation is simply, "What are you doing?" An inquiry as to what the suspects are doing is consistent with the objective of the general inquiry. Now back to the man hiding under the bush.

On the Street

The General Inquiry

Our police officer has now told the man hiding under the bush to come out with his hands in the air. It would be logical, reasonable, and legal at this juncture for the officer to ask him what in the world he is doing underneath that bush at three in the morning. It would also have been OK if he asked for identification.

"Just curious, dude, but why are you hiding under these folks' bushes?" ▪

Legal Issue: Are There Any *Miranda* Problems Associated with Asking the Suspect Questions?

No. The general inquiry posed as part of a *Terry v. Ohio* stop and frisk is not considered a custodial interrogation. At the point of the general inquiry, the suspect has only been temporarily detained. His freedom of action has not been deprived in a significant manner; therefore, the police do not have to give the *Miranda* warnings when they talk to him. That would, of course, change in the event the suspect is arrested.

Is the Suspect Required to Answer the Officer's Questions?

No. The Fifth Amendment protects us from self-incrimination. The suspect does not have to say anything. However, silence is not without consequences. As you will see in our discussion of the next step, failure to respond would also fail to relieve the officer's fears and give rise to a frisk. If the suspect was driving a motor vehicle, he or she would be required to produce a driver's license upon request. A nonresponse to that request could result in the driver being arrested and charged with the appropriate driver's license violation. A few states have Stop and Identify offenses that require persons subjected to a stop as a result of reasonable suspicion to identify themselves.

Step Five: The Officer's Fears Are Not Dispelled

A suspect's response to an officer's general inquiry must relieve the officer's fears that the suspect could be dangerous. When Officer McFadden asked Terry, Chilton, and Katz for their names, they responded with indiscernible mumbling. Their nonresponse failed to dispel the detective's fears that the men might have weapons or that they may pose a danger to McFadden or others. At that point, he was authorized to take further action.

Could the suspects have dispelled his fears? Maybe. They could have provided their personal information and identification. They could have told the detective who they were and perhaps explained further that one of them was simply waiting for a girlfriend to get off work at the store because they were all going to the movies and that she was late but her boss didn't want them in the store. Had that been their response, McFadden could have easily verified the information and sent them on their way. Instead their response was one that confirmed rather than denied their likely criminal involvement.

In some situations, it would be impossible to reasonably explain the suspect's conduct. In that event, the officer can proceed to the frisk stage.

On the Street

Are the officer's fears dispelled?

Let's go back to the man hiding under the bush. Our officer has brought him out from under the bush, maybe even at gunpoint, and asked him why he was hiding. This may be one of those situations in which the suspect is unable to say anything that would dispel the fears. What could he possibly say? "I'm waiting on a bus." Nope, a reasonable person waiting on a bus doesn't run from the police and hide in the bushes. "Uh . . . officer . . . uh . . . I live here." Nope. A reasonable person doesn't run from the police at 3:00 A.M. and hide in the bushes of his own home unless he is up to no good. "Uh . . . what . . . you mean this isn't my house?" In this case, it is hard to imagine a viable response. So just like Detective McFadden, our officer is now going to the next step. ▦

Step Six: Frisk

Frisk
A pat down of the outer part of a suspect's clothing.

A **frisk** is a pat down of the outer part of the suspect's clothing for weapons. The concern here is for the officer's personal safety. The suspect has already failed to co-operate or offer a reasonable explanation for his or her conduct. The officer needs to determine if the suspect has a weapon.

The Court has been clear that reasonable suspicion only justifies a frisk for weapons in this circumstance. There is a legal distinction between a "frisk" and a "search." A search is not allowed. A search involves a greater and impermissible intrusion into the suspect's privacy. It would be considered a search if the officer went beyond a pat down by actually intruding into the suspect's clothing. This would include the officer inserting his or her hands inside of pockets to determine what was there or to remove whatever was found. It would also be considered a search if the officer checked inside the suspect's waistband or took off the suspect's hat and looked inside. Reaching inside the suspect's socks or shoes would be a search. Examining the contents of a bag or purse would be considered a search.

The objective of the frisk is to feel for potential weapons. It is not a frisk for evidence other than weapons. The Court was clearly concerned about officer safety. Consider the Court's language:

> The crux of this case, however, is not the propriety of Officer McFadden's taking steps to investigate petitioner's suspicious behavior, but rather, was there justification for McFadden's invasion of Terry's personal security by searching him for weapons in the course of that investigation.
>
> We are now concerned with more than the governmental interest in investigating crime; in addition, there is the more immediate interest of the police officer in taking steps to assure himself that the person with whom he is dealing is not armed with a weapon that could unexpectedly and fatally be used against him. Certainly it would be unreasonable to require that police officers take unnecessary risks in the performance of their duties.

American criminals have a long tradition of armed violence, and every year in this country many law enforcement officers are killed in the line of duty, and thousands more are wounded. Virtually all of these deaths and a substantial portion of the injuries are inflicted with guns and knives.

On the Street

The Frisk for Weapons

As our story continues, the officer now has the suspect out from under the bush. His attempts at explaining why he was hiding have failed, so the officer can now frisk him for weapons. That is perfectly consistent with the Court's holding in *Terry v. Ohio*. But suppose when he pats him down, he feels what would reasonably feel like a butcher knife slid inside the suspect's sock? ▪

Step Seven: If Weapon Found, Search

In the event an officer feels what he or she could reasonably believe to be a weapon, the officer may search that area to determine if the item is, in fact, a weapon.

Upon feeling a gun in Terry's pocket, McFadden searched it. He first took some tactical precautions to make sure he was safe. He apparently could not easily retract the gun so he placed Terry between himself and the other two men. He ordered them inside Zucker's store presumably to give him a safer environment and to protect any outside pedestrians from danger. He then pulled off Terry's coat, inserted his hand in the pocket, and pulled out the gun. He then frisked Chilton. Again, once he felt a gun through Chilton's clothes as well, he was justified in conducting a search. The more intrusive search was allowable at the moment the detective could feel what he reasonably believed to be a weapon. He did not feel a weapon under Katz's clothing so he did not search further.

On the Street

The Frisk Leads to a Search

If our officer ran his hand down the outside of the suspect's sock and felt what reasonably seemed like a long butcher knife, the officer could legally reach inside his sock and pull it out. If it turned out to be a butcher knife, then he could make an arrest for a weapons charge. ▪

The Expansion of Stop and Frisk

The *Terry* stop and frisk steps may unfold quickly. In the 1972 case of *Adams v. Williams*, 407 U.S. 143, Sergeant John Connelly of the Bridgeport, Connecticut, police department conducted such a stop. Early one morning, an individual known to the sergeant informed him that there was a man sitting in a nearby vehicle and that the man had narcotics in his car and a gun stuck inside his waistband. The officer tapped on the car's window and told the driver, Robert Williams, to open his door. Instead of complying, Williams partially rolled the window down. Sergeant Connolly immediately reached in and grabbed William's waistband and discovered a pistol. He retrieved it and arrested Williams on the weapons charge. Subsequent searches of William's vehicle revealed narcotics, a machete, and another gun. The Court concluded that the steps of *Terry v. Ohio* had been followed. Reasonable suspicion was established by the informant. The uniformed officer was in a marked police car. Sergeant Connolly conducted a general inquiry by reasonably asking the suspect to open the door and get out of the car. The suspect's failure to respond to that lawful order constituted a failure to dispel. The grabbing of the suspect's waistband was the obvious target for the frisk since the officer already had information that a gun was present.

The behaviors that lead to reasonable suspicion may not be illegal. The police officer must consider them as a whole. Courts describe this as the totality of circumstances. In a sense, it is the viewing of all of the factors into a combined big picture. The 1989 case of *United States v. Sokolow* provides an excellent illustration of how a combination of behaviors can give rise to reasonable suspicion. As you examine the detailed facts of the case, keep in mind that the rules of travel have changed considerably in the post-911 era. Today, the rules of the Transportation and Safety Administration would not have allowed Sokolow to board a plane.

UNITED STATES v. SOKOLOW

490 U.S. 1 (1989)

The Facts: On Sunday, July 22, 1984, Andrew Sokolow bought two round-trip tickets on board a United Airlines flight from Honolulu, Hawaii, to Miami, Florida. The tickets were open ended, meaning there was no defined date for the return flight. He paid $2,100 in cash for the tickets and peeled the money from a wad of $20 bills described as at least $4,000. He purchased the tickets in the name of Andrew Kray and Janet Dorian. The ticket agent, who subsequently contacted the police, stated that Sokolow was about 25 years of age, dressed in a black jumpsuit with gold jewelry, and that he was extremely nervous. He left a phone number. Neither he nor his female companion checked any of their four pieces of luggage. After their departure, the agent contacted the Honolulu Police Department. The police determined that the phone number was subscribed to Karl Herman. It would later be discovered that Herman and Sokolow were roommates. The ticket agent was able to identify Sokolow's voice on the answering machine. There were no listings for Andrew Kray. Drug Enforcement Administration (DEA) officials and airline officials determined that "Kray" and Norian booked their return from Miami three days later with a layover in Los Angeles. DEA agents set up surveillance in Los Angeles and observed that Sokolow was still wearing the same clothing and was pacing around the terminal in a nervous manner.

Upon his arrival at the Honolulu Airport, he was followed by law enforcement agents as he walked through the terminal. Just as he and Dorian were about to hail a taxi, the DEA agents grabbed his arm and pulled him back to the sidewalk. They asked for his airline ticket and identification. He said that he had none, that his name was Sokolow, and that he was traveling under his mother's maiden name, "Kray." At this point, the agents moved him to a security office. "Donker," a dog trained to sniff drugs, alerted the agents to one of the couple's bags. Sokolow was arrested, and a search warrant was obtained for the bag. However, no illicit drugs were found. Donker then sniffed luggage again and alerted to another bag. Now, too late to obtain another warrant, the agents allowed the couple to leave but kept their luggage. The next morning, another trained dog sniffed the luggage and confirmed there were drugs present. A second warrant was obtained and the subsequent search resulted in the discovery of 1,063 grams of cocaine.

Drug courier profile
A compilation of behaviors typical of drug smugglers.

The Decision: The issue before the Supreme Court was whether the agents had reasonable suspicion to stop Sokolow in the airport. Sokolow argued that he did not engage in any specific illegal conduct that would have led to such suspicion. He also argued that the agents reached their conclusions based on **drug courier profiles** that identified common behaviors of individuals engaged in drug smuggling rather than Sokolow's specific actions. The Supreme Court rejected those arguments and determined that reasonable suspicion was established. "Any one of these factors is not by itself proof of any illegal conduct and is quite consistent with innocent travel. But we think taken together they amount to reasonable suspicion." The Court allowed the stop and subsequent search of Sokolow's bags.

Stop and Frisk and Motor Vehicles

The investigative procedure provided by *Terry v. Ohio* investigative tools does not only apply to situations involving pedestrians. As indicated in *Adams v. Williams*, it is a procedure used to investigate people who may be involved in criminal activity whether they are alone on the street, in a car, on a boat, on a plane, or slithering along on a Segway.

On the Street

Reasonable Suspicion Stop

A police officer is patrolling in her police car at 2 A.M. She is working in an industrial area that includes several small manufacturing businesses as well as the local utility power station. She notices an old brown Honda Civic pull out quickly from the power station and head east on Johnson Road. The power station is surrounded by tall, heavy, galvanized steel fencing, and the gate is always locked. The only vehicles she has ever seen enter or leave the facility have been white utility trucks with clear markings of the utility company name. Whoever was driving the Honda left the gate wide open when he or she left. She also knows that there is seldom anyone inside the facility at night unless there is some kind of problem in the area such as a power outage.

Does she have reasonable suspicion? Yes. While there may be some type of reasonable explanation for this driver's conduct, it is obvious based on her training, experience, and knowledge of this particular facility that whoever is driving that brown car is either committing or has committed a crime.

So she calls for backup and also requests a car to check out the power station. As she pursues the Honda, she asks the dispatcher to contact the utility company to determine if anyone would be inside at this time of night.

After flashing blue lights and sounding the siren, she pulls the Honda over to the curb. It is clear that she is a police officer, and she has now made the stop. She demands that the driver get out of the car and walk back to her police vehicle. As he is walking back she asks him why he was in the power station. He denies that he was. Now she has conducted her general inquiry and the driver has certainly failed to relieve her fears. She may frisk.

It is always important to realize that one legal justification may lead to another. On-the-street confrontations are dynamic and fluid actions. In this scenario involving the power plant, the officer would also be conducting a plain view look at the interior of the car. There might be evidence discovered such as copper stolen from the power plant. Assuming that her suspect did not have authority to be inside the plant, she would likely be arresting him for at least criminal trespass. That would result in the towing of his vehicle and a subsequent inventory search as well. If there was a discovery that copper had been stolen, that would give her probable cause to search his vehicle. If she had arrested him, she would be able to search him incident to arrest. But all of these possibilities began with her observations and reasonable suspicion determination. These additional search considerations will be addressed in subsequent chapters.

The Frisk and Probable Cause

In determining the scope and extent of a *Terry* stop, the courts have been clear in stating that the frisk is a pat down of the outer clothing for the purpose of determining if there is a weapon present. But questions abound:

- How much pressure can the officer place on the clothing?
- Is the officer allowed to squeeze the clothing during the frisk?
- What feels "reasonably" like a weapon?
- What happens if the officer feels something else such as drugs or other evidence?

Many of these questions were answered by the U.S. Supreme Court decision in 1993.

MINNESOTA v. DICKERSON

508 U.S. 366 (1993)

The Facts: Police had approached a suspect who was leaving a "notorious crack-house" where illicit drug sales were often made in the hallways. When the suspect saw the police he turned around quickly and headed in the opposite direction. The police ultimately conducted a stop and frisk. The frisk did not disclose any weapons. However, when the officer patted the suspect's pants pocket, he did feel what he believed to be cocaine. He said it felt like a cellophane bag that slid inside the suspect's pocket when he touched it. He reached inside of the suspect's pocket and retrieved cocaine.

The Decision: The U.S. Supreme Court considered whether plain feel would allow an officer to go beyond the frisk and actually search. They answered yes but with a very important focused caution.

They first addressed the issue of plain feel:

> To this Court, there is no distinction as to which sensory perception the officer uses to conclude that the material is contraband. An experienced officer may rely upon his sense of smell in DWI stops or in recognizing the smell of burning marijuana in an automobile. The sound of a shotgun being racked would clearly support certain reactions by an officer. The sense of touch, grounded in experience and training, is as reliable as perceptions drawn from other senses. "Plain feel," therefore, is no different than plain view, and will equally support the seizure here.
>
> These principles were settled 25 years ago when, on the same day, the Court announced its decisions in Terry and Sibron. The question presented today is whether police officers may seize nonthreatening contraband detected during a protective patdown search of the sort permitted by Terry. We think the answer is clearly that they may, so long as the officers' search stays within the bounds marked by Terry.

The Court agreed that probable cause to arrest could result from a frisk. If the plain feel from the frisk provided a reasonable belief that contraband was present, the officer would have the right to search further and seize the illegal evidence. However, there was an additional critical issue. How much tactile manipulation of the clothing is allowed in the frisk? They noted that in the Minnesota incident, the officer determined only that the item he was feeling was contraband after "squeezing, sliding and otherwise manipulating the contents of the defendant's pocket." The Court concluded that had the officer immediately realized during the initial pat down for weapons that the item he felt was contraband, he could have seized it. However, once there was a determination that no weapon was present, he could not manipulate the clothing further. The Court would not allow a fishing expedition to determine the contents of the suspect's pocket. The officer is not allowed to manipulate the clothing beyond what is necessary to find a weapon.

Obviously many objects could be used as weapons. Common items such as pens, keys, or cell phones could be utilized to harm an officer. The key issue in these circumstances is, of course, reasonableness. The "stop and frisk" procedure has been designed in part to ensure an officer's safety during the limited investigation. Unless other factors are present, it is unlikely that a court would approve an intrusive search of a person's pocket based simply on the presence of a set of keys or a pencil.

It should also be noted that the actions of a suspect during a stop and frisk may quickly turn into a dangerous arrest situation. If the suspect assaults the officer when the stop is attempted, then the rules of stop and frisk no longer apply. The situation is now one of arrest and self-defense. Likewise, the discovery of a dangerous weapon or evidence that clearly links the suspect to a serious offense would provide probable cause to arrest.

Summary

The Fourth Amendment does not protect citizens from all government intrusion, rather only that which is unreasonable. In the landmark case of *Terry v. Ohio*, the U.S. Supreme Court determined that if reasonable suspicion exists, then the stop is reasonable. The procedure does, at times, result in the stopping of innocent people. However, the procedure involves a limited and temporary intrusion, and if there is no further evidence of criminal activity, then the citizen is free to leave. As with most criminal procedure decisions, the Court has balanced the need to protect citizens from crime, to provide protection for police officers, and our desire for our individual privacy.

The *Terry* stop and frisk is not without controversy. A common misunderstanding is that it gives the police the right to stop and confront individuals without a reason. As you can see, that is not true. The police must, through their observations, possess reasonable suspicion and then follow certain proscribed steps. The criminal justice student should also understand that the procedure is used by law enforcement in any situation in which reasonable suspicion exists, such as traffic stops. If the information gained from a *Terry* stop gives rise to probable cause, it may result in an arrest and a more extensive search.

Review Questions

1. Define *reasonable suspicion*.
2. Identify and describe the steps required in conducting a *Terry v. Ohio* stop and frisk.
3. Explain the distinction between an arrest and a temporary detention.
4. Under what circumstances is an officer allowed to go beyond a frisk, and search a suspect's pockets during a stop and frisk?
5. Describe a situation in which a stop and frisk could lead to probable cause to arrest.

Legal Terminology

Articulate
Drug courier profile
Frisk

Plainclothes
Reasonable suspicion

References

Adams v. Williams, 407 U.S. 143 (1972)
Minnesota v. Dickerson, 508 U.S. 366 (1993)
United States v. Sokolow, 490 U.S. 1 (1989)
Terry v. Ohio, 392 U.S. 1 (1968)

Chapter 7

Investigative Detentions and Searches

In addition to *Terry v. Ohio* stop and frisks, there are a number of other situations in which the government may temporarily detain individuals or their vehicles without the necessity of legal justification for an arrest. These detentions include traffic stops, impaired driving checkpoints, entry into the country, and immigration checkpoints.

Traffic Stops

The traffic stop scenario involves a police officer engaging the lights and siren of the police vehicle in order to pull over a motor vehicle. This may occur simply because the driver has committed a traffic violation such as speeding or driving with a broken headlight. An officer may also detain a vehicle if he or she has reasonable suspicion that the occupants are committing or are about to commit a criminal act. Probable cause would also justify the stop of the vehicle. However, law enforcement cannot pull over a vehicle without a reason.

Traffic Offenses

When a police officer observes the driver of a vehicle committing a traffic offense, the officer may pull over the driver and detain the driver for a reasonable amount of time in order to investigate the offense; obtain the driver's license, insurance, and vehicle documentation; and complete any legal action such as writing a ticket or making an arrest. This is considered a temporary detention. The subject can be detained only for a reasonable period of time. The courts have not specifically identified a number of minutes since it would vary greatly depending upon the circumstances of the stop. It may take a longer period of time to examine the documents required by an over-the-road trucker than it would to address a traditional traffic stop. Likewise, the

Field sobriety test
A test conducted on the street in an effort to determine if a motorist is intoxicated. It usually evaluates the suspect's motor and cognitive skills.

investigation of a drunk driving violation might involve a number of **field sobriety tests** to determine the level of impairment and may ultimately lead to an arrest. In some situations, the stop may evolve into a more extensive criminal investigation. However, if an officer stopped a vehicle for a minor traffic offense, the individual could not be detained longer than reasonably necessary to investigate and administer the traffic citation. The officer could not detain the person beyond that time frame in order to have a drug-sniffing dog come to the scene unless other suspicious factors were discovered.

Often citizens who are stopped by the police complain that they were either pulled over for no reason or were not informed of the reason. As previously stated, the police may not pull someone over without legal justification. However, they are not required to disclose to the driver their reason for the stop. Traffic stops are considered dangerous encounters by police, and in some situations the disclosure of the reason for the stop would increase the level of danger. If the detained individual is aware that he or she has been stopped for the investigation of a robbery as opposed to a regular traffic stop, the reaction might be entirely different. The police often ask drivers if they know why they were stopped. Those types of questions provide information about the driver's intention and demeanor. Of course, if criminal charges should result from the encounter, the reason for the stop would have to be disclosed in court.

The police also have the right to require the driver and all other passengers to exit the vehicle. Law enforcement agencies vary in their methods in this regard. The tactics may also vary according to the circumstances of the stop. Some officers may ask the driver to step to the other side of the vehicle; others require the motorist to remain in the vehicle. A few agencies will place the driver in the police cruiser while they are completing the investigation.

In 1997, the U.S. Supreme Court addressed the issue of removing the driver and passengers from a car during a traffic stop.

MARYLAND v. WILSON

519 U.S. 408 (1997)

The Facts: Maryland state trooper David Hughes spotted a car traveling at 64 miles per hour on I-95. The posted speed limit was 55 mph. The vehicle did not have a license plate but rather a torn piece of paper reading "Enterprise Rent-A-Car." When the trooper engaged his lights and siren, the driver failed to comply and continued driving for another mile and a half. During the pursuit, the trooper noticed that the three occupants of the car continually turned to look at him and also repeatedly ducked below sight level. When the car was finally stopped, the driver got out and walked back toward the officer. He was trembling and appeared extremely nervous. The trooper told him to return to the car to retrieve the rental documents. At this point, Trooper Hughes noticed that passenger Jerry Lee Wilson was sweating and was also nervous. Hughes ordered Wilson out of the car. When Wilson slid out of the front passenger seat a quantity of crack cocaine fell to the ground. Wilson was arrested and charged with possession of cocaine with the intent to distribute.

Wilson argued that the cocaine should not be admissible because the officer did not have the right to demand that he get out of the car.

The Decision: The Court had previously ruled that a police officer may require a driver to get out of the car during a traffic stop [*Pennsylvania v. Mimms,* 434 U.S. 106 (1977)]. In *Maryland v. Wilson,* they extended the rule to include passengers:

> On the personal liberty side of the balance, the case for the passengers is in one sense stronger than that for the driver. There is probable cause to believe that the driver has committed a minor vehicular offense, but there is no such reason to stop or detain the passengers. But as a practical matter, the passengers are already stopped by virtue of the stop of the vehicle. The only change in their circumstances which will result from ordering them out of the car is that they will be outside of, rather than inside of, the stopped car. Outside the car, the passengers will be denied access to any possible weapon that might be concealed in the interior of the passenger compartment. It would seem that the possibility of a violent encounter stems not from the ordinary reaction of a motorist stopped for a speeding violation, but from the fact that evidence of a more serious crime might be uncovered during the stop. And the motivation of a passenger to employ violence to prevent apprehension of such a crime is every bit as great as that of the driver.

After balancing the privacy interests of the passengers against the public safety concerns of the officers conducting the stop, the court ruled that the intrusion was minimal. They held that the passengers may be removed from the vehicle for the duration of the traffic stop.

Reasonable Suspicion Stops

As previously discussed in Chapter 6, *Terry v. Ohio* justifies the stop of a motor vehicle if the officers have reasonable suspicion that a crime is being committed or is about to be committed. Consider the following case.

ALABAMA v. WHITE

496 U.S. 325 (1990)

The Facts: On April 27, 1987, Corporal B.H. Davis of the Montgomery, Alabama, police department received an anonymous tip that Vanessa White would be leaving her apartment at 235-C Lynnwood Terrace at a particular time. The informant further stated that White would then drive to Dobey's Motel in a brown Plymouth station wagon with a broken right taillight lens and that she would be transporting cocaine in a brown briefcase. Officers went to the apartments and waited. At the specified time, Ms. White came out of the apartment and got into a brown Plymouth station wagon. She was not carrying anything. She then drove the obvious route to Dobey's Motel. The police stopped on the Mobile Highway just short of the motel. After confronting her, she consented to a search of her vehicle. In a brown attaché case they discovered marijuana. They also found 3 milligrams of cocaine in her purse after she was arrested on the marijuana charge.

The Decision: The U.S. Supreme Court determined that the Alabama police had reasonable suspicion sufficient to justify pulling over Ms. White's station wagon. They indicated that the anonymous tip along with the corroborative information gathered by the police provided sufficient "indicia of reliability" to justify a Terry stop. They suggested that the tip alone was not enough, but reasonable suspicion was achieved when it was combined with accurate information regarding the time, place, car, and direction. It was obvious that the information was offered by someone familiar with the suspect's behavior. They considered the totality of circumstances in making their decision.

Pretextual Stops

Pretextual stop
The police use the legal justification of a traffic violation stop to conduct an investigation for other criminal activity.

A **pretextual stop** occurs when the police pull a vehicle over for a traffic violation although their true motive is the investigation of additional criminal activity. For example, they may wish to check out a suspect for drug smuggling so they observe the suspect's vehicle until a traffic violation is committed. Once the vehicle is stopped, the officers are able to talk with the suspect and conduct a plain view examination of the vehicle. They might even obtain consent to search. Police officers often conduct these types of stops as part of **drug interdiction programs**. The U.S. Supreme Court has ruled that the procedure does not violate the Fourth Amendment.

Drug interdiction program
A law enforcement program designed to detect and apprehend offenders engaging in illegal drug activities.

In *Whren v. United States*, 517 U.S. 806 (1996), they upheld the practice. District of Columbia plainclothes police officers, working a high drug area, noticed Brown and Whren sitting at a stop sign for an unusually long period of time. They also noticed the driver, Brown, staring down at the lap of the passenger, Whren. When the officers made a U-turn to investigate, the vehicle abruptly turned right without giving a turn signal and sped away at an "unreasonable" rate of speed. The officers pulled them over when they stopped at a red light. As they approached the driver's window, they viewed Whren holding two plastic bags of what appeared to be cocaine. After arresting both men, the officers discovered more illegal drugs during a search of the car. Both were convicted of multiple counts of drug possession in violation of the U.S. Code. The defendants argued on appeal that the real reason for the original stop by the police was to investigate drug possession, not the alleged traffic violations. Upholding their conviction, the Supreme Court held that an officer may stop a vehicle if the officer has probable cause to believe that a traffic violation has occurred. It does not matter if the officer is also concerned about additional criminal activity.

Sobriety Checkpoints

Many law enforcement agencies in the United States conduct periodic vehicle roadblocks for the purpose of identification and apprehension of impaired drivers. They typically set up as roadblocks in which approaching cars are temporarily stopped as they pass through. The officers will briefly speak with the driver while assessing the possibility of impaired driving due to drugs or alcohol. This practice was authorized by the U.S. Supreme Court in 1990.

MICHIGAN DEPARTMENT OF STATE POLICE v. SITZ

496 U.S. 444 (1990)

Sobriety checkpoint
A police roadblock at which motorists are randomly stopped and investigated for the offense of driving while intoxicated.

The Facts: In 1986, the Michigan Department of State Police established a **sobriety checkpoint** pilot program. The checkpoints were conducted within the parameters set by a committee established by the state police director. The committee, comprised of state and local police officers, state prosecutors, and representatives from the University of Michigan Transportation Research Institute established guidelines for checkpoint operations, site selection, and publicity. Per the guidelines, the checkpoints were located along state roads. All approaching vehicles would be stopped. The drivers would be briefly examined for signs of intoxication. If the driver was suspected of impairment, he or she would be directed out of the traffic lane for further investigation. The officers would then check the driver's license and registration and, if warranted, conduct a field sobriety test. An arrest would be made if there was probable cause to believe the driver was intoxicated.

The state police along with the Saginaw County Sheriff's Department conducted one sobriety checkpoint. During the 75-minute operation, 126 drivers passed through the checkpoint. The average per driver delay was 25 seconds. Only two drivers were detained for further sobriety testing, one of which was arrested. In addition, one driver drove through the roadblock without stopping and was apprehended and arrested for driving under the influence.

The Decision: The argument against the use of a sobriety checkpoint was that it allowed the temporary detention of a suspect without the establishment of reasonable suspicion. However, the Court approved the use of the DUI checkpoint procedure. In their discussion, they weighed the impact on society against the privacy intrusion of the checkpoint procedure. They determined that the intrusion was minimal when compared to the government's need to protect the traveling public. The Court stated the following:

> No one can seriously dispute the magnitude of the drunken driving problem or the States' interest in eradicating it. Media reports of alcohol-related death and mutilation on the Nation's roads are legion. The anecdotal is confirmed by the statistical. "Drunk drivers cause an annual death toll of over 25,000 and in the same time span cause nearly one million personal injuries and more than five billion dollars in property damage." 4 W. LaFave, Search and Seizure: A Treatise on the Fourth Amendment 10.8(d), p. 71 (2d ed. 1987). For decades, this Court has "repeatedly lamented the tragedy." *South Dakota v. Neville*, 459 U.S. 553, 558 (1983); see *Breithaupt v. Abram*, 352 U.S. 432, 439 (1957) ("The increasing slaughter on our highways . . . now reaches the astounding figures only heard of on the battlefield").

"In sum, the balance of the State's interest in preventing drunken driving, the extent to which this system can reasonably be said to advance that interest, and the degree of intrusion upon individual motorists who are briefly stopped, weighs in favor of the state program. We therefore hold that it is consistent with the Fourth Amendment."

Most jurisdictions that conduct sobriety checkpoints comply with the guidelines of the National Highway Safety and Transportation Board. The checkpoints are not only designed to provide an enforcement mechanism but also to act as **deterrence**. While the actual deterrence success may be difficult to measure, the presence of a sobriety checkpoint arguably impacts those motorists who must make the driving decision. The Governor's Highway Safety Association indicates that 38 states currently conduct sobriety checkpoints. The checkpoints are prohibited in some states due to their statutes or constitutions.

The *Sitz* case did not give police the right to randomly pull over a vehicle with a reason. It does allow them to randomly stop the cars that, in essence, come to them. The police may pull over a vehicle for the investigation of impaired driving if the driver is operating in a manner which would indicate possible intoxication or is otherwise committing a traffic violation. Individual states may impose specific statutory requirements such as warning signs, public service announcements, or escape routes for drivers who do not wish to go through the checkpoint. Though not required by the *Sitz* case, some states have elected to include such restrictions.

Deterrence
The theory that an action by law enforcement or the courts will discourage another from engaging in criminal activity.

Drug Checkpoints

In *City of Indianapolis v. Edmond*, 531 U.S. 32 (2000), the U.S. Supreme Court ruled that roadblocks conducted for the purpose of narcotics detection were unconstitutional. In their decision, they held that the objectives of the drug roadblocks were general crime control as opposed to a specific public safety interest. Therefore, the use of roadblocks to detect the possession or use of illegal drugs violates the Fourth Amendment. The Indianapolis Police Department established checkpoints at which they randomly stopped motorists to investigate for the possession or use of illegal drugs. As the motorists entered the checkpoint, they were asked for their license and vehicle registration. As the officers conducted a visual examination from outside the car, a drug detection canine would walk around the vehicle. Some drivers were asked for consent to search. Signs leading up to the checkpoints stated the following: "NARCOTICS CHECKPOINT ___ MILE AHEAD, NARCOTICS K-9 IN USE, BE PREPARED TO STOP." During the 1998 drug interdiction program, the police utilized six drug roadblocks between August and November. They stopped 1,161 vehicles resulting in 104 arrests—55 drug-related offenses.

In ruling that the drug roadblocks violated the Fourth Amendment, the Court stated the following:

The primary purpose of the Indianapolis narcotics checkpoints is in the end to advance "the general interest in crime control," *Prouse,* 440 U.S., at 659, n. 18. We decline to suspend the usual requirement of individualized suspicion where the police seek to employ a checkpoint primarily for the ordinary enterprise of investigating crimes. We cannot sanction stops justified only by the generalized and ever-present possibility that interrogation and inspection may reveal that any given motorist has committed some crime.

Criminal Apprehension Roadblocks

Courts have never allowed roadblocks or checkpoints for the general purpose of detecting crime, gathering evidence, or apprehending criminals. In *Michigan v. Sitz,* the use of limited-purpose checkpoints was allowed for a specific and focused public safety interest. However, law enforcement agencies may set up roadblocks in emergency situations in order to detect and apprehend a dangerous criminal. The practice would have to meet the requirements of an exigent circumstance that was necessary to protect the public from a dangerous and possibly fleeing suspect. The uses of these roadblocks are rare and controversial. If the police discovered plain view evidence from a third party as a result of an emergency roadblock, the court would have to be convinced that the need to protect the public outweighed the privacy intrusion. In the previously discussed drug checkpoint case, *Indianapolis v. Edmonds,* the Court suggested that "the Fourth Amendment would almost certainly permit an appropriately tailored roadblock set up to thwart an imminent terrorist attack or to catch a dangerous criminal who is likely to flee by way of a particular route."

The emergency justification was used during the highly publicized Beltway Sniper case in 2002. Two snipers terrorized the citizens around the Washington, D.C., Virginia, and Maryland areas. The suspects randomly shot and killed ten people between October 2 and October 22. The police had received information that the suspects may have been driving a white van or a box truck. Roadblocks were set up in the Washington, D.C., area in an effort to apprehend the suspects. As a result, the already cumbersome traffic was snarled at many locations in the beltway area. However, the roadblocks were unsuccessful. John Allen Muhammad and Lee Boyd Malvo were arrested while sleeping at an I-70 rest area in Maryland on October 24. They were found in a blue 1990 Chevrolet Caprice which had been customized into a rolling sniper's nest. They had built a shooting platform and cut holes in the trunk lid from which they could fire. It was also determined that they were responsible for murders in Montgomery, Alabama, a few months earlier. Muhammad and Malvo were convicted of multiple counts of murder in Maryland and Virginia. Muhammad was executed by lethal injection in a Virginia prison November 10, 2009. Malvo, who was 17 at the time of the shootings, was sentenced to six consecutive life terms and remains in prison.

Immigration checkpoint
A roadblock established to determine the immigration status of passing motorists and pedestrians at or near the U.S. border.

Immigration Checkpoints

In an effort to combat illegal immigration and combat terrorism, the U.S. Border Patrol has established permanent fixed **immigration checkpoints** on a variety of roads and highways within 100 miles of the Mexican border. Approaching vehicles are warned of the checkpoints by posted highway signs. Vehicles entering the checkpoints are stopped and briefly examined by the U.S. Border Patrol agents. U.S. citizens are not required to provide passports, but noncitizens must provide documentation of legal entry into the United States. If agents believe there is reason for further investigation after the initial stop, the suspect vehicle will be directed to a secondary inspection area. The Border Patrol also conducts tactical or moving roadblocks on the side roads near the checkpoints to identify vehicles attempting to avoid the fixed checkpoints. Those stops must be justified by reasonable suspicion. The U.S. Supreme Court affirmed the constitutionality of the permanent warrantless checkpoints in *United States v. Martinez-Fuerte*, 428 U.S. 543 (1976). They balanced the minimal intrusion of the stop against the specific need to enforce the immigration laws of the United States and to detect and apprehend illegal immigrants attempting to enter the country.

The enactment and enforcement of our nation's immigration laws are often impacted by political consideration. Efforts by individual states to enforce federal immigration statutes have given rise to considerable litigation and political maneuvering in recent years. Discussions about the enforcement of immigration laws have focused on efforts by both federal and state agencies. The debate has examined the building of security fences, the location of checkpoints, and the ability of local jurisdictions to enact laws that impact immigration status.

Border Searches

The government has the right to temporarily detain and search anyone who is entering the United States. These searches occur at all entry points such as airports, ocean ports, and actual geographical borders. For example, if an international flight made its initial arrival to the country at the Chicago airport, travelers would be subject to the customs search. The searches are also conducted whether the entering traveler is an American citizen or from a foreign country. These types of border search procedures and laws are enacted all over the world. The searches generally involve a routine and brief detention in which government agents will examine the traveler's passport and visa documents, ask some basic questions concerning the reasons for their international travel, and conduct a cursory search of their luggage and property. If the agents have additional concerns, they may conduct a more thorough inquiry and search. The extent of those more intrusive investigations was addressed in the following case.

UNITED STATES v. MONTOYA DE HERNANDEZ

473 U.S. 531 (1985)

The Facts: Rosa Elvira Montoya de Hernandez, referred to as the respondent, traveled to the United States from Bogota, Colombia, and was subjected to an extensive search by U.S. Customs agents. Upon discovering drugs, she was prosecuted and convicted for federal drug violations. The following is the actual description of the facts from the U.S. Supreme Court decision:

Respondent arrived at Los Angeles International Airport shortly after midnight, March 5, 1983, on Avianca Flight 080, a direct 10-hour flight from Bogota, Colombia. Her visa was in order so she was passed through Immigration and proceeded to the customs desk. At the customs desk she encountered Customs Inspector Talamantes, who reviewed her documents and noticed from her passport that she had made at least eight recent trips to either Miami or Los Angeles. Talamantes referred respondent to a secondary customs desk for further questioning. At this desk Talamantes and another inspector asked respondent general questions concerning herself and the purpose of her trip. Respondent revealed that she spoke no English and had no family or friends in the United States. She explained in Spanish that she had come to the United States to purchase goods for her husband's store in Bogota. The customs inspectors recognized Bogota as a "source city" for narcotics. Respondent possessed $5,000 in cash, mostly $50 bills, but had no billfold. She indicated to the inspectors that she had no appointments with merchandise vendors, but planned to ride around Los Angeles in taxicabs visiting retail stores such as J. C. Penney and K-Mart in order to buy goods for her husband's store with the $5,000.

Respondent admitted that she had no hotel reservations, but stated that she planned to stay at a Holiday Inn. Respondent could not recall how her airline ticket was purchased. [473 U.S. 531, 534] When the inspectors opened respondent's one small valise, they found about four changes of "cold weather" clothing. Respondent had no shoes other than the high-heeled pair she was wearing. Although respondent possessed no checks, waybills, credit cards, or letters of credit, she did produce a Colombian business card and a number of old receipts, waybills, and fabric swatches displayed in a photo album.

At this point Talamantes and the other inspector suspected that respondent was a "balloon swallower," one who attempts to smuggle narcotics into this country hidden in her alimentary canal. Over the years Inspector Talamantes had apprehended dozens of alimentary canal smugglers arriving on Avianca Flight 080. See App. 42; *United States v. Mendez-Jimenez*, 709 F.2d 1300, 1301 (CA9 1983).

The inspectors requested a female customs inspector to take respondent to a private area and conduct a pat down and strip search. During the search the female inspector felt respondent's abdomen area and noticed a firm fullness, as if respondent were wearing a girdle. The search revealed no contraband, but the inspector noticed that respondent was wearing two pairs of elastic underpants with a paper towel lining the crotch area.

When respondent returned to the customs area and the female inspector reported her discoveries, the inspector in charge told respondent that he suspected she was smuggling drugs in her alimentary canal. Respondent agreed to the inspector's request that she be x-rayed at a hospital but in answer to the inspector's query stated that she was pregnant. She agreed to a pregnancy test before the x ray. Respondent withdrew the consent for an x ray when she learned that she would have to be handcuffed en route to the hospital. The inspector then gave respondent the option of returning to Colombia on the next available flight, agreeing to an x-ray, or remaining in detention until she produced a monitored bowel movement that would confirm or rebut the inspectors' [473 U.S. 531, 535] suspicions. Respondent chose the first option and was placed in a customs office under observation. She was told that if she went to the toilet she would have to use a wastebasket in the women's restroom, in order that female customs inspectors could inspect her stool for balloons or capsules carrying narcotics. The inspectors refused respondent's request to place a telephone call.

Respondent sat in the customs office, under observation, for the remainder of the night. During the night customs officials attempted to place respondent on a Mexican airline that was flying to Bogota via Mexico City in the morning. The airline refused to transport respondent because she lacked a Mexican visa necessary to land in Mexico City. Respondent was not permitted to leave, and was informed that she would be detained until she agreed to an x ray or her bowels moved. She remained detained in the customs office under observation, for most of the time curled up in a chair leaning to one side. She refused all offers of food and drink and refused to use the toilet facilities. The Court of Appeals noted that she exhibited symptoms of discomfort consistent with "heroic efforts to resist the usual calls of nature." 731 F.2d, at 1371.

At the shift change at 4:00 o'clock the next afternoon, almost 16 hours after her flight had landed, respondent still had not defecated or urinated or partaken of food or drink. At that time customs officials sought a court order authorizing a pregnancy test, an x ray, and a rectal examination. The Federal Magistrate issued an order just before midnight that evening, which authorized a rectal examination and involuntary x ray, provided that the physician in charge considered respondent's claim of pregnancy. Respondent was taken to a hospital and given a pregnancy test, which later turned out to be negative. Before the results of the pregnancy test were known, a physician conducted a rectal examination and removed from respondent's rectum a balloon containing a foreign substance. Respondent was then placed [473 U.S. 531, 536] formally under arrest. By 4:10 a.m. respondent had passed 6 similar balloons; over the next four days she passed 88 balloons containing a total of 528 grams of 80% pure cocaine hydrochloride.

The Decision: The U.S. Supreme Court upheld the conviction and overturned the previous decision of the Court of Appeals which had excluded the evidence. The Supreme Court ruled that a traveler entering the United States may be detained beyond the customary search and inspection if there is reasonable belief that the traveler is smuggling contraband in his or her **alimentary canal** (digestive system). In this case the U.S. Customs officials based their suspicions on the facts and reasonable inferences based on their knowledge of the operation of drug smugglers. The Court also acknowledged that a cursory search and brief routine detention would not be sufficient to determine if the defendant was hiding drugs inside of her body. The detention, though uncomfortable for the suspect, was a reasonable alternative to allowing her to leave and disseminate the drugs into the population. The search and detention was reasonable, and the drugs were admissible in evidence.

Alimentary canal smuggler
One who smuggles drugs by swallowing condoms filled with narcotics and passing them through his or her digestive system upon arrival at the intended destination.

Summary

As discussed in this chapter, the courts have affirmed a number of investigative detention situations that allow limited searches. Law enforcement officers may certainly temporarily detain vehicles when a criminal or traffic violation has occurred. The police may also stop vehicles when the circumstances give rise to reasonable suspicion. Occupants of the vehicles may be required to step out of the car during the temporary investigation.

In 1990, the U.S. Supreme Court approved traffic checkpoints designed to investigate impaired driving. Today, these DUI checkpoints are used as crime prevention tools all over the nation. The Court has, however, declined to approve vehicle roadblocks for the general investigation of criminal activity. Absent exigent circumstances, the checkpoints may only be utilized for the prevention of drunk driving.

This chapter also included a discussion of the laws that protect the borders of the United States. Government officials are authorized to search all individuals attempting to enter the borders of the United States. In a more controversial opinion, the Court has also approved roving checkpoints within reasonable proximity to the borders.

Review Questions

1. Define *pretextual stop*.
2. Explain why the U.S. Supreme Court allows sobriety checkpoints but not drug interdiction checkpoints.
3. Under what circumstances could the police set up a roadblock for the apprehension of a criminal suspect?
4. Define *border search*.
5. What are the objectives of an immigration checkpoint?

Legal Terminology

Alimentary canal smuggler

Deterrence

Drug interdiction program

Field sobriety test

Immigration checkpoint

Pretextual stop

Sobriety checkpoint

References

Alabama v White, 496 U.S. 325 (1990)

City of Indianapolis v. Edmond, 531 U.S. 32 (2000)

Governors Highway Safety Association. (2013, October) *Sobriety Checkpoint Laws.* Retrieved from http://www.ghsa.org/html/stateinfo/laws/checkpoint_laws.html

Maryland v. Wilson, 519 U.S. 408 (1997)

Michigan Department of State Police v. Sitz, 496 U.S. 444 (1990)

National Highway Safety and Transportation Board. (2002, December) *Saturation Patrols and Sobriety Checkpoints.* Retrieved from http://www.nhtsa.gov/people/injury/alcohol/saturation_patrols/index.html

Pennsylvania v. *Mimms,* 434 U.S. 106 (1977)

United States v. Martinez-Fuerte, 428 U.S. 543 (1976)

United States v. Montoya de Hernandez, 473 U.S. 531 (1985)

Chapter 8
Search and Seizure
Evidence

When making a decision that impacts the search and seizure of evidence, the U.S. Supreme Court always considers the Fourth Amendment. They must determine whether the search was reasonable. The Fourth Amendment does not protect citizens from all searches but rather only those that are considered unreasonable. The court balances privacy interests against the government's duty to protect its citizens and enforce the laws.

As discussed previously, there are many circumstances in which the police may reasonably search for a person and those resulting seizures may also result in the discovery of evidence. This section examines the issues surrounding the search for evidence. What is considered private? When may the government intrude on our private property? When is a search warrant required? What are the requirements of a valid consent search? What privacy interests do we have in our cars? How does the Fourth Amendment apply to the use of modern technology? These and many other questions will be addressed in this section.

Police officers conduct searches in a variety of situations. They might conduct the search of a motor vehicle after the driver has been pulled over for a traffic violation or for committing a more serious criminal offense. They might search a person's house or apartment for drugs or evidence. Upon arresting a suspect, they may search his or her clothing. The forensic search of a computer, smartphone, or social media history might come into play. There have been some national political discussions over the use of drone technology and satellite imagery to monitor activities. The evidence that police search for will fall within one or more of the following categories.

Categories of Items Subject to Search

Contraband

Contraband
An item that is illegal to possess.

Criminal laws may prevent the possession of specific items such as illegal drugs or unlawfully possessed firearms. Often the issue of whether an item is **contraband** is determined by the specific situation. For example, the possession of the drug oxycodone is not illegal if the person has a valid prescription. A handgun would not be considered contraband if the possessor was carrying the weapon pursuant to a valid concealed carry permit. In most circumstances, it is not contraband to have a grapefruit. However, if a person was illegally transporting a grapefruit into the United States from another country, it would be considered contraband. In prisons and jails, there are rules against the possession of certain items. It might be contraband for a prisoner to possess a cell phone.

Instrumentalities of a Crime

Instrumentalities of a crime
An item used to commit a crime.

The police might be searching for the tools used to perpetuate a criminal act: the murderer's gun or the screwdriver a burglar used to break into a building. In the Boston Marathon Bombing, Tamerlan Tsarnaev and Dzhokhar Tsarnaev allegedly used pressure cookers to encase their explosive materials. Those cookers were **instrumentalities of a crime**. A computer would be the instrumentality for a predator using the Internet to solicit sex from children.

Fruits of a Crime

Fruits of a crime
The benefit derived from the commission of a crime.

The most common **fruit of a crime** would be the money or items gained from theft or robbery crimes. Examples would include the money obtained from a robbery or the property stolen in a burglary. A computer hacker might illegally obtain data. The data would be the fruit of the crime.

Evidence

Evidence
An item or information that could be used to prove or support a fact.

Contraband, fruits of a crime, and instrumentalities certainly fall under this category as well. However, police often must search for items that link a perpetrator to a crime such as blood, fingerprints, hair fibers, or other trace evidence. A blanket with traces of semen might be **evidence** in a sexual assault case. Photographs on a cell phone might link a stalker to his victim.

Reasonable Expectation of Privacy

The Fourth Amendment guaranteed the protection against unreasonable governmental intrusion. It did not, however, identify what was actually protected from intrusion. The U.S. Supreme Court tackled that question in the 1967 case of *Katz v. United States* and provided the touchstone for many search and seizure issues.

KATZ v. UNITED STATES

389 U.S. 347 (1967)

The Facts: Charles Katz was convicted of transmitting wagering information via telephone in violation of federal law. He used a public telephone booth in Los

Angeles to conduct his illegal gambling business in other cities including Boston and Miami. As part of their investigation, the FBI hid an electronic listening device on the top of a public outdoor phone booth. The device would transmit the sound to a receiver positioned in a nearby vehicle. They could hear only the ambient noise from the phone booth. It was not a wiretap so it did not allow them to hear what the person on the other end of the line was saying. They could only hear Katz. They used his captured statements to prosecute him in the U.S. District Court of Southern California. Katz appealed to the U.S. Court of Appeals, but they upheld his conviction. Ultimately, Katz appealed to the U.S. Supreme Court.

The Decision: The FBI argued that they did not violate the Fourth Amendment. Their contention was that Katz was operating in a public space, thus waiving any privacy rights. There was no physical trespass of Katz's person or any of his property, and anything that he said was in public. Katz contended that the government had violated his rights because they were listening to his private conversation. The U.S. Supreme Court overturned Katz' conviction and provided clarification to the protections provided by the Fourth Amendment.

Writing for the majority, Justice Stewart stated the following:

> For the Fourth Amendment protects people, not places. What a person knowingly exposes to the public, even in his own home or office, is not a subject of Fourth Amendment protection. See *Lewis v. United States*, 385 U.S. 206, 210; *United States v. Lee*, 274 U.S. 559, 563. But what he seeks to preserve as private, even in an area accessible to the public, may be constitutionally protected. [389 U.S. 347, 352] See *Rios v. United States*, 364 U.S. 253; Ex parte Jackson, 96 U.S. 727, 733.

Justice Harlan stated the following in his concurring opinion:

> I join the opinion of the Court, which I read to hold only (a) that an enclosed telephone booth is an area where, like a home, *Weeks v. United States*, 232 U.S. 383, and unlike a field, *Hester v. United States*, 265 U.S. 57, a person has a constitutionally protected reasonable expectation of privacy; (b) that electronic as well as physical intrusion into a place that is in this sense private may constitute a violation of the Fourth Amendment; [389 U.S. 347, 361] and (c) that the invasion of a constitutionally protected area by federal authorities is, as the Court has long held, presumptively unreasonable in the absence of a search warrant.

The Court said that even though Katz was in a public telephone booth, he would have still reasonably expected some privacy. He could not have assumed that someone standing next to the booth could not have heard him. He would have also understood that the person to whom he was talking would hear him. However, he could not have reasonably expected that the government would be listening to him via an electronic eavesdropping device. The court said that the government had violated his reasonable expectation of privacy, therefore violating the Fourth Amendment. The evidence was excluded.

The *Katz* case is considered a landmark case because it modified the view that the Fourth Amendment protected only private property from an intrusion by trespass. The reasonable expectation of privacy standard erased some of the distinctions between private and public property. As a result, a citizen might still expect privacy in a public setting. Likewise, the expectation of privacy might not exist in an ordinarily private setting if it is reasonable to believe that a person's conduct or evidence would be viewed by others.

In 2000, the Court reviewed a case involving luggage that was stored in the overhead bin of a Greyhound bus. They determine whether the traveler had a reasonable expectation of privacy in the stashed bag.

BOND v. UNITED STATES

529 U.S. 334 (2000)

The Facts: The U.S. Border Patrol had established a permanent checkpoint in Sierra Blanca, Texas, for the purpose of conducting immigration checks. Agent Cantu boarded a Greyhound bus stopped at the checkpoint and conducted a walk-through check of the immigration status of the passengers. After he completed the checks, he reached into the overhead bins that carried the passengers' carry-on luggage. He squeezed a soft-sided bag belonging to Steven Bond. He felt a brick-like object. Agent Cantu then asked Bond if he could search the bag. Bond consented. Upon searching the bag, Cantu discovered a brick of methamphetamine. As a result, Bond was convicted of possession with intent to distribute and sentenced to 57 months in prison.

The Decision: Upon appeal, the U.S. Supreme Court ruled that the search violated the Fourth Amendment and overturned his conviction. They stated the following:

> Our Fourth Amendment analysis embraces two questions. First, we ask whether the individual, by his conduct, has exhibited an actual expectation of privacy; that is, whether he has shown that "he [sought] to preserve [something] as private." *Smith v. Maryland,* 442 U.S. 735, 740 (1979) (internal quotation marks omitted). Here, petitioner sought to preserve privacy by using an opaque bag and placing that bag directly above his seat. Second, we inquire whether the individual's expectation of privacy is "one that society is prepared to recognize as reasonable." *Ibid.* (internal quotation marks omitted). When a bus passenger places a bag in an overhead bin, he expects that other passengers or bus employees may move it for one reason or another. Thus, a bus passenger clearly expects that his bag may be handled. He does not expect that other passengers or bus employees will, as a matter of course, feel the bag in an exploratory manner. But this is exactly what the agent did here. We therefore hold that the agent's physical manipulation of petitioner's bag violated the Fourth Amendment.

The key issue in the Bond case was the passenger's reasonable expectation of privacy. The bus passengers did not expect that government agents would be conducting exploratory searches of their carry-on bags. The decision does not mean that all luggage is immune from government search. Passengers flying on commercial airlines are given notice that their bags will be examined. Carry-on bags are searched by Transportation and Safety Administration (TSA) employees at the security checkpoints, and checked luggage is searched by TSA and airline employees in the baggage-handling facilities. If the bus company had warned passengers in advance that their bags would be searched, then they would not have had the privacy expectation.

Abandoned Property

On the Street

Is garbage fair game?

Officer Frizzell is driving down a residential street on trash pickup day. One of the homes has a large collection of cardboard boxes alongside their trash cans. Frizzell notices that there is a hockey stick poking out of one of the boxes. Thinking the homeowner is throwing out a perfectly good hockey stick, the officer stops to check it out. His son could use a better stick for his local youth league team. The officer pulls open the top of the box to examine the stick and discovers several hypodermic needles and some other evidence of drug usage. Is he permitted to seize the syringes and the other paraphernalia?

Abandoned property
Property in which the original possessor has disposed of in a manner which indicates that their privacy interest has been abandoned.

If it is reasonable to believe that an individual has given up his or her possessory interest in property, the police may seize it without a search warrant. There is no reasonable expectation of privacy in property that a person has abandoned. **Abandoned property** is considered as such when a person gives up possession of that property in a manner that indicates to the public that it has been abandoned, such as placing it in a trash bag for curbside pickup, throwing it into a public trash can, or tossing it out of a car. The U.S. Supreme Court addressed the issue in the landmark case of *Greenwood v. California*.

GREENWOOD v. CALIFORNIA

486 U.S. 35 (1988)

The Facts: In February 1984, a criminal informant told police that a truck carrying illegal narcotics was en route to the home of Billy Greenwood in Laguna Beach, California. They also had complaints from a neighbor concerning constant traffic in front of the Greenwood's house where cars would stop for just a few minutes and then leave. This activity went on all during late night and early morning hours. Acting on the information, Officer Jenny Stracner of the Laguna Beach Police Department asked Greenwood's trash collector to give her the plastic garbage bags that Billy had taken to the curb of his home. Upon searching the bags, Officer Stracner discovered evidence that provided probable cause for her to obtain a search warrant for Greenwood's house. Armed with the search warrant, police obtained hashish and cocaine at the house. As a result, police arrested Greenwood and another defendant, Van Houten. Both defendants posted bail, and the late night activities continued. On May 4, Laguna Beach Officer Robert Rahaeuser again obtained Greenwood's trash bags and discovered additional evidence of drug trafficking. Once again, a search warrant was obtained and executed resulting in the seizure of more illegal narcotics.

The Decision: Greenwood argued that the search of his trash was a violation of his reasonable expectation of privacy and the Fourth Amendment. His contention was that the police conducted an intrusion of his personal property without first obtaining a search warrant. However, the U.S. Supreme Court ruled that once Greenwood had placed his trash bags on the street for pickup, he had abandoned the property, thus giving up any reasonable expectation of privacy. The Court stated the following:

> They assert, however, that they had, and exhibited, an expectation of privacy with respect to the trash that was searched by the police: The trash, which was placed on the street for collection at a fixed time, was contained in opaque plastic bags, which the garbage collector was expected to pick up, mingle with the trash of others, and deposit at the garbage dump. The trash was only temporarily on the street, and there was little likelihood that it would be inspected by anyone.
>
> It may well be that respondents did not expect that the contents of their garbage bags would become known to the police or other members of the public. An expectation of privacy does not give rise to Fourth Amendment protection, however, unless society is prepared to accept that expectation as objectively reasonable.
>
> Here, we conclude that respondents exposed their garbage to the public sufficiently to defeat their claim to Fourth Amendment protection. It is common knowledge that plastic garbage bags left on or at the side of a public street are readily accessible to animals, children, scavengers, snoops, and other members of the public. Moreover, respondents placed their refuse at the curb for the express purpose of conveying it to a third party, the trash collector, who might himself have sorted through respondents' trash or permitted others, such as the police, to do so. Accordingly, having deposited their garbage "in an area particularly suited for public inspection and, in a manner of speaking, public consumption, for the express purpose of having strangers take it," respondents could have had no reasonable expectation of privacy in the inculpatory items that they discarded.

Do you ever have an expectation of privacy in your trash? Yes. The Court was clear in Greenwood that the defendant had disposed of his trash in a manner that exposed it to the public and indicated intent to abandon. Greenwood could have retrieved it but that did not negate the fact that he had already placed it at the curb. However, a citizen who places his or her garbage in trash cans behind his or her house that will be ultimately taken to the curb on a scheduled trash day has not yet given up a reasonable expectation of privacy.

Vehicles may be considered abandoned if the owner has left the car without any intention to return. If a car owner drives his or her car to some secluded woods, takes off the license plates, and leaves it without any intention of returning, the car is abandoned and the police can search it without a warrant. However, leaving a car on the side of the road because it has broken down is not consistent with the intention to abandon.

Police pursuits often result in the seizure of evidence due to abandonment. If a suspect throws contraband or evidence out of a window during a police chase, those items are considered abandoned, and the police may retrieve them without a warrant. They are often found within plain view as well.

Plain View, Plain Hearing, and Plain Touch

A reasonable expectation of privacy does not exist when evidence or actions are exposed to the public. If a police officer is in a place where he or she has a legal right to be, the officer may employ his or her ordinary senses of smell, sight, touch, and hearing to discover evidence. The premise is that if the evidence or actions are exposed and a person would not reasonably expect privacy, then they are fair game. If the evidence can be reasonably detected by the ordinary senses, then it is admissible. In most circumstances an officer may not trespass or otherwise violate a person's privacy to employ the use of the senses.

Plain View

On the Street

The Eyes Have It

One bright, sunny, summer afternoon, Officer Foster observes Lucinda roll past a stop sign without making any effort to stop. He pops on his blue lights and siren and quickly pulls her over. As he approaches the driver's side of her car, he notices her frantically digging through her purse. Upon reaching the driver's door, he asks her for her license and registration. Lucinda hands him her license but says she hasn't found her registration yet. She then opens the console compartment. Inside the compartment is a plastic bag that contains what appears to be marijuana. The officer sees the bag and immediately asks Lucinda to step out of the car. He then grabs the bag of marijuana and places Lucinda under arrest. Is the marijuana admissible? ■

Evidence that can be reasonably seen by law enforcement may be seized. The traffic stop often provides a common setting for such an action. When an officer stops a vehicle for a traffic violation or other legal reason, the officer is then able to visually scan the interior of the car. This often results in the discovery of evidence. The plain view scan does not allow the officer to search closed areas such as glove compartments, trunks, or other areas that are not visible from the officer's vantage point outside the car. Suspects in vehicles may toss evidence such as drugs or guns out of the car during the pursuit. Those items are in plain view and may be seized.

There are many other circumstances that give rise to plain view seizures. Officers are often invited into a person's home to investigate a crime or take a report. If they are invited into the home, any evidence that they observe is admissible. If a person called the police to report a barking dog and invited the officer inside to discuss the problem, the person's prize marijuana plant growing in the corner of the living room would be in plain view. It could be seized and used as evidence.

The execution of a search warrant often provides an opportunity for a plain view discovery of evidence. When executing a search warrant, officers have the right to search any area in which the evidence described in the search warrant could likely be found. If the officers observe other evidence during that search, that evidence can also be seized. For example, if officers were searching a home for a stolen gun pursuant to a search warrant, they can search any place that the gun could be hidden. If they opened a nightstand drawer and found cocaine, the cocaine would be admissible because of plain view. The officer would have been justified by the search warrant to examine the drawer for the gun. In doing so, he found the cocaine. In *United States v. Montgomery Gray*, the U.S. Court of Appeals examined the scope of a search warrant's impact on plain view.

UNITED STATES v. MONTGOMERY GRAY

78 F.Supp.2d 524 (1999)

The Facts: As part of a 1999 investigation for hacking into the National Library of Medicine of the National Institutes of Health computers, the FBI obtained a warrant for the search of Montgomery Gray's home in Arlington, Virginia. The warrant authorized the search of Gray's computers for evidence of the unauthorized computer intrusions. They seized four computers and took them to the FBI offices to conduct the forensic searches. During the methodical search of the computer files, an FBI agent opened two files—one named "Teen" and the other "Little Teen"—and realized that they included child pornography. Armed with that information, the agents obtained additional search warrants for evidence of child pornography. The defendant, Gray, argued that the evidence should have been excluded because the photographs from the initial two files were not described in the original warrant. The U.S. District Court Trial Judge allowed the evidence.

The Decision: The U.S. Court of Appeals agreed. They ruled that the photographs were admissible because they fell within the plain view doctrine. The agent's actions in opening the files were justified by the original search warrant that provided for the search of all files in Gray's computers for evidence of the computer hacking crime. While conducting that authorized search, the FBI agent observed the child pornography. Therefore, the photographs were in "plain view" and admissible.

A police officer may also use common tools to enhance the senses, such as a flashlight or binoculars. It is not a violation of one's reasonable expectation of privacy for an officer to use a flashlight or car lights to illuminate a dark area. An officer cannot, however, utilize advanced technology to bring something into plain view if the use of the technology is not in reasonably common usage. The use of more advanced technology is also discussed later in this chapter.

Plain Hearing

Noise or voices that can be easily heard by others are not within one's reasonable expectation of privacy. As with plain view, if an officer can hear another's voice from a legal vantage point, the audible sound is admissible. In the Katz case, the FBI could have used an agent posing as another citizen waiting to use the phone. If the agent could have overheard Katz's conversations without the use of the bugging device, the statements would have been admissible. It is not uncommon to overhear another's conversation in a public place such as a restaurant or a store. Those conversations fall within plain hearing. A police officer is allowed to go undercover to listen to another's conversation so long as he or she is not trespassing. Unfortunately, we have all been annoyed by a person talking loudly on a cell phone. If the overheard conversation included evidence of criminal activity, it is admissible in evidence.

On the Street

The Loud Mouth

Candace is a police officer attending classes at the local university. She is sitting in a grassy common area provided for studying in the center of the campus. Unfortunately, there is another student on a nearby bench who is talking loudly on his cell phone. Not only is he annoying, everyone can hear his somewhat frantic conversation. Candace hears the annoying student threaten to kill the person with whom he is talking. "I'm gonna kill you. You don't break up with me. Nobody breaks up with me. You are a dead woman. Dead . . . hear me . . . . dead!" Are his threats admissible? Does he have a reasonable expectation of privacy in his words? ■

Plain Smell

An odor cannot be seized, but its detection and identification may be a determining factor in establishing probable cause for an arrest or search. Its presence may also be used as evidence at trial under some circumstances. The law of plain view and hearing applies in the same manner to plain smell. If an officer is in a legal vantage point, his or her detection of an odor is admissible. An officer who smells the odor of marijuana during a vehicle stop would have probable cause to believe there is marijuana in the car. It should be noted that not all jurisdictions allow warrantless vehicle searches based on evidence of smell. The smell of a rotting corpse would be evidence that leads a reasonable person to believe that a dead victim may be present, and the odor of a toxic substance might lead emergency personnel to investigate or evacuate a premises.

The odor of a substance which is a by-product or source material for contraband is not alone sufficient for probable cause. For example, acetone is an ingredient that is often used in the manufacture of methamphetamine. Acetone is also legally used in other chemical and cleaning applications. Thus, the smell of acetone alone would not be sufficient for probable cause to believe that a meth lab was present. However, combined with other evidence, the odor may contribute to establishment of probable cause.

As indicated previously in the discussion of exigent circumstances, police may enter a premises without a warrant if there is reason to believe someone is in danger. The presence of a toxic odor may provide that justification. In *United States v. Cervantes*, 219 F.3d 882 (9th Cir. 2000), police in Garden Grove, California, were summoned by firefighters who were concerned about a strong chemical odor coming from a unit in an apartment building. The officers recognized the odor as acetone which is used in the manufacture of methamphetamine. The residents of the apartment refused entry to the police and firefighters when they knocked on the door where the odor was the strongest. The police, concerned that there was a meth lab in the apartment, entered the apartment without a warrant. The existence of a meth lab would have been dangerous to all of the building residents. Once inside, they discovered a meth lab. The Ninth Circuit Federal Appeals Court determined that the strong smell of a chemical odor justified the warrantless entry into the apartment. They ruled that the odor provided the officer with reasonable cause to believe their emergency entry was necessary. The warrantless entry was not based on probable cause to believe there was contraband but, rather, probable cause to believe that there were dangerous chemicals inside.

Plain Feel

The concept of plain feel operates the same as plain view. If a law enforcement officer has the right to touch or feel property, then the information gathered from the touch might lead to probable cause. As a practical matter, the plain feel seizure of evidence is less common. In *Minnesota v. Dickerson*, discussed in Chapter 6, the Supreme Court indicated that the frisk for weapons conducted during a *Terry v. Ohio* stop and frisk might result in a probable cause determination that contraband was present. However, they also ruled that the initial "feel" could not exceed what was necessary to determine if a weapon was present. The information gathered from touch is usually not as informative as plain view, smell, or hearing.

Open Fields Doctrine

Open fields
The open spaces and land that do not immediately surround a person's home.

Curtilage
Buildings in close proximity to a dwelling, which are continually used for carrying on domestic employment; or such place as is necessary and convenient to a dwelling and is habitually used for family purposes.

In some circumstances law enforcement may conduct warrantless searches in the open lands and fields that do not immediately surround a person's home. Warrantless searches pursuant to the **open fields** doctrine are usually conducted in rural and farm settings. The term *open fields* refers to the open spaces and land that are not part of the property that is used for intimate home activities. The open fields surround the curtilage which is the immediate area surrounding a home. In *United States v. Potts*, 297 F2d. 68 (Sixth Circuit, 1961), **curtilage** was defined as "all buildings in close proximity to a dwelling, which are continually used for carrying on domestic employment; or such place as is necessary and convenient to a dwelling and is habitually used for family purposes." The family home and adjacent outbuildings would fall within the curtilage, while the outlying fields and woods would be considered as open fields. While one has a reasonable expectation of privacy in their curtilage, they do not in the surrounding open fields. Thus, law enforcement officers may enter an open field without consent or a warrant.

OLIVER v. UNITED STATES

466 U.S. 170 (1984)

The Facts: Narcotics agents of the Kentucky State Police went to Oliver's farm to investigate information that marijuana was being grown on the property. When they arrived at the farm, they encountered a locked gate with a "No Trespassing" sign. However, the agents walked around the gate on a footpath and continued onto the farm. They walked past a barn and a parked camper. At one point, someone standing in front of the camper shouted that no hunting was allowed and demanded that the agents "come back up here." The officers shouted back that they were Kentucky State Troopers. When they approached the camper no one was present. They discovered marijuana growing in a field over a mile from Oliver's house. Oliver was arrested and indicted for manufacturing a controlled substance in violation of federal law. The agents did not have a search warrant.

The Decision: The Court ruled that Oliver's marijuana patch did not fall within the protection of the Fourth Amendment and that the evidence was admissible. They agreed that the officers did not have a search warrant and that they were, in fact, trespassing. However, they identified the search area as open fields and ruled that Oliver did not have a reasonable expectation of privacy. The Court stated the following:

> Open fields do not provide the setting for those intimate activities that the Amendment is intended to shelter from government interference or surveillance. There is no societal interest in protecting the privacy of those activities, such as the cultivation of crops that occur in open fields. Moreover, as a practical matter these lands usually are accessible to the public and the police in ways that a home, an office, or commercial structure would not be. It is not generally true that fences or "No Trespassing" signs effectively bar the public from viewing open fields in rural areas. And both petitioner Oliver and respondent Thornton concede that the public and police lawfully may survey lands from the air. For these reasons, the asserted expectation of privacy in open fields is not an expectation that "society recognizes as reasonable."

The Court indicated that efforts by an individual to protect their privacy, such as planting marihuana on secluded land, erecting fences and signs designed to deter trespassing, does not establish reasonable expectations of privacy in an open field environment. They stated, "the test of legitimacy is not whether the individual chooses to conceal assertedly 'private' activity. Rather, the correct inquiry is whether the government's intrusion infringes upon the personal and societal values protected by the Fourth Amendment. As we have explained, we find no basis for concluding that a police inspection of open fields accomplishes such an infringement." The Court also indicated that the common law of trespass had little or no relevance to the applicability of the Fourth Amendment.

While the Court did not provide exact parameters for the distinction between curtilage and open fields, its guidance suggests that the area of a farm in which the family activities are conducted would be considered curtilage and thus is protected by the Fourth Amendment. Many farms are designed so there is a farmhouse with a nearby garage for the family car as well as a workshop or storage area. It is usually clear by the fact that the property has a closely cut lawn as opposed to the fields where crops may be tended. A fence may help distinguish the curtilage from the open field. The Court, while suggesting that each case would provide its own unique circumstances, provided a commonsense approach to the determination.

Technology and Privacy

In 2013, Edward Snowden, an employee of a national defense contractor, revealed the existence of a massive National Security Agency surveillance program. In the aftermath, the U.S. Government admitted that it was conducting domestic surveillance of some cell phone and e-mail transmissions though it denied that it was actually listening to personal conversations. The framers of the U.S. Constitution could not have envisioned such technology. They could not have imagined that a private citizen would be able to sit in a coffeehouse and connect with a worldwide Internet. Satellite technology now allows live imagery broadcast of a backyard barbeque. A **global positioning system** (GPS) unit can provide navigation instructions from an automobile or phone. A golfer can purchase a product at his or her local pro shop which allows them to determine the exact yardage from their ball to the hole. While all of these advancements have connected us in unimaginable ways, they have also stretched the limits of the Fourth Amendment. Advances in technology have also altered the concept of one's reasonable expectation of privacy.

As technology has advanced, the interpretation of the term "plain" to describe sensory perception has evolved. The Supreme Court has never indicated that technology could not be used to enhance the senses. Common devices such as flashlights, hearing aids, and binoculars may be used to view evidence that could not otherwise be seen or heard. These are items in common use and are easily accessible to the general population. One would not reasonably expect that these common items would not be available to law enforcement. The police may not, however, utilize high-tech devices that exceed one's reasonable expectation of privacy in order to enhance their abilities without first obtaining a search warrant. The difficulty occurs in determining where the line is drawn. As technology has advanced, the concept of common usage has changed. The majority of Americans now carry electronics devices that store information, access the Internet, and link with GPS. One thing is certain, change is constant. Courts must also consider the method and manner in which the technology is used. One of the early cases in which the Court addressed the use of technology to enhance plain view was decided in 1983.

Global positioning system (GPS)
A navigational system that uses satellite technology to determine a geographic location.

UNITED STATES v. KNOTTS

460 U.S. 276 (1983)

The Facts: The Knotts case began when officials from the 3M Company in St. Paul, Minnesota, informed law enforcement that one of their employees, Tristan Armstrong, had been stealing chemicals that may be used in the manufacture of illegal drugs. Further investigation revealed that Armstrong had been purchasing similar chemicals from the Hawkins Chemical Company in Minneapolis. With the permission of Hawkins Chemical, police inserted an electronic beeper device inside a container of chloroform, a precursor chemical used in the manufacture of meth-amphetamines. The beeper would transmit a signal to the police so they could more easily track Armstrong. When Armstrong picked up the container, the police fol-lowed him using both visual surveillance and the beeper signal. Armstrong drove to the home of Darryl Petschen and moved the container to Petschen's car. The police then followed him across the St. Croix River into Wisconsin. At that point, Petschen apparently spotted the police and made evasive maneuvers causing the police to lose sight of the car. About an hour and a half later, the police picked up the beeper signal. The car was now stationary. With the assistance of a helicopter, they were able to determine that the car and beeper were now at a secluded cabin occupied by Knotts. That information combined with other evidence from their investigation allowed the police to obtain a search warrant for Knotts' cabin. The search revealed a fully operable drug laboratory along with $10,000 worth of equipment and chemi-cals as well as recipes for the manufacture of amphetamine and methamphetamine. There were enough chemicals to manufacture 14 pounds of amphetamine. Police discovered the marked chloroform container under a barrel outside of the cabin.

The Decision: The Court allowed the evidence discovered in Knott's cabin. Armstrong and Petschen had no reasonable expectation of privacy of their route on public streets or through open fields. The beeper did not provide the police with any information that they could not have legally obtained through visual surveil-lance. The Court stated:

> But no such expectation of privacy extended to the visual observation of Petschen's automobile arriving on his premises after leaving a public highway, nor to movements of objects such as the drum of chloroform outside the cabin in the "open fields." *Hester v. United States*, 265 U.S. 57 (1924).
>
> Visual surveillance from public places along Petschen's route or adjoining Knotts' premises would have sufficed to reveal all of these facts to the police. The fact that the officers in this case relied not only on visual surveillance, but also on the use of the beeper to signal the presence of Petschen's automobile to the police re-ceiver, does not alter the situation. Nothing in the Fourth Amendment prohibited the police from augmenting the sensory faculties bestowed upon them at birth with such enhancement as science and technology afforded them in this case.

Thermal imaging device
A device that detects the heat emitted from a person or object.

In 2001, the Supreme Court decided a landmark technology case involving the warrantless use of a **thermal imaging device** to examine the heat signature emanating from a residence.

KYLLO v. UNITED STATES

533 U.S. 27 (2001)

The Facts: Suspecting that Danny Kyllo was growing marijuana inside of his Oregon home, agents of the U.S. Department of Interior used a thermal imaging device known as an Agema Thermovision 210 to scan the heat signature of his home. The agents determined that unusually high heat levels were emanating from Kyllo's garage and roof. The detected levels were higher than those of the rest of his house or his neighbors and were consistent with the heat from marijuana grow lights. Armed with this information, the officers requested and obtained a federal search warrant. Their search of Kyllo's home revealed a marijuana growing operation and over 100 marijuana plants. Kyllo was convicted of manufacturing marijuana in violation of the U.S. Code.

The Decision: The evidence was excluded by the U.S. Supreme Court. The Court stated, "Where, as here, the Government uses a device that is not in general public use, to explore details of the home that would previously have been unknowable without physical intrusion, the surveillance is a 'search' and is presumptively unreasonable without a warrant."

On the Street

Plain hearing or violation of privacy?

The police suspect three men are running a meth lab in a barn in a rural farm area. With the permission of an adjacent landowner, the police set up a parabolic microphone that allows them to focus on a small and distant target and amplify the sound. They can see the suspects milling around outside the barn. By directing the microphone, they hear the suspects' conversation. The men are openly discussing the manufacture of methamphetamine in the barn. Armed with the evidence of the conversation, the police seek a search warrant for the barn. May the statements be used? Was this a violation of their reasonable expectation of privacy? ▧

In *Kyllo*, the Supreme Court used the description "general public use" to describe acceptable technology. However, devices that were once available only to the military can now be purchased in a department store. Global positioning technology is now included in most cell phones. May the police track your whereabouts using the cell phone GPS? Automotive manufacturers now sell vehicles with built-in GPS. The General Motors OnStar system can determine the location of your vehicle at any time. Do you have a reasonable expectation of privacy in this information? In 2012, the Supreme Court addressed the use of a GPS device placed on a vehicle without a warrant.

UNITED STATES v. JONES

565 U.S. ___, 132 S.Ct. 945 (2012)

The Facts: As stated by the Court:

> In 2004 respondent Antoine Jones, owner and operator of a nightclub in the District of Columbia, came under suspicion of trafficking in narcotics and was made the target of an investigation by a joint FBI and Metropolitan Police Department task force. Officers employed various investigative techniques, including visual surveillance of the nightclub, installation of a camera focused on the front door of the club, and a pen register and wiretap covering Jones's cellular phone. Based in part on information gathered from these sources, in 2005 the Government applied to the United States District Court for the District of Columbia for a warrant authorizing the use of an electronic tracking device on the Jeep Grand Cherokee registered to Jones's wife. A warrant issued, authorizing installation of the device in the District of Columbia and within 10 days.
>
> On the 11th day, and not in the District of Columbia but in Maryland, agents installed a GPS tracking device on the undercarriage of the Jeep while it was parked in a public parking lot. Over the next 28 days, the Government used the device to track the vehicle's movements, and once had to replace the device's battery when the vehicle was parked in a different public lot in Maryland. By means of signals from multiple satellites, the device established the vehicle's location within 50 to 100 feet, and communicated that location by cellular phone to a Government computer. It relayed more than 2,000 pages of data over the 4-week period.

Jones was convicted of trafficking cocaine and received a life sentence at his original trial.

The Decision: The Court ruled that the agents committed a trespass and conducted a search when they placed the device on Jones' car without a warrant. The Justices, though in agreement on the issue of trespass, were divided in their reasoning. They excluded the evidence because the police actions violated the Fourth Amendment, but they did not agree that the defendant's reasonable expectation of privacy was violated.

In May 2013, Antoine Jones pleaded guilty rather than face a new trial. He was sentenced to 15 years in federal prison.

Public Exposure to Technology

Closed-circuit technology
Cameras that broadcast, monitor, or record events and transmit to another receiving source.

Law enforcement's use of advanced technology is acceptable when the target of the monitoring activity is knowingly exposing his or her activities to the public. In those situations, the individual cannot reasonably expect his or her conduct or evidence to be private. The use of closed-circuit video is becoming increasingly common in the United States. The Turkish National Police have developed an advanced system of video surveillance which allows them to monitor public activities all across the city of Istanbul. The use of such **closed-circuit technology** is now becoming increasingly common in the United States. With such technology, the police are able to monitor and video citizen activity in public places. The videos from these surveillances allow the police to investigate and apprehend individuals involved in criminal activity. If a person engages in criminal activity on a public street corner, that person does not have a reasonable expectation that his or her conduct is not being videotaped. If a citizen is on another person's private property, that citizen may be subject to video monitoring. Video of criminal behavior is commonly used in evidence in our nation's criminal courts. News media institutions now play crime videos in order for the members of the public to provide information regarding the crime. Closed-circuit video was instrumental in identifying the suspects in the Boston Marathon bombings.

On the Street

The Nanny Cam

Betsy works for the Elliot family as a nanny. She provides care for their four-year-old son, Jeremy. One fall afternoon, Jeremy was continually complaining about being hungry. Betsy offered him a healthy snack, but he demanded leftover Halloween candy. He continued to scream and call Betsy names. Frustrated, she locked Jeremy in a closet with the family cat. She then kicked the door several times to agitate the cat. The cat scratched Jeremy all over his face requiring a trip to the hospital. Betsy claimed that Jeremy grabbed the cat by the tail and the cat attacked him. Unknown to Betsy, the Elliot family had installed video cameras throughout their home. The video clearly showed the course of events including Betsy telling the injured Jeremy that he deserved it for calling her names. Would the video be admissible as evidence if Betsy is prosecuted for assault? ▪

Social media is now being used by law enforcement to identify and apprehend people involved in criminal organizations. By researching the network of friends and contacts, investigators have been able to identify criminal affiliations. When a suspect posts information or evidence on the Internet, the suspect has waived his or her privacy interests.

In August 2013, a Florida man posted a murder confession along with a photo of his wife's bloody corpse on the social media site, Facebook. He purportedly stated, "I'm going to prison or death sentence for killing my wife love you guys miss you guys take care Facebook people you will see me in the news." He then went to a police station and admitted killing her. The Miami-Dade police went to his house and discovered the woman's body. Would his social media confession be admissible? Yes. He has no reasonable expectation of privacy that his writings would not be seen by others.

One month later, Matthew Cordle posted a three-minute YouTube video in which he confessed to killing a man while he was driving while intoxicated. Cordle was convicted of Aggravated Vehicular Homicide and sentenced to six years in prison in the Franklin County, Ohio, Court of Common Pleas.

Pen registers
Technology that records the outgoing numbers called or texted on a communication device such as a phone.

Trap and tap
Technology that records the numbers received by a communication device such as a phone.

Biometric technology
Technology used to detect and recognize human physical characteristics.

Aeronautical drones
Unmanned aircraft used primarily in military operations to conduct surveillance or deliver weapons.

Pen registers allow the recording of the numbers dialed by a telephone. **Trap and tap** devices record the number received by a phone. These devices do not listen to the contents of a conversation. In *Smith v. Maryland*, 442 U.S. 735 (1979), the Supreme Court ruled that there was no expectation of privacy in a person's phone number since the public was aware that telephone service providers recorded the numbers called and received for billing purposes. However, in 1986, the U.S. Congress enacted legislation requiring a warrant to obtain such information but provided that warrant could be based on law enforcement's assertion that the information would be material to an ongoing investigation.

A caller does not have a reasonable expectation of privacy that the receiver of the call will not disclose the information to the police. If a person sends a text message to others, the sender does not have a reasonable expectation that the recipient would not disclose the text to law enforcement. Likewise, a search warrant that results in the seizure of a cell phone allows the police to examine the date recorded in that phone.

A number of states are now using **biometric technology** to detect and identify offenders. The technology detects and recognizes human physical characteristics. The technology is being used in some states to identify suspects caught on camera by comparing their biometric data to state driver's license photographs. This technology could allow police to more easily identify suspects in crowd situations. The Federal Bureau of Investigation is developing a surveillance initiative based on biometric data. The billion dollar Next Generation Identification (NGI) program utilizes facial recognition and new technologies allowing the identification of fingerprints, palm prints, tattoos, and DNA. The use of the technology continues to incite controversy. While advocates argue that an individual does not have a reasonable expectation of privacy if the individual exposes his or her facial features to the general public, critics allege that the advanced technology exceeds a person's privacy interests.

Police are also using cameras to measure and record traffic events such as speeding and red light violations. One such Maryland company, Optotraffic, provides traffic enforcement cameras that record speeding violations. Photographs are taken of speeding vehicles and their license plates. The government jurisdiction then issues a civil liability ticket to the registered owner of the vehicle. The owner is responsible for paying the ticket unless the owner identifies another as the driver. These programs are administrated by the private company in exchange for a portion of the collected revenues. In some jurisdictions there have been both lawsuits and legislation designed to prevent the use of such technology. Citizenry often argue that the objective of the camera usage is more about revenue generation than traffic safety.

Courts have consistently agreed that observation from an airplane or helicopter does not violate one's expectation of privacy. However, the use of **aeronautical drones** to monitor activity by domestic government agencies may be on the horizon. This technology, developed for military functions such as monitoring and weapons delivery, is becoming more commonly available to local governments as well as private enterprises. Does your reasonable expectation of privacy include surveillance by drones and satellite systems? Google Maps allow a private citizen to view a satellite image of almost anywhere in the world, sometimes in real time. Is that plain view?

Summary

In *Katz v. United States*, the U.S. Supreme Court delineated one of the most important concepts in criminal procedure: the premise that the Fourth Amendment protected one's reasonable expectation of privacy. This standard changed the view that the Fourth Amendment only barred unreasonable intrusion or trespass. At the same time, it expanded warrantless plain view searches to private areas in some circumstances.

The concepts of plain view, plain hearing, and plain smell are also discussed in detail in this chapter. Based on the theory that a person does not have a reasonable expectation of privacy in his or her conduct or property which is exposed to the public, plain view allows the police to seize evidence that they view from a legally allowed standpoint. The concept was expanded even more when the Court allowed that the police could actually trespass on private lands if the property was considered an "open field."

Rapid advances in technology have continued to test the courts. As devices such as GPS and smartphones become more common, the bounds of what is reasonably private are changing. Many of the future search and seizure cases are likely to revolve around these technology issues.

Review Questions

1. May the police use binoculars in order to bring targeted property within plain view? Why or why not?
2. Describe a situation in which plain smell could be used to establish probable cause to search?
3. Explain the distinction between open fields and curtilage.
4. May the police use a thermal imaging device from a flying helicopter to determine if there are marijuana grow lights being used in a private home? Why or why not?
5. Does an individual have a reasonable expectation of privacy in a statement or photograph posted on a social media site such as Facebook or Instagram? Why or why not?
6. What is protected from an unreasonable search by the government?
7. A conversation you have with another during lunch in a public restaurant may not be protected. Why?
8. The U.S. Supreme Court ruled that the evidence in *Katz* was inadmissible. What could the government have done differently in order to have legally listened to Katz's conversation?
9. The TSA may search your bags before you board an airplane. The police may not board a bus and search your bags stowed in an overhead compartment without a warrant. Explain the difference.
10. Under what circumstances is property considered abandoned and thereby subject to a warrantless search or seizure?

Legal Terminology

Aeronautical drones
Biometric technology
Closed-circuit technology
Contraband
Curtilage
Evidence
Fruits of a crime

Global positioning system (GPS)
Instrumentalities of a crime
Open fields
Pen registers
Thermal imaging device
Trap and tap

References

Alsup, D., & Brumfield, B. (2013, August 11). Florida Man Allegedly Kills Wife, Posts Confession, Photo of Body on Facebook. CNN. Retrieved from http://www.cnn.com/2013/08/09/us/florida-facebook-confession

Bond v. United States, 529 U.S. 334 (2000)

CNN Library. (2013, June) *Boston Marathon Terror Attack Fast Facts.* Retrieved from http://www.cnn.com/2013/06/03/us/boston-marathon-terror-attack-fast-facts

Greenwood v. California, 486 U.S. 35 (1988)

Katz v. United States, 389 U.S. 347 (1967)

Oliver v. United States, 466 U.S. 170 (1984)

Pen Registers and Trap and Trace Devices, 18 U.S.C.A. §§3121–3127

Silva, S. (2013, November 23). Driver Who Confessed to DUI Killing in YouTube Video Gets 6 Years, 6 Month in Jail. NBC News. Retrieved from http://usnews.nbcnews.com/_news/2013/10/23/21096393-driver-who-confessed-to-dui-killing-in-youtube-video-gets-6-years-6-months-in-jail

Smith v. Maryland, 442 U.S. 735 (1979)

United States v. Cervantes, 219 F.3d 882 (9th Cir. 2000)

United States v. Jones, 565 US ___, 132 S.Ct. 945 (2012)

United States v. Montgomery Gray, 78 F.Supp.2d 524 (1999)

United States v. Potts, 297 F2d. 68 (Sixth Circuit, 1961)

WJLA.com. (2013, May 1). Antoine Jones Pleads Guilty; Accepts Fifteen Year Sentence. Retrieved from http://www.wjla.com/articles/2013/05/antoine-jones-pleads-guilty-accepts-15-years-sentence-88229.html

Chapter 9
Consent Searches

Officer: "Do you mind if I search your car? It would sure make me feel safer."

Suspect: "Sure, go ahead."

Law enforcement officers often discover and seize evidence simply because a person gives them permission to search. This is considered a consent search. The police ask an individual if they can search the individual's property. Amazingly, suspects will give consent even though they know that they are hiding evidence or contraband. If the consent is obtained in a valid manner, no other legal justification is needed for the search. They do not need a warrant, probable cause, or arrest. In many situations, the police will ask for consent when they have no other legal justification to search. There are, however, legal requirements that must be met for a valid consent. A valid consent to search must meet three specific requirements: standing, voluntary, and knowing.

Standing

Standing
The authority to grant consent to search.

The authority to grant consent to a search is called **standing**. In order for a consent search to be valid, the consenting person must have that authority. In many situations, the standing may be obvious. The police pull over a car for a traffic violation. They ask the driver if they can search his car and he says yes. Upon searching the car, the police discover marijuana hidden under the back seat. The evidence is admissible. The driver has the authority to give consent because he has control and custody of the vehicle. Thus, he has standing. A woman who gives consent to search her purse has standing. A student would have standing to give consent to search her book bag. It is also common that the consenting party becomes the defendant because the contraband or evidence discovered is used to prosecute them for a crime. The more troublesome issues come from third-party consents. A third-party consent occurs when someone other than the defendant grants the consent to search. In a third-party situation, the consenting party must have standing. If not, the defendant may have the evidence excluded. Can your neighbors give the police consent to search your house? Of course they can't. Why not? They do not have standing. If you were involved in a car wreck could the police ask a passerby if they could search your car? No. Those standing decisions are rather easy. However, the determination of standing for third-party consents is not always so simple.

Landlord and Tenant

Ownership of property does not always guarantee standing to consent. The owner of property may have conveyed the standing to a tenant who actually has the reasonable expectation of privacy. A tenant who rents an apartment or house has the privacy interest, not the owner or landlord. Most state laws and rental contracts allow landlords to enter premises to perform reasonable inspections for damage, termites, or maintenance. A landlord may not, however, grant permission to the police to search his or her tenant's home. The person renting the apartment or house has the same reasonable expectation of privacy as that of a homeowner. A search based on the consent of the landlord would not be valid, and any evidence discovered would be inadmissible.

On the Street

The Consenting Landlord

Jermaine lives in an eight-unit apartment building just east of his college campus. The building is owned by Walter and Edna who also live in one of the apartment units. Walter and Edna bought the property for their retirement income. One afternoon, the local police approach Walter and Edna and explain to them that they suspect that Jermaine might be selling drugs. The police do not have a warrant, but they would like to check out Jermaine's apartment while he is in class just to make sure everything is alright. Walter and Edna readily agree and give a key to the police. Edna says, "He seems like a sweet kid but I don't want anyone selling drugs in our building. We live here too, you know. Just bring the key back down when you finish." The police open Jermaine's apartment and enter without a warrant. They search it thoroughly and discover two-gallon storage bags stuffed with marijuana under Jermaine's fish tank. They seize them, wait for Jermaine to return, and arrest him for the possession of illegal drugs. Is the marijuana admissible? Did the police have the right to search?

Hotels

The issue of standing also arises when the police seek consent to search a hotel or motel room. Though the hotel is owned by an individual or company, guests still have reasonable privacy interests that protect them from police intrusion. The manager or clerk of a hotel does not have standing to consent to a police search. The U.S. Supreme Court addressed the issue in a California armed robbery case.

STONER v. CALIFORNIA

376 U.S. 483 (1964)

The Facts: On October 25, 1960, two armed men robbed the Budget Town Food Market in Monrovia, California. During the police investigation, an eyewitness indicated that one of the men had a gun and was wearing a gray jacket and horn-rimmed glasses. While the police were still on the scene, a checkbook was found in a nearby parking lot. The checkbook register indicated that recent checks had been written to the Mayfair Hotel in nearby Pomona. The name on the checkbook was Joey Stoner. Further investigation revealed that Joey Stoner had a criminal record. The Pomona Police provided a photograph of Stoner to the Monrovia officers. After viewing the photograph, two eyewitnesses identified Joey Stoner as the man who held the gun during the robbery of the market. Acting upon this information, the police went to the Mayfair Hotel on the night of October 27. They did not have an arrest or search warrant. The hotel desk clerk confirmed that Stoner was registered in Room 404 but that he wasn't in at the time. All guests were required to leave their keys at the desk if they left the hotel premises. The police told the clerk that Stoner was wanted for the robbery, and they asked if they could search his room. The clerk consented and gave them the room key. The police searched the room and found a pair of horn-rimmed glasses, a gray jacket, a .45-caliber semi-automatic pistol, and ammunition. Stoner was arrested in Las Vegas, Nevada, two days later, and the evidence discovered in the hotel room was admitted at his trial. Stoner was convicted and ultimately appealed his case to the U.S. Supreme Court.

The Decision: The Court, in overturning Stoner's conviction, stated, "It is important to bear in mind that it was the petitioner's constitutional right which was at stake here, and not the night clerk's nor the hotel. It was a right, therefore, which only the petitioner could waive by word or deed, either directly or through an agent. It is true that the night clerk clearly and unambiguously consented to the search. But there is nothing in the record to indicate that the police had any basis whatsoever to believe that the night clerk had been authorized by the petitioner to permit the police to search the petitioner's room." The Court excluded the evidence from the hotel room ruling that the clerk did not have standing to consent to the search. While the court acknowledged that an individual who rents a room would reasonably expect that "maids, janitors, or repairmen" might enter the room, the guest would not reasonably expect that the hotel clerk would allow the police to search.

Shared Standing

A person has standing to consent to a search if he or she shares common authority over the area to be searched. The police officer seeking consent has the responsibility of determining whether a person has the standing to consent. In *Illinois v. Rodriquez,* 497 U.S. 177 (1990), the U.S. Supreme Court held that the police officer obtaining consent to search must make an objective decision based on the facts available at the moment of consent as to whether the consenting party had authority. It must be a reasonable consideration of the circumstances known at the time of consent. There are a variety of situations in which two or more people might share standing to consent.

The U.S. Supreme Court addressed the concept of shared standing in *United States v. Matlock*, 415 U.S. 164 (1974):

> Common authority is, of course, not to be implied from the mere property interest a third party has in the property. The authority which justifies the third-party consent does not rest upon the law of property, with its attendant historical and legal refinements but rests rather on mutual use of the property by persons generally having joint access or control for most purposes, so that it is reasonable to recognize that any of the co-inhabitants has the right to permit the inspection in his own right and that the others have assumed the risk that one of their number might permit the common area to be searched.

Cotenants

The determination of who has the authority to grant consent to search is often difficult in situations in which people share a residence. Americans live together in a variety of arrangements. They may be married. They may be college roommates. They may be brother and sister sharing a home. People share personal property as well. A couple of people might share luggage or even a vehicle. These shared situations pose a number of problems in the determination of standing.

The general rule is that any party who shares the care, custody, and control over the property has standing to consent to a search. They each have a privacy interest in the property. They can, however, only consent to search those areas they either share or in which they have an individual privacy interest.

Consider the following: Brenda and Linda are college roommates. They have rented a two-bedroom apartment together. The apartment has one bathroom that they share. It also has a small kitchen, living room, and utility room. They share all of those common areas. However, they have separate bedrooms. While they do not usually lock their bedroom doors, both Brenda and Linda understand that those are their individual private rooms. Of course, they will occasionally go into each other's rooms to visit or to borrow some clothing, but they generally respect one another's privacy. One evening, Brenda is home alone. Linda is out on a date. The local police knock on the door. When Brenda answers, the officer tells her that they have some strong suspicion that her roommate, Linda, has been selling drugs, and they would like to search the apartment. Brenda tells them that Linda is not here. The police say, "That's ok. You live here. Just tell us we can come in and search. You don't want to live with a drug dealer, do you?" Brenda opens the door. The police search the entire apartment. They discover a bag of cocaine underneath the kitchen sink. They also find marijuana in Linda's bedroom closet.

Is the Cocaine Admissible?

Yes. Brenda had the authority to consent to a search for all commonly shared areas in the apartment as well as her own room. The cocaine was discovered in the kitchen that she shared with Linda.

Is the Marijuana Admissible?

No. The marijuana was found in Linda's room. Though Brenda and Linda were room-mates, they did not share common control over each other's bedrooms. They retained their individual privacy interests. Therefore, Brenda did not have the authority to consent to a search of Linda's bedroom.

What are the common areas? To identify standing to consent, there must be a determination of what common areas are shared. In the roommate scenario, the arrangements may vary. Roommates may share the logical common areas such as living room, kitchen, bathrooms, and utility areas. Officers would need to investigate whether they shared bedrooms or other private areas. There might be individual private property that, while located in a common area, is considered private by only one roommate. It is reasonable to presume that the husband and wife are cotenants of all areas and property within their home and share care, custody, and control. When that occurs, either party would have standing to consent.

In *Georgia v. Randolph*, 547 U.S. 103 (2006), the Supreme Court addressed the problem that occurs when one joint tenant consents and the other refuses. The police requested consent to search the Americus, Georgia, home of Janet and Scott Randolph. The husband and wife both had standing. Janet explained to the police that they had been having marital problems and that her husband used drugs. Scott denied it and accused his wife of abusing alcohol and drugs. Janet consented to a police search of the home but her husband refused. The police searched the house based on the wife's consent and her claim that her husband had some "items of drug evidence" in the house. The police found a drinking straw with cocaine residue. Armed with that information, the police then obtained a search warrant. When they searched the house with the warrant, they found additional drugs. Scott Randolph was indicted for possession of cocaine. The U.S. Supreme Court overturned the conviction stating, "We therefore hold that a warrantless search of a shared dwelling for evidence over the express refusal of consent by a physically present resident cannot be justified as reasonable as to him on the basis of consent given to the police by another resident."

As a result of the Randolph decision, the police may not conduct a search if a party who has standing is physically present to object even under circumstances where there is another consenting party with valid standing. The decision does not, however, mandate that the police seek the consent of a party who is not present. Had Scott Randolph not been present, the consent of his wife would have been valid. The police would not have been required to find Scott and ask for his consent.

On the Street

Waldo Isn't Here

Carly and her boyfriend, Waldo, live together in a mobile home. Waldo travels almost every week for his work as a fertilizer salesman. When Waldo left for his weekly sales trip this past Monday morning, he told Carly, "Honey, the police have been snooping around here. If they come by, whatever you do, don't let 'em in. It's my home too, and I don't want those fools coming inside my home looking around. OK, honey bunny?" Carly nodded, "yes." The next afternoon, the local sheriff knocks on the door of the trailer. When Carly answers, he asks her if he can come in and talk to her about her boyfriend. She nervously says, OK. She offered him some sweet tea but he declined. He then tells her that her boyfriend is a suspect in a meth lab operation. He goes on to say he doesn't want Carly to get caught up in it when it all comes falling down. At that point, he tells her that there might be some evidence of the drug operation in the trailer and that he would like to look around if it is OK with her. She says, "hell, go ahead. I don't think he would do anything in here anyway." Carly was wrong. When the sheriff searched the trailer he found several items associated with the illegal manufacture of methamphetamine. Is the evidence admissible? Did the sheriff need Waldo's consent to search? ▧

Consent to Search Motor Vehicles

On the Street

Consenting cousins?

Verlon, after obtaining his learner's permit, asked his older cousin Buford to teach him how to drive. Buford said "sure thing, cousin" and off they went. Verlon was driving Buford's new Dodge Challenger down Hollytree Drive when he failed to stop at a stop sign. The police pulled him over. The officer, upon realizing that Verlon only had a learner's permit, asked him who the car belonged to. Buford explained the situation. The officer then asked Buford if they could search the car. Buford said, "I don't know why you would want to but go ahead. We don't have anything to hide." Unfortunately they did. Apparently, Verlon had stuffed his bag of weed between his seat and console when he got into the car. The cops found it. Is the marijuana admissible? Did Buford have standing to consent to the search of the car even though Verlon was driving and the marijuana belonged to Verlon? ▧

Generally, the owner, the driver, or anyone else who had permission by the owner to drive the car, all have the authority to consent to a search. An exception would occur if the car was rented and the driver was still operating under the rental agreement. In that circumstance, the privacy interest and standing would belong to the driver or the person who rented the vehicle. The consent would allow the officers to search the entire vehicle including any containers within the vehicle so long as it is reasonable to believe they are within the scope of the authority to consent. However, if it is obvious that a container is not the property of or controlled by the consenting party, then the police could not search that item. For example, in *United States v. Welch*, 4 F.3d 761 (9th Cir. 1993), Las Vegas Police obtained consent to search from the male driver of a rental car. His female passenger was also in the car. When they opened the trunk, the police discovered a clasped purse in which they found counterfeit bills. The U.S. Court of Appeals ruled that the defendant's purse was not within the scope of the consent given by the driver of the car.

Voluntary

Valid consent to search must be **voluntary**. Law enforcement cannot obtain consent through **coercion**. They may not threaten a person with physical harm. They are also forbidden from lying about the existence of a warrant or from threatening arrest if they do not have legal justification for a valid arrest. They cannot threaten any other legal action such as the removal of the person's child or exposure to blackmail in order to gain the consent. The mere presence of the police is not considered coercion. While it may be true that a person is intimidated or scared by the presence of law enforcement, the individual still has the ability to exercise his or her own free will and refuse to consent. Likewise, the fact that the person has been legally arrested does not mean that that person cannot voluntarily consent.

In *Schneckloth v. Bustamonte*, 412 U.S. 218 (1973), the U.S. Supreme Court examined the issue of voluntary consent.

SCHNECKLOTH v. BUSTAMONTE

412 U.S. 218 (1973)

The Facts: Early one morning, Sunnyvale, California, Police Officer James Rand pulled a vehicle over for having only one headlight and no license plate light. There were six men in the car. Robert Bustamonte was sitting in the middle of the front seat; Joe Alcala was next to the passenger door; and Joe Gonzales was driving. The driver, Gonzales, did not have a driver's license. When Officer Rand asked for identification from the other five men, only Alcala was able to produce anything. He explained that his brother had loaned him the car. At that point the officer called for backup. After two other officers had arrived, the officer asked Alcala if he could search the car. He replied, "Sure, go ahead." Officer Rand testified that everything was "congenial" during the search. Alcala actually helped him open the doors and the glove compartment. When Rand asked him about the trunk, Alcala opened it himself. The police discovered three wadded checks that had been stolen from a car wash stuffed under the backseat. At no point prior to the discovery of the evidence was anyone threatened with arrest.

The Decision: The Court ruled that all of the facts and circumstances should be examined in order to determine whether the consent was voluntary. They stated:

> We hold only that when the subject of a search is not in custody and the State attempts to justify a search on the basis of his consent, the Fourth and Fourteenth Amendments require that it demonstrate that the consent was in fact voluntarily given, and not the result of duress or coercion, express or implied. Voluntariness is a question of fact [412 U.S. 218, 249] to be determined from all the circumstances, and while the subject's knowledge of a right to refuse is a factor to be taken into account, the prosecution is not required to demonstrate such knowledge as a prerequisite to establishing a voluntary consent.

Knowingly

A person who consents to a search must also understand that he or she is granting permission to search. While a fairly simple premise, there are circumstances in which a person would not meet the knowing requirement. The person may not be able to **knowingly** consent if there is a language barrier. Likewise, a speech or hearing impairment or disability might prevent the person from understanding the nature of the consent. A person who is suffering from a disability or mental impairment to the extent it would diminish his or her ability to understand might also be unable to knowingly consent. The decision to grant consent does not have to be a wise one. The consenting individual does not have to understand the legal consequences that might be suffered from the discovery of evidence. The individual must simply understand that the police are going to search his or her person or property if granted permission. As previously discussed, the police are not required to advise a person that he or she can refuse.

Knowingly
Understanding the nature of one's actions. A person consenting to a search must understand that he or she is granting permission for the police to search a particular area or property.

On the Street

Consenting while Intoxicated

Della was heartbroken. Her boyfriend, Jerry, had just dumped her rather publicly on Facebook. He also announced that he was heading for greener pastures with one of Della's best friends. Della lined up four bottles of her favorite wine on her front porch and proceeded to chug them. After she succeeded in draining the bottles, she heaved them onto the sidewalk in front of her house. Apparently, someone called the police. When the police arrived, they discovered the empty wine bottles on the sidewalk. Della was crying and mumbling incoherently on the steps. The officers asked her if she needed help. She just continued to cry. It was also apparent that she had urinated on her clothing. The officer suggested that she move her pity party indoors. She started crawling toward the door. The officer then said, "I would like to make sure you are gonna be OK. Can I come in and look around your apartment just to make sure everything is cool?" Della growled, "Do what you gotta do." The officer walked into the house and found cocaine lying on the kitchen table. Is the cocaine admissible? Was Della's consent voluntarily and knowingly given? ■

Scope of the Consent

The extent or scope of the permission is determined by both the question and the response to the request for consent. The decision as to what can be searched lies with the consenting party. If the consenting party says yes when the police ask to search their home, then the police are allowed to search the entire house. However, the consenting person could give permission to search everything except the bedrooms. In that situation, the police could not search the bedrooms but could search all other areas of the house. In most situations, the consent is obtained in general terms such as a house, a car, or a garage. The consenting party may also withdraw consent during the search. For example, if the officers were searching a person's home, the consenting individual could change his or her mind and stop the search. While any evidence that had already been seized would be admissible, the officers would be required to stop searching. In some situations, the police will ask if they can search an individual. That issue was addressed in the 2012 decision from the Ninth Circuit of the U.S. Court of Appeals.

UNITED STATES v. RUSSELL

664 F.3d 1279 (2012)

The Facts: As the Court stated:

> Officer Matt Bruch is a Port of Seattle Police Officer assigned as a task force officer with the Drug Enforcement Administration group at the Seattle–Tacoma International Airport. On August 12, 2010, Bruch received a phone call from an Alaska Airlines ticket agent reporting that Russell, described as a black male wearing a leather jacket and a large necklace, had paid cash for a last-minute, one-way ticket to Anchorage, Alaska. The Alaska Airlines agent also reported that Russell was traveling alone and did not check any luggage. In light of these circumstances, Bruch was suspicious that Russell might be a drug courier. Bruch, together with an assisting officer, proceeded to the departure gate for Russell's flight. En route to the gate, Bruch learned that Russell had prior drug and firearm-related convictions, and had also been implicated in a prior drug investigation in Alaska.
>
> Once he approached Russell, Bruch displayed his badge and identified himself as a police officer investigating narcotics. Bruch told Russell that he was "free to go and he wasn't under arrest." Bruch asked Russell for permission to search his bag and his person; Russell consented. After taking possession of Russell's bag and handing it to the assisting officer to search, Bruch asked for permission to search Russell a second time. Russell again consented verbally and spread his arms and legs to facilitate the search.
>
> Russell was wearing baggy pants. Bruch testified that he searched Russell beginning from the ankles and working his way up, using his "standard operating procedure" for a frisk. He squeezed the shin, knee and thigh. When Bruch reached into Russell's groin area he "lifted up to feel." After feeling something hard and unnatural, Bruch arrested Russell. The entire search occurred outside the clothing; Bruch never patted or reached inside the pants.

The Decision: The Appeals Court allowed the search and admitted the evidence. They determined that the search was reasonable and within the scope of Russell's voluntary consent. In their opinion, they discussed the fact that narcotics are often hidden on the body in locations that make discovery difficult. They stated, "Not only would a reasonable person in Bruch's situation understand that the general consent for a narcotics search of the person included a pat-down of all areas of the body, including the groin area, Russell's unrestricted consent to the search and conduct during the search suggested nothing different."

The judges also stated that Russell could have easily stopped the search when the officers started working their way up his pants leg by simply telling the officer not to search his crotch. Russell did not take advantage of this clear opportunity to withdraw consent.

Written Consent

Consent to search does not have to be in writing. As discussed in *Schneckloth,* the police must show that the consent was made voluntarily and not under duress or coercion. While a signed written document may provide some evidence that the consent was voluntarily and knowingly given, it is neither required nor absolute proof. Many police departments provide written consent forms to their officers. The use of police in-car video often assists in proving that consents were voluntarily and knowingly given as well.

Consent by Notice

Individuals may be searched when they are given notice of or are aware of the impending search if they place themselves in the situation. Anyone boarding a commercial airline in the United States may have both their person and their belongings searched. An individual has the option of not flying. Privately owned facilities also have the right to search individuals entering their premises if they provide advance notice. Concert venues and nightclubs often require limited searches and the passage through security detectors prior to entry. Sports fans are now searched prior to entry at some sporting events, including the National Football League. The U.S. government has the right to search anyone who enters a military base. The notification is given by both federal statute and by signage posted on the military reservations.

K-12 schools often conduct searches of school lockers and student book bags. Some actually request local law enforcement to use drug-sniffing dogs to search lockers and vehicles in the school parking lots. Employers may search their employees as a matter of policy and as a condition of employment. This is a form of consent. The individual consents to the search by entering the specified premises. Private employers conduct drug testing based on the same premise. As a condition of employment, the employees must consent to drug testing. The police could, of course, not order an employer to conduct a search of employee's property or a drug test for the purposes of a criminal investigation.

Administrative Searches

In some circumstances, the government may conduct administrative searches for purposes other than investigating criminal activity. Regulated businesses such as liquor, firearms, waste management, or nuclear power often are subject to government regulations that provide search powers to determine if the business is in compliance with industry rules and laws. Most of these administrative searches still require a warrant for involuntary entry; however, the probable cause standards are less stringent in that they require only that the search meets reasonable regulatory standards. For example, a food and health inspector would need only to show that the regulations are reasonably necessary to ensure that the business is complying with health and food standards. Warrantless searches may be allowed in specific public safety situations such as fire inspections.

Summary

A powerful search tool, consent to search allows the police to search a person or property with only the permission of the person authorized to grant such consent. They do not need a warrant, probable cause, or any other legal justification other than the proper permission. Many situations arise when the police will simply ask for permission to search realizing that citizens often agree. Valid consent searches must meet specific requirements. Consenting parties must have proper standing, and the permission must be given voluntarily and knowingly. Collateral issues impacted by consent searches have also been examined in this chapter. The discussions include the scope of consent, implied consent, and consent by notice.

Review Questions

1. The manager of a hotel may allow the police to search a guest's room so long as the guest is not present in the room at the time of the search. True or False? Why or why not?
2. Heather and Cheryl are roommates. Heather returns home from a trip, drops her luggage in their living room, and heads to bed. About an hour later, the police knock on the door and ask if they can search the apartment for drugs. Cheryl says, "Come on in, I've got nothing to hide. My roommate is asleep so please don't bother her. This is her luggage. I'll move it out of the way for you." They then ask if they can search it. Cheryl says, "sure go ahead." The police search the luggage and find heroin. Is the heroin admissible? Did Cheryl have common authority over Heather's luggage?
3. Jack and Jill are married. When asked by the police for consent to search their home, Jill says no. However, Jack tells them to ignore her and to come on in. May the police search? Why or why not?
4. Describe a situation in which a person would not be able to grant a valid consent to search because his or her consent would not be knowingly given?
5. In order to combat a chronic problem with shoplifters, a local grocery store posts a sign at their entrance indicating that everyone entering and leaving their store will be subjected to a search. Can they do that? Why or why not?

Legal Terminology

Coercion   Standing
Knowingly   Voluntary

References

Georgia v. Randolph, 547 U.S. 103 (2006)
Illinois v. Rodriquez, 497 U.S. 177 (1990)
Schneckloth v. Bustamonte, 412 U.S. 218 (1973)
Stoner v. California, 376 U.S. 483 (1964)
United States v. Matlock, 415 U.S. 164 (1974)
United States v. Russell, 664 F.3d 1279 (2012)
United States v. Welch, 4 F.3d 761 (9th Cir. 1993)

Chapter 10
Vehicle Searches

Motor vehicles often play a role in criminal activity. Cars and trucks are used to commit murder and assaults, escape from apprehension, hide evidence, and smuggle contraband. They are also prevalent in the transportation of illegal immigrants. Almost forty thousand people are killed annually as a result of traffic accidents, and that doesn't begin to account for the multiple injuries and property damage. Timothy McVeigh murdered 168 people by transforming a rental truck into an explosive device. He was arrested later that day while driving a car with an illegal license plate. Many Americans watched former NFL football star, O.J. Simpson, elude the police for hours in the infamous white Ford Bronco. The difficulty in apprehending the famous murdering duo of the 1930s, Bonnie and Clyde, has been attributed to their fast V-8–powered Ford getaway cars. Police receive focused training concerning the dangers involved when conducting traffic stops. The involvement of the motor vehicle in criminal activity has posed a number of constitutional problems for the courts. Yet those judges must apply the U.S. Constitution and Bill of Rights to those ever-evolving situations. The constitutional forefathers could not have envisioned the search of a motor vehicle. They could not have imagined a federal building being leveled by a homemade bomb delivered in a box truck.

Because of their mobility and considerable involvement in crime, motor vehicles have been given special consideration by the courts. The expectation of privacy in a motor vehicle is certainly diminished when compared to that enjoyed in a home. Many of the legal justifications that have been addressed previously apply to vehicle searches. Those include the following:

- *Consent:* Searches based on permission apply to the search of automobiles. Police may search a vehicle based upon the voluntary and knowing consent of a person who has legal standing. Police often ask for consent to search from drivers while conducting a traffic stop.
- *Search warrant:* The police may conduct a search of a vehicle if they have a valid search warrant.

- *Plain view:* Police who are standing in a legally allowed location may observe evidence or contraband by simply looking in the windows of a vehicle. This is quite common during traffic stops or accident investigations. These situations often lead to the discovery of contraband or other evidence. For example, a police officer on routine patrol may observe a driver smoking a marijuana cigarette while stopped at a red light. The drug may be seized and used as evidence.
- *DUI and immigration checkpoints:* These roadblock settings place officers in a position to conduct visual inspections of the interior of motor vehicles. These plain view searches may lead to the discovery of evidence or contraband.
- *Border search:* Vehicles are also subject to search when they cross an international border into the United States. Criminals often attempt to smuggle drugs, weapons, and other contraband inside hidden compartments. Some border checkpoints employ technicians skilled in dismantling vehicles in order to discover evidence.
- *Exigent circumstances:* Fresh pursuit, danger to persons, imminent escape, and the immediate destruction of evidence may provide justification for the warrantless search of a vehicle.

There are, however, several legal circumstances that uniquely apply to motor vehicle searches. These situations include probable cause, area within immediate control, and inventory searches.

Probable Cause Search—Motor Vehicle

Law enforcement may conduct a warrantless search of a motor vehicle which is likely to be moved if there is probable cause to believe there is evidence of criminal activity inside the car. This exception to the warrant requirement was originally determined in *Carroll v. United States,* 267 U.S. 132, (1925). In 1982, the U.S. Supreme Court clarified it in detail.

UNITED STATES v. ROSS

456 U.S. 798 (1982)

The Facts: As stated by the Court,

In the evening of November 27, 1978, an informant who had previously proved to be reliable telephoned Detective Marcum of the District of Columbia Police Department and told him that an individual known as "Bandit" was selling narcotics kept in the trunk of a car parked at 439 Ridge Street. The informant stated that he had just observed "Bandit" complete a sale and that "Bandit" had told him that additional narcotics were in the trunk. The informant gave Marcum a detailed description of "Bandit" and stated that the car was a "purplish maroon" Chevrolet Malibu with District of Columbia license plates.

Accompanied by Detective Cassidy and Sergeant Gonzales, Marcum immediately drove to the area and found a maroon Malibu parked in front of 439 Ridge

Street. A license check disclosed that the car was registered to Albert Ross; a computer check on Ross revealed that he fit the informant's description and used the alias "Bandit." In two passes through the neighborhood the officers did not observe anyone matching the informant's description. To avoid alerting persons on the street, they left the area. [456 U.S. 798, 801]

The officers returned five minutes later and observed the maroon Malibu turning off Ridge Street onto Fourth Street. They pulled alongside the Malibu, noticed that the driver matched the informant's description, and stopped the car. Marcum and Cassidy told the driver—later identified as Albert Ross, the respondent in this action—to get out of the vehicle. While they searched Ross, Sergeant Gonzales discovered a bullet on the car's front seat. He searched the interior of the car and found a pistol in the glove compartment. Ross then was arrested and handcuffed. Detective Cassidy took Ross' keys and opened the trunk, where he found a closed brown paper bag. He opened the bag and discovered a number of **glassine** bags containing a white powder. Cassidy replaced the bag, closed the trunk, and drove the car to headquarters.

At the police station Cassidy thoroughly searched the car. In addition to the "lunch-type" brown paper bag, Cassidy found a zippered red leather pouch in the trunk. He unzipped the pouch and discovered $3,200 in cash. The police laboratory later determined that the powder in the paper bag was heroin. No warrant was obtained.

The Decision: The U.S. Supreme Court ruled that if the police have probable cause to believe there is contraband inside a motor vehicle, they may search the entire vehicle including any containers that are inside the vehicle. Their decision confirmed *United States v. Carroll* and the warrantless search of automobiles based on probable cause. They also addressed the scope of the search. They indicated that the police could only search in those areas of the car in which the items could be reasonably found.

The probable cause exception allows the police to skip the trip to the courthouse to obtain a search warrant when they possess probable cause to search a motor vehicle. The Court extended the ruling in *Wyoming v. Houghton*, 526 U.S. 295 (1999) by holding a probable cause search could also include the property of a passenger so long as the objects that were the subject of the search could be located within the container. In *Houghton*, the police searched a passenger's purse after they had established probable cause that drugs may have been in the vehicle. They found drugs in the purse and the search was upheld. In the same year, the Supreme Court allowed the search of a vehicle after the police saw a suspect place a bag of what they reasonably believed to be marijuana in the trunk of a car. *California v. Acevedo,* 500 U.S. 565 (1991).

The exception does not apply in all cases. The warrantless probable cause search is only justified if the vehicle is likely to be moved before it is reasonable to obtain a search warrant. For example, a car parked in a driveway or legally parked on the street is not likely to be moved. The police can easily place the vehicle under surveillance until a warrant can be obtained. Of course, they could immediately search if someone

---

Glassine
A thin, water-resistant, translucent paper product that is occasionally used to transport illegal narcotics.

attempted to access the vehicle. If the police had probable cause to believe there were illegal drugs hidden in a car that was locked in a private garage, a search warrant would be required. They would be allowed to secure the garage to make sure that the car was not moved or tampered with until they obtained a warrant.

The vehicle probable cause exception also applies if the vehicle is in police custody. If the police have probable cause to conduct a warrantless search of a vehicle, they may move that vehicle to the police station, impound lot, or a safer location in order to conduct a more thorough search.

CHAMBERS v. MARONEY

399 U.S. 42 (1970)

The Facts: On May 20, 1963, two men robbed a gas station in North Braddock, Pennsylvania, by gunpoint. After taking the money from the cash register, they directed the attendant, Stephen Kovacich, to stuff the coins in his right-hand glove. Witnesses saw a blue compact station wagon circling the station before the robbery and also observed it speeding away from the scene with four men inside. Within an hour, police stopped four men in a light blue compact station wagon. The car, the men, and the clothing matched the descriptions provided by witnesses. Inside the car, police found a trench coat that also had been described by the station attendant. The men were arrested and the car was driven to the police station. At the stationhouse, the police conducted a thorough search of the station wagon and found two .38-caliber handguns (one loaded with **dumdum bullets**), and a right-hand glove containing small change. They also discovered some cards bearing the name of Raymond Havicon, a gas station attendant from McKeesport, Pennsylvania, who had been robbed at gunpoint seven days earlier. After presenting information concerning the evidence found in the car, police also obtained a search warrant for the home of the defendant. During that search they seized more .38-caliber dumdum bullets similar to those taken from the station wagon. The materials were introduced at trial. Havicon identified the cards, and Kovacich identified the glove. Maroney was convicted of both robberies and sentenced to prison.

The Decision: The Court first determined that the police had probable cause to arrest the subjects for the robbery and to believe that there was evidence in the vehicle. The vehicle, the men, and their clothing matched the detailed descriptions provided by several witnesses including the gas station attendant, Kovacich. The Court's prior decision in *Carroll* clearly would have allowed the police to search the car on the street where they pulled it over without first obtaining a warrant. The auto exception allows the police to conduct a warrantless probable cause search of a vehicle that is likely to be moved. The only difference in this case was that the police moved the vehicle to the police station before they engaged in a more thorough search. That didn't matter. The probable cause still existed. They had the right to search any area of the car where the targeted items could have been hidden. The evidence was allowed and Chamber's conviction stood.

Dumdum bullets
A slang term referring to bullets that are either designed or altered to expand upon striking their target resulting in fragmentation and more serious damage or injury.

Inventory Searches

Motor vehicles are towed and impounded for a variety of reasons. Vehicles that have been rendered inoperable as a result of an accident must be removed from the roadway. Likewise, the vehicle may be towed if the driver has been injured and is unable to drive. The police may **impound** a vehicle when the driver is arrested, and they cannot leave the car unattended along the roadway. They may also impound a car because it was used in a crime. In many jurisdictions, cars are towed if they park in specific no parking zones or if they have multiple unknown parking tickets. In almost all jurisdictions, it is standard procedure for the police to perform an **inventory search** of the car either prior to towing or when the car arrives at the impound lot in order to identify any personal property that may be in the car. Jurisdictions vary greatly as to how the property is subsequently managed and stored once in police custody. People commonly leave valuables in their cars, and it is not unusual for the police to find contraband or other evidence.

Impound
The procedure in which police tow and store a vehicle in a secure facility until it is released to the owner. The area in which the vehicle is stored is referred to as an impound lot.

Inventory search
A search conducted by law enforcement to determine the contents of a vehicle that is being towed and impounded.

SOUTH DAKOTA v. OPPERMAN

428 U.S. 364 (1976)

The Facts: Opperman had parked his car in a no parking/tow-away zone in downtown Vermillion, South Dakota. The city restricted parking between 2:00 and 6:00 A.M. The police first ticketed the vehicle at 3:00 A.M. Later at 10:00 A.M. they wrote another ticket for overtime parking. At that point, the police towed it to the impound lot. At the impound lot, an officer noticed a watch lying on the dashboard as well as other personal items in the backseat. Pursuant to the agency's standard procedure, the officer had the door unlocked and conducted an inventory search for additional personal property. The officer discovered a bag of marijuana in the unlocked glove compartment. The contraband and other personal property were identified on the inventory list and secured in the property room. Later that afternoon, when Opperman came to claim his car and property, he was arrested and charged with possession of marijuana. He attempted to **suppress** the evidence at trial, but it was allowed. He was convicted and sentenced to 14 days in jail and a fine of $100. He ultimately appealed his case to the U.S. Supreme Court.

Suppress
To exclude the evidence from use at trial.

The Decision: The Supreme Court upheld the admissibility of the marijuana pursuant to an inventory search of an automobile. They first discussed the community caretaking responsibilities of law enforcement regarding vehicles:

> In the interests of public safety and as part of what the Court has called "community caretaking functions," *Cady v. Dombrowski*, supra, at 441, automobiles are frequently taken into police custody. Vehicle accidents present one such occasion. To permit the uninterrupted flow of traffic and in some circumstances to preserve evidence, disabled or damaged vehicles will often be removed from the highways or streets at the behest of police engaged solely in caretaking and traffic-control

activities. Police will also frequently remove and impound automobiles which violate parking ordinances and which thereby jeopardize both the public safety and the efficient movement of vehicular traffic. The authority of police to seize and remove from the streets vehicles impeding traffic or threatening public safety and convenience is beyond challenge.

They then provided three reasons for police inventory searches:

1. Protection of the owner's property while in police custody
2. Protection of the police against false claims or disputes over lost or stolen property
3. The protection of the police from potential danger

They further stated, "On this record we conclude that in following standard police procedures, prevailing throughout the country and approved by the overwhelming majority of courts, the conduct of the police was not 'unreasonable' under the Fourth Amendment."

Area Within Immediate Reach and Control— Motor Vehicles

Courts have clearly stated that the police may search a person whom they have placed under a legal arrest. They have extended this premise to the area within their immediate reach and control of the arrestee. The scope of immediate reach and control as it applies to vehicles was examined by the U.S. Supreme Court in 2009.

ARIZONA v. GANT

556 U.S. 332 (2009)

The Facts: On August 25, 1999, Tucson police officers encountered Rodney Gant during the investigation of some suspected drug trafficking. They determined later in the day that Gant's driver's license had been suspended and that he had an outstanding warrant for driving under a suspended license. Later that evening, they returned to the residence and arrested two other people on unrelated charges. As they were securing their prisoners in the police car, Gant pulled into the driveway. He stepped out of his car, closed the door, and walked toward the officers. At that point the officers arrested Gant and placed him in handcuffs. They then called for backup because they already had two prisoners in their car. When the other officers arrived, Gant was placed in the locked backseat of the police car. Then, the police officers went back to his car, searched it, and found cocaine in the pocket of his jacket that was lying on the backseat. They also found a gun. As a result, Gant was convicted of possession of illegal narcotics and sentenced to three years in prison.

The Decision: The Court ruled that the search of the vehicle was a violation of the Fourth Amendment and overturned Gant's conviction. Their decision was extraordinary in that it was a reversal of a ruling they made 28 years earlier in *New York v. Belton*, 453 U.S. 454 (1981). The *Belton* rule allowed police to search even though the suspect had been removed and placed in a police car. In *Gant*, the Court stated the following:

> Police may search a vehicle incident to a recent occupant's arrest only if the arrestee is within reaching distance of the passenger compartment at the time of the search or it is reasonable to believe the vehicle contains evidence of the offense of arrest. When these justifications are absent, a search of an arrestee's vehicle will be unreasonable unless police obtain a warrant or show that another exception to the warrant requirement applies.

As a result of the Gant decision, the police may only justify a search as immediate reach and control if the suspect was still in the car at the time of the search. This would be unlikely as police are generally trained to remove a person whom they have arrested from the car for safety reasons before commencing a search. The *Gant* rule does not prevent the police from conducting a warrantless search justified by probable cause, inventory, or consent.

Recreational Vehicles

Is it a vehicle or a home? That question is sometimes difficult to answer. The answer, however, may be critical in determining the legality of a warrantless police search. The courts have been clear in stating that a person's home provides a greater expectation of privacy than their motor vehicle. As discussed in this chapter, there are a number of circumstances in which law enforcement may conduct warrantless searches of motor vehicles that do not apply to houses, buildings, and homes. There are many recreational vehicles that provide accommodations such as beds, kitchens, living rooms, and the other amenities associated with one's home. Many are capable of connecting to electricity, gas, and sewage facilities and/or providing those functions on-board. The courts look not at the size or the capabilities, but rather at the use at the time of the legal action. It is clear that a recreational vehicle that is in motion is considered a motor vehicle. It is equally clear that a nonmotorized mobile home that sits in a trailer park connected to sewage and utility systems would be treated as a fixed home. The motor home that may be used as either takes a more focused look.

On the Street

On the Road Again

Carissa decided to take the Great American Road Trip. She bought a 32-foot-long motor home to drive from New York City to San Francisco. Her new home had two bedrooms, a full kitchen, a wine cabinet, a dining area, a bathroom with a full stand-up shower, and a Ford V-8 engine. She packed it with plenty of food and clothes and hit the road. At night, she would pull into interstate rest areas to sleep. Many of the rest areas also had pump stations where she could empty her sewage system and replenish her water tanks. What Carissa didn't know was that the Kentucky State Police regularly patrolled the rest areas with drug-sniffing dogs. One night while she was dreaming about the open road, a police drug dog sniffed around her motor home in a rest stop near Lexington, Kentucky. The dog alerted its handler that there were illegal narcotics present. The police knock on her door, wake her up, and then search the interior of her motorhome. Sure enough, they found Carissa's stash of marijuana that she kept under the kitchen sink. Is it admissible? If the motor home was a motor vehicle, the police may search it without a warrant based on probable cause. Consider the following case of *California v. Carney* to determine the answers. ▪

CALIFORNIA v. CARNEY

471 U.S. 386 (1985)

Acting on information that a Dodge mini motor home was being used to exchange marijuana for sex, a Drug Enforcement Administration agent watched Charles Carney approach a young man and then take him inside. The motor home was parked in a lot in downtown San Diego. When the young man left, the agents stopped him. The youth admitted that he was given marijuana in exchange for engaging in sexual activity. The boy agreed to return to the motor home and knock on the door. When he did, Carney stepped outside, and the agents arrested him. The agents then entered the motor home without a warrant and discovered marijuana.

The Decision: The Court allowed the marijuana. They stated that when a vehicle is being used on the highways or is capable of such use and is sitting stationary in a place not regularly used for residential purpose, the automobile warrant applies. Although a motor home has many attributes of a home, it is considered a vehicle, and there is a reduced expectation of privacy.

Federal Appellate Courts have extended the warrant exception to houseboats as well as citing the same considerations as with motor homes. If the houseboat is readily mobile and being used as a movable boat, then it may be searched without a warrant if probable cause exists.

Summary

The motor vehicle was invented long after the drafting of the Fourth Amendment, yet today law enforcement officers and the courts must apply the constitutional requirements to the searches and seizures of cars and trucks. In previous chapters, many legal justifications for searches have been discussed. This chapter, however, has examined how many of those justifications apply uniquely to the search of vehicles.

Of particular note is the ability of law enforcement to conduct warrantless searches on vehicles based on probable cause. In a fairly recent case, the U.S. Supreme Court revised their previous rules on immediate reach and control searches. The chapter also addressed the determination of whether recreational and other large vehicles would be treated as homes or vehicles for the purpose of search. In *South Dakota v. Opperman*, the Court affirmed inventory searches for vehicles that are towed and impounded for a variety of reasons.

Review Questions

1. The police pull over a car that they have probable cause to believe was just used as a getaway vehicle in an armed robbery of a jewelry store. The occupants, who had used firearms in the robbery, also took jewelry and cash from the store. May the police search the vehicle? Why or why not? What areas may they search?
2. Under what circumstances may police search a motor vehicle without a warrant?
3. The U.S. Supreme Court, in allowing the use of inventory searches of motor vehicles, based their decision on three reasons. What are they?
4. *Arizona v. Gant* restricted searches of motor vehicles based on the area within the suspect's immediate reach and control. On what other legal justifications might a police officer base the search of a motor vehicle?
5. What factors should be considered in determining whether a search of a recreational vehicle is considered that of a home or a motor vehicle?

Legal Terminology

Dumdum bullets
Glassine
Impound

Inventory search
Suppress

References

Arizona v. Gant, 556 U.S. 332 (2009)
Carroll v. United States, 267 U.S. 132 (1925)
South Dakota v. Opperman, 428 U.S. 364 (1976)
United States v. Ross, 456 U.S. 798 (1982)

Section III
Self-Incrimination

The previous chapters examined the search and seizure of primarily tangible physical evidence and its use in criminal prosecution. However, the spoken testimony of individuals also provides critical evidence on which judges and juries must base their decisions. Police investigators rely on the statements of suspects, witnesses, and informants as they attempt to unravel the mysteries of a criminal case. Some of these oral exchanges simply provide clues and avenues for investigation. Other statements may become the evidence on which the case outcome will be determined. The spoken word is powerful, and it may carry even more weight when offered under oath in a courtroom.

Criminal defendants are also identified by their personal appearance. They may be recognized by witnesses via eyewitness identification procedures such as lineups, showups, photographic or video presentations, or even in-court identification. Eyewitness identifications are often problematic because they may be impacted by both human fallibility and suggestive investigative procedures. While the personal appearance of an individual is not protected directly by the Fifth Amendment protection from compelled self-incrimination, courts have provided procedures to ensure fairness.

What is testimonial evidence? Simply, testimonial evidence is an oral statement that may be used to prove a fact in a court of law. It may come as an answer to a question, a description of an event, or even from words spoken during a criminal event. An armed robber who says to a cashier, "Give me all of your money" has made a statement that may be presented later in court. A suspect who is being interrogated by the police about his or her involvement in a crime may say something that can be used later as evidence to prove his criminal conduct. Testimonial evidence might be offered without any prompting or questioning at all. People sometimes make spontaneous statements about an event or provide evidentiary information during a casual conversation. Interactions between police and citizens often result in the obtaining of oral evidence.

On the Street

Confessions at a Traffic Stop

Ashley was texting her boyfriend to discuss their plans for the evening. Unfortunately, she was also driving and didn't see the stop light changed from green to red. Luckily, she did not have an accident, but as soon as she passed through the intersection, she heard the sirens of a police car behind her. The officer pulled her over. She rolled down her window as the officer approached the left side of her car. "License and registration, please," he sternly demanded. After she gave the officer the documents, he asked her if she knew why he pulled her over. Ashley said, "I guess I ran that red light. I'm so sorry. I just wasn't paying attention. I might have been using my phone." Has Ashley made an incriminating statement? Can her statement be used in court? ▪

Just like Ashley's traffic stop, there are many situations in which the police interact with citizens in a manner designed to gather evidence. People may call 911 to report a crime. They may talk to the police because they are the victim of a criminal act. They may be a witness to a crime.

People not only make incriminating statements to the police, they also talk to others. Best friends may swear each other to secrecy and confess to criminal behavior. An individual may brag to his friends about his criminal conduct. They may engage in conversations that are overheard by third parties.

Chapters 11 and 12 examine the various ways in which oral evidence is obtained and the admissibility of such evidence in court. Chapter 13 addresses the rules impacting eyewitness identification of suspects.

Chapter 11
The Spoken Word as Evidence

The Fifth Amendment of the U.S. Constitution states in part,

> No person . . . shall be compelled in any criminal case to be a witness against himself, nor be deprived of life, liberty, or property, without due process of law.

Self-incrimination
The act of a defendant making a statement that could be used as incriminating evidence against them in a criminal prosecution.

These powerful words provide the constitutional foundation for the laws and rules that govern the use of oral statements as evidence in a criminal prosecution. The constitutional protection from compelled **self-incrimination** is based on the Fifth Amendment. Our right to remain silent is deeply ingrained in American culture, yet oral statements often provide key pieces of evidence in many criminal cases. The fact that a criminal suspect has a right to remain silent does not always prevent the person from making incriminating statements. And, in spite of the popularity of television shows depicting the importance of physical evidence, the words that come from an individual's lips still carry tremendous weight in a criminal courtroom. The words spoken by a defendant may offer the most damning evidence against him or her. This chapter examines the laws and rules that impact the use of such evidence.

The *Miranda* Rights

The foundation for the determination of the admissibility of oral evidence was set in the landmark case of *Miranda v. Arizona*. In arguably their most famous criminal procedure case, the U.S. Supreme Court created the *Miranda* warnings and provided instruction as to their application and consequences. The terms *Miranda rights* and *Miranda warnings* are often used interchangeably. Technically, they are warnings that are provided to suspects by the police. The police are advising the suspect of the rights to which they are entitled.

MIRANDA v. ARIZONA

384 U.S. 436 (1966)

The Facts: On March 13, 1963, the Phoenix police arrested 18-year-old Ernesto Miranda for rape and kidnapping. He was arrested at his home and transported to a Phoenix police station for questioning. Prior to the questioning, he was identified by the victim as her assailant. He was then interrogated by two police officers in "Interrogation Room No. 2" of the detective bureau. Miranda did not have an attorney present nor was he advised that he had a right to have one. He was questioned for approximately two hours during which time he admitted the sexual assault. Miranda provided a handwritten confession. On the top of the paper on which he wrote his statement were the typed words that the confession was made voluntarily, without threats or promises of immunity, and "with full knowledge of my legal rights, understanding any statement I make may be used against me." The interrogation was not remarkable or unusual. The officers did not physically coerce the suspect in any way.

Miranda's statement was used in evidence against him at his criminal trial. Additionally, the victim and Miranda's girlfriend both testified against him. He was convicted of rape and kidnapping.

The Decision: In a landmark decision, the Court took a comprehensive look at the history of police interrogation in the United States. Their examination considered the emotional and psychological techniques used to gain an advantage over suspects in interrogation settings. They acknowledged that police are trained in the use of such techniques in order to obtain incriminating oral evidence. Their discussion also included the importance of the Fifth Amendment protection against self-incrimination. The opinion included a discussion of the sordid history of police interrogation abuses. In order to ensure that suspects subjected to police interrogation were provided due process and their Fifth Amendment protection, the Court attempted to level the playing field. They created a rule designed to apprise all suspects subjected to police custodial interrogations of their basic rights. The Court stated the following:

> To summarize, we hold that when an individual is taken into custody or otherwise deprived of his freedom by the authorities in any significant way and is subjected to questioning, the privilege against self-incrimination is jeopardized. Procedural safeguards must be employed to [384 U.S. 436, 479] protect the privilege, and unless other fully effective means are adopted to notify the person of his right of silence and to assure that the exercise of the right will be scrupulously honored, the following measures are required. He must be warned prior to any questioning that he has the right to remain silent, that anything he says can be used against him in a court of law, that he has the right to the presence of an attorney, and that if he cannot afford an attorney one will be appointed for him prior to any questioning if he so desires. Opportunity to exercise these rights must be afforded to him throughout the interrogation. After such warnings have been given, and such opportunity afforded him,

the individual may knowingly and intelligently waive these rights and agree to answer questions or make a statement. But unless and until such warnings and waiver are demonstrated by the prosecution at trial, no evidence obtained as a result of interrogation can be used against him.

In addition to its decision to protect the rights of an interrogated suspect, the Court also dictated the content of the warnings, when they must be advised, and how and when they may be waived. The Justices also clearly identified the consequence for failing to comply with the decision. Statements obtained as a result of an unlawful interrogation would be excluded from evidence.

As a result of the case, the following warnings must be given to a suspect prior to the custodial interrogation by law enforcement.

The *Miranda* Warnings
1. You have the right to remain silent.
2. Anything you say may be used against you in a court of law.
3. You have the right to an attorney.
4. If you cannot afford an attorney, one will be appointed for you by the Court.

One could argue that the circumstances of Ernesto Miranda's arrest created the perfect storm for the court's ruling. Miranda was young, Hispanic, and uneducated. He was certainly ignorant of the complexities of criminal procedure. Under arrest and without an attorney, he faced two police detectives trained in the art of interrogation. The playing field was not fair. Thus, the Supreme Court decided that in order to protect a suspect's rights in these situations, the police must inform the suspect of those rights. The warnings themselves are quite clear.

Prophylactic rule
A rule designed to protect the rights of everyone facing a specific issue.

The *Miranda* requirement is also considered a **prophylactic rule**, meaning it is designed to protect every suspect subjected to a custodial interrogation. The warnings must be given prior to all custodial police interrogations, not just those with a disadvantaged suspect. If the police arrested a law professor, they would still be required to advise him or her of the *Miranda* warnings prior to any interrogation.

The wording of the warnings does not have to be exact nor is a specific order required. It would be satisfactory if the officer stated, "you have the right to not talk to the police. You don't have to say anything." The substantive meaning of the warnings must be conveyed. Likewise, all four warnings are required. The *Miranda* requirement has not been met if the officer only offered three of the warnings. Many police departments provide cards to their officers so they can read the exact words every time. Officers will often refer to those cards when asked in court to restate exactly what they said to a suspect when advising them of their rights.

Waiver of Rights

Once a suspect has been given the *Miranda* warnings, the suspect may either waive or invoke his or her rights. A **waiver** may often be obtained by asking the following questions:

Waiver
Waiving one's rights means that a person is giving up his or her rights. In *Miranda* situations, the suspect who waives his or her rights may agree to talk to the police without an attorney present.

■ *Do you understand these rights as they have been stated to you?*
■ *Having heard and understood these rights, do you wish to waive them and make a statement?*

By waiving their rights, suspects are agreeing to give up their right to remain silent and/or their right to an attorney. Suspects often talk to the police even with an attorney present. When that occurs, the suspect has waived his or her right to remain silent but has not waived his or her right to an attorney. A common misconception is that a suspect cannot talk to the police if the suspect has been advised by his or her attorney to refuse to answer any questions. The rights belong to the suspect, not the attorney. Thus, a suspect could ignore his attorney's advice and speak anyway. A waiver of the *Miranda* rights must be voluntarily, knowingly, and intelligently given.

Voluntary

Voluntary
An individual acts or refrains from acting on his or her own free will, free from any undue coercion.

The waiver is considered **voluntary** if the individual is acting on his or her own free will, free from any undue coercion. The police may not use any physical force or threat of harm in an effort to encourage a suspect to talk. Likewise, they cannot interrogate the suspect under physical conditions that would be unduly coercive. They cannot place the suspect in a harsh environment such as extreme temperature or in unsanitary conditions. The individual cannot be denied food, water, or bathroom privileges or be interrogated for an unreasonably long period of time.

Unfortunately, there have been several instances of abuse of prisoners for the purpose of interrogation in our nation's history. The torture of three murder suspects during their questioning in *Brown v. Mississippi* was discussed in Chapter 3. In that 1936 case, the U.S. Supreme Court emphatically ruled that physical abuse could not be used to coerce a suspect to talk. While cases that severe are now rare, a horrendous case occurred in New York City in 1997.

True Story of Abuse: The Abner Louima Story

The New York City Police arrested 30-year-old Abner Louima on August 9, 1997, during the investigation of a fight that occurred at the Club Rendez -Vous in the East Flatbush neighborhood. They charged Louima with disorderly conduct, resisting arrest, and obstructing government administration. One of the arresting officers claimed Louima struck him with a sucker punch, but the officer later admitted he was mistaken.

Louima was transported to the 70th Precinct. The officers struck him with their fists, nightsticks, and radios during the ride to the station. Once at the precinct, they strip-searched him and placed him in a holding cell. During the "interrogation," the officers kicked Louima in the testicles, and Officer Justin Volpe sodomized him with a toilet plunger. Volpe also damaged some of his teeth by shoving the toilet plunger in his mouth. Louima suffered serious injuries and was hospitalized for two months.

The case attracted national media attention. Ultimately the charges against Louima were dropped. Officer Volpe was convicted for the assault and sentenced to 30 years in prison. Another officer, Charles Schwartz, was sentenced to five years in federal prison for perjury during the investigation of the incident. Louima sued the City of New York and the police union and received an $8.7 million settlement several years later.

While tortuous conduct such as the Brown and Louima cases are obviously coercion, the unlawful conduct during an interrogation may be more subtle. The test is whether the police tactics led the suspect to involuntarily incriminate himself or herself.

On the Street

Interrogation by dog?

Police respond to a break-in at Bronson's Bakery. Upon their arrival they spot two men coming out of the back door, their arms loaded with white bakery bags. The police yell for them to stop. Randall stops but the other suspect drops his bags and begins running through the yards behind the store. The police pursue on foot but are unable to apprehend him. The police then place Randall in the back seat of a police cruiser but they leave the door open. They then bring a German shepherd police dog to the car. The dog lays his nose on Randall's leg very close to his crotch. The dog sits quietly without growling or biting but continues to press his nose down on Randall's leg. He occasionally bares his teeth. The police advise Randall of his *Miranda* rights and question him regarding his involvement in the burglary. Randall says that it was all his friend's idea, tells them where his friend lives, and says that the only reason he broke in was to keep his friend from being mad at him. Is Randall's statement admissible? Did he voluntarily waive his *Miranda* rights? ▪

May the police lie to a suspect? The answer is yes and no. The police cannot lie about a person's legal rights and cannot lie about an official document or the potential consequences that the suspect may be facing. It would be considered unlawful coercion if the interrogating officer told a suspect that he or she could be sentenced to five years in prison for a misdemeanor charge that, in truth, had a maximum penalty of only 60 days. A threat to take away a mother's child when there is no truth to the threat would also be considered coercive. An officer could not lie about an official report such as a medical examiner's report or a drug test in order to obtain a confession.

Police are generally allowed to lie about their evidence or knowledge of the crime. They may lie about statements made by witnesses or other suspects who may have been involved in the crime. In *Oregon v. Mathiason*, 429 U.S. 492 (1977), a state trooper falsely told a suspect that his fingerprints had been discovered at the scene of a burglary. This disclosure to the suspect led him to confess, and the court allowed the defendant's confession.

The police may also inform the suspect of the maximum possible penalties available. Describing the vagaries of prison life is generally not considered coercive. Offering a reduced sentence or even simply a better situation in exchange for a confession is not considered coercive. However, it should be noted that every suspect and situation are different. The judge must ultimately determine if a person voluntarily waived his or her *Miranda* rights.

Knowingly and Intelligently

A valid waiver of the *Miranda* rights must not only be voluntary, it must also be knowingly and intelligently given. That does not require that the decision to waive be a sound legal strategy but rather only that the suspect understands the rights that he or she is relinquishing and that the suspect's statements may be used against him or her in a court of law. In *Moran v. Burbine*, 475 U.S. 412 (1986), the U.S. Supreme Court stated the following:

> Miranda holds that "the defendant may waive effectuation" of the rights conveyed in the warnings "provided the waiver is made voluntarily, knowingly and intelligently." 384 U.S., at 444, 475. The inquiry has two distinct dimensions. First, the relinquishment of the right must have been voluntary in the sense that it was the product of a free and deliberate choice rather than intimidation, coercion, or deception. Second, the waiver must have been made with a full awareness of both the nature of the right being abandoned and the consequences of the decision to abandon it. Only if the "totality of the circumstances surrounding the interrogation" reveals both an uncoerced choice and the requisite level of comprehension may a court properly conclude that the Miranda rights have been waived.

In the *Moran* case, the suspect had agreed to confess after being apprised of his *Miranda* rights. He provided a handwritten confession to murder. Unknown to the suspect, his sister had obtained an attorney for him. The attorney had contacted the police and been told that they did not yet plan to conduct an interrogation. The Court, while critical of the police conduct, held that Burbine's confession was given voluntarily, knowingly, and intelligently and that the police were under no obligation to apprise the suspect of any external events that might affect his decision.

So what circumstances might prevent the waiver from being knowing and intelligent? Consider the following.

On the Street

The Language Barrier

Two men walked into Tom's Taco Palace late one afternoon, pulled a gun on the clerk, and demanded all of the cash and three of Tom's chimichanga specials. After obtaining the food and money, they ran outside, hopped in a slime green 1998 Pontiac Aztec, and drove east on Elvis Presley Boulevard. Within 15 minutes, they were apprehended by the police. Sitting in the backseat of the vehicle was Enrique. The police placed him in the backseat of their cruiser, advised him of his *Miranda* rights, and began questioning him. They first asked him if he wished to waive his rights. Enrique stated, "Si, Senor." They then asked him if he was involved in the robbery. Same response, "Si, Senor." Enrique gave the same response to every question he was asked. It was later determined that he did not speak any English but had been taught by his parents to always be respectful of the police. Thus, he knew to say "yes, sir" in Spanish. Has Enrique knowingly and intelligently waived his *Miranda* rights? ■

Obviously, a language barrier could prevent a suspect from understanding the warnings. Mental defects, hearing and speech impairments, age, and diminished learning capacities might all impact a suspect's ability to understand and comprehend the nature of the warnings. A defendant might not even understand the legal term "waiver."

Impairment due to drug or alcohol intoxication might also inhibit an individual's ability to knowingly waive his or her rights. Situations involving chemical impairment may offer difficult situations. The degree of intoxication becomes the determining factor. It is certainly possible for an individual to ingest alcohol or drugs and still comprehend the *Miranda* warnings. However, if the person is so intoxicated that he or she cannot understand, then the waiver would not be valid. It is common for suspects involved in criminal activity to also be under the influence of alcohol or drugs. If an officer is going to conduct an interrogation, it is imperative that the officer make an accurate assessment of the suspect's ability to understand. If the behavior of the suspect indicates the inability to understand, then it is wise for the officer to delay the interrogation.

Age may also be a factor. While the U.S. Supreme Court has not identified a bright line rule setting a specific age required for a valid waiver, some states have enacted legislation that requires the presence of an attorney or a parent prior to the custodial interrogation of a juvenile. Even in those states where a parent's presence is not required, caution must be exerted to ensure that the interrogation is conducted in a noncoercive manner and that the juvenile has the capacity to understand the waiver of rights. It may be obvious that a ten-year-old could not and that a 17-year-old could understand the warnings, but every child and circumstance are different. The burden is on the prosecution to show that the child understands the rights.

Must the waiver be in writing? No. Many law enforcement agencies will ask suspects to sign a written waiver. These documents usually reiterate the *Miranda* rights and indicate that the suspect understands the rights and wishes to waive them and respond to the officer's questions. While these written waivers may provide some evidence of a voluntary and knowing waiver, they are not required by law. The waiver is, of course, worthless if the suspect is forced to sign it or cannot understand its content. Figure 11-1 shows a written waiver used by the Springfield Township, Ohio, police department.

Springfield Township Police Department
1130 Compton Road, Cincinnati, Ohio 45231
513/729-1300
WARNING

BEFORE YOU ARE ASKED ANY QUESTIONS
YOU MUST UNDERSTAND YOUR RIGHTS.

- YOU HAVE THE RIGHT TO REMAIN SILENT.
- ANYTHING YOU SAY COULD BE USED AGAINST YOU IN COURT.
- YOU HAVE THE RIGHT TO TALK TO A LAWYER FOR ADVICE BEFORE WE ASK YOU ANY QUESTIONS AND TO HAVE HIM/HER PRESENT WITH YOU DURING QUESTIONING.
- IF YOU CANNOT AFFORD A LAWYER, ONE WILL BE APPOINTED FOR YOU BEFORE QUESTIONING IF YOU WISH.
- IF YOU DECIDE TO ANSWER QUESTIONS NOW WITHOUT A LAWYER PRESENT, YOU WILL STILL HAVE THE RIGHT TO STOP ANSWERING AT ANY TIME.
- YOU ALSO HAVE THE RIGHT TO STOP ANSWERING AT ANY TIME UNTIL YOU TALK TO A LAWYER.

WAIVER

I HAVE READ THIS STATEMENT OF MY RIGHTS (THIS STATEMENT OF MY RIGHTS HAS BEEN READ TO ME) AND I UNDERSTAND WHAT MY RIGHTS ARE. I AM WILLING TO DISCUSS SUBJECTS PRESENTED AND ANSWER QUESTIONS. I DO NOT WANT A LAWYER AT THIS TIME. I UNDERSTAND AND KNOW WHAT I AM DOING. NO PROMISES OR THREATS HAVE BEEN MADE TO ME AND NO PRESSURE OR COERCION OF ANY KIND HAS BEEN USED AGAINST ME.

SIGNATURE: _____

TIME: _____

DATE: _____

WITNESSED BY: _____

TITLE: _____

Courtesy of Springfield Township Police Department

Figure 11-1   Written Waiver

Though verbal waivers are allowed, the burden of proof lies with the police to convince the judge that the statements were voluntarily and knowingly given. That may be accomplished through the officer's testimony, other witness statements, or video technology. "He said, she said" situations certainly occur in which the judge must make a factual decision as to whether the suspect truthfully waived his or her rights.

Invoking the Rights

Invoking one's *Miranda* rights means that the individual wishes to accept his or her rights and is unwilling to waive them. A suspect invokes the *Miranda* rights by either asking for an attorney or indicating that he or she wishes to exercise the right to remain silent. If a suspect invokes his or her rights, the interrogation must stop. The police may no longer question the suspect and cannot encourage the suspect to change his or her mind. The slang phrase "lawyering up" refers to a suspect invoking his or her *Miranda* rights by demanding a lawyer. Silence, however, does not constitute an invocation of the rights. If a suspect simply does not speak, there has been no invoking of the rights and the police may continue to ask questions. The suspect must actually say or otherwise constructively indicate that he or she is refusing to talk or wants an attorney.

Invoking
In *Miranda* situations, the suspect who invokes his or her rights is accepting his or her rights and refusing to respond to police questioning.

On the Street

Is silence golden?

Rashid is arrested for rape. The police bring him to an interrogation room at the police station. They advise him of his rights and ask if he wishes to waive them and make a statement. He just stares at the cops. He doesn't say anything. So they begin by showing him a photo of the victim. They then ask him questions about the sexual assault. He just stares. Finally they tell him that they have all night and they know that he raped her so he might as well tell his side of the story. All of a sudden, he starts yelling, "Yeah, I raped her, so what? Get over it. She wasn't my first. You can't prove it. I ain't saying nothing else 'til I get a lawyer!" Is his statement admissible?

In the 2010 case of *Berghuis v. Thompkins*, the U.S. Supreme Court considered whether a suspect had invoked his rights by remaining silent for an extended period of time. A police detective and another Michigan officer interrogated Van Chester Thompkins concerning a shooting. Thompkins just sat silently during almost all of the entire three-hour interrogation. He never said that he wanted to remain silent or talk to an attorney. However, near the end of the three-hour period, the detective asked him if he prayed to God for forgiveness for "shooting that boy down" and Thompkins answered, "Yes." The Court allowed Thompkins' statement indicating that in order to invoke the *Miranda* rights the suspect must make an unambiguous request for an attorney or a refusal to speak.

A suspect may also retract his or her waiver and invoke his or her rights. In the On the Street box involving Rashid, his original statements would be admissible, but the police would then have to terminate the interrogation at the moment that he indicated he was not going to talk anymore and wanted an attorney.

Termination of Interrogation

Law enforcement must terminate the interrogation at the moment the suspect invokes his or her rights. If the suspect asks for an attorney or indicates a refusal to answer questions, the police must immediately halt all questioning. Should they continue, any further responses on the part of the defendant would be inadmissible in court. The Supreme Court addressed this issue in their *Miranda* opinion:

> Once warnings have been given, the subsequent procedure is clear. If the individual indicates in any manner, at any time prior to or during questioning, that he wishes to remain silent, the interrogation must cease. At this point he has shown that he intends to exercise his Fifth Amendment privilege; any statement taken after the person invokes his privilege cannot be other than the product of compulsion, subtle or otherwise. Without the right to cut off questioning, the setting of in-custody interrogation operates on the individual to overcome free choice in producing a statement after the privilege has been once invoked. If the individual states that he wants an attorney, the interrogation must cease until an attorney is present. At that time, the individual must have an opportunity to confer with the attorney and to have him present during any subsequent questioning. If the individual cannot obtain an attorney and he indicates that he wants one before speaking to police, they must respect his decision to remain silent.

Reinitiating the Interrogation

Once the interrogation has been halted, the suspect may reinitiate the question by requesting that it resume. The suspect must act of his or her own free will and agree to waive his or her rights. Prior to 2010, the police could never act to reinitiate the questioning; it had to be the act of the suspect. However, the rule was modified in a sexual assault case arising in Maryland. The U.S. Supreme Court decided that upon a break in *Miranda* detention lasting at least 14 days, the police could renew their efforts to interrogate.

MARYLAND v. SHATZER

559 U.S.98, 130 S.Ct. 1213 (2010)

The Facts: In 2003, a Child Advocacy Center social worker working for the Hagerstown, Maryland, police department referred allegations that Michael Shatzer, Sr., had sexually abused his three-year-old son. At the time, Shatzer was incarcerated in the Maryland Correctional Institution on an unrelated sexual abuse conviction. Detective Shane Blankenship interviewed Shatzer, Sr., at the prison on August 7, 2003. He advised him of his *Miranda* rights and obtained a written waiver. When Shatzer realized that the detective wanted to question him about a new crime, he refused to talk without an attorney. The detective ended the interview, and Shatzer was released back into the general prison population. At that point, the detective closed the investigation.

Two and a half years later, the agency received more detailed information in regard to the sexual abuse of Shatzer's son who was now eight years old. On March 2, 2006, Detective Paul Hoover and the social worker went to the Roxbury Correctional Institute, where Shatzer was now being held. They questioned him in a maintenance room that had a desk and three chairs. Again they read him his rights and obtained a written waiver. Shatzer seemed surprised because he thought the investigation had been closed. During a 30-minute interview, Shatzer denied ordering his son to perform fellatio on him but admitted that he masturbated in front of his son less than three feet away. He also agreed to submit to a **polygraph** examination. Five days later, detectives returned to the prison to administer the polygraph examination. Again they read Shatzer his *Miranda* rights and obtained a waiver. The detectives determined that he failed the test and questioned him further. Shatzer became upset, started to cry, and stated, "I didn't force him. I didn't force him." Shatzer then demanded an attorney and ended the interrogation. Shatzer was then prosecuted for several child sexual assault charges regarding his son. At trial, he asked the court to suppress the statements taken during the interrogations at the prison, but the trial court allowed them. He was convicted of sexual child abuse of his son.

The Decision: In the 1981 case of *Edwards v. Arizona*, 451 U.S. 477, the Supreme Court had clearly indicated that the renewal of an interrogation could only occur at the initiation of the defendant. "He is not subject to further interrogation by the authorities until counsel has been made available to him, unless the accused himself initiates further communication, exchanges, or conversations with the police." A violation of this rule would result in the exclusion of the testimonial evidence. However, the Court modified the *Edwards* rule in *Maryland v. Shatzer*. After the initial interrogation with Detective Blankenship, Shatzer was released back into the general institution population and resumed his normal prison life. The Court considered this a break in the *Miranda* detention. While Shatzer was still detained in a correctional facility, he was not being detained for the purposes of the investigation of his son's abuse case. Thus, the coercive environment of a *Miranda* custody had ended. The Court ruled that law enforcement could attempt to interrogate a defendant so long as there had been a break in the *Miranda* custody and at least 14 days had passed. The Court stated the following:

> Because Shatzer experienced a break in *Miranda* custody lasting more than two weeks between the first and second attempts at interrogation, *Edwards* does not mandate suppression of his March 2006 statements. Accordingly, we reverse the judgment of the Court of Appeals of Maryland, and remand the case for further proceedings not inconsistent with this opinion.

Polygraph
A device that measures and records several physiological indices such as blood pressure, pulse, respiration, and skin conductivity in order to determine if a subject is making truthful responses to prescribed questions.

The Supreme Court's decision in *Maryland* was considered extraordinary. They not only modified a previous U.S. Supreme Court decision, they clearly created a bright line rule by identifying a specific number of days which must pass before the renewal of an interrogation. In a sense, they went from never to fourteen days. There may still be confusion over what constitutes a break in *Miranda* custody, but the case certainly provided law enforcement with a valuable interrogation tool.

Admissibility Versus Truthful Evidence

The decisions as to whether oral statements are admissible are based on whether the procedures involved complied with the due process standards of the Fifth and Fourteenth Amendments. Those admissibility decisions are not determinations of whether the evidence proves a truthful fact but only whether the fact-finder in a case (judge or jury) may consider the statements. If a statement is admitted into evidence, it is then the responsibility of the jury (or judge if bench trial) to determine the truthfulness of the statement and how much weight to give the specific evidence. A judge might allow the statement of a defendant obtained through an interrogation, but the jury may still decide to ignore it.

On the Street

Author's Note

I once represented a 19-year-old Asian American woman in a criminal forgery case. She was interrogated by two detectives for several hours concerning her involvement and made incriminating statements. The statements were not confessions but were certainly damaging to our defense. During the preliminary hearing, I cross-examined the two detectives concerning their interrogation and asked the judge to exclude the statements of my client. The judge refused. I cross-examined the two detectives again at a pretrial hearing in an effort to suppress her statements. Once again, I lost. Then at the jury trial, in a rather intense cross-examination, I took a shot at the detectives again. The officers openly displayed their agitation at me during the exchange. Again, the judge refused to exclude the statements of my client and ruled them admissible. Ultimately, the jury found my client not guilty. After the jury was discharged, I had the opportunity to talk with members of the jury. They indicated that they ignored the incriminating statements made by my client. They thought the only reason she made them was because the two large, well-dressed, angry detectives berated her in an unfair manner. Though the statements were admitted, they were not believed. ■

The Consequences of an Illegal Interrogation

Testimonial evidence
An oral statement that may be used to prove a fact in a court of law.

Ultimately, the entire discussion presented in this section concerns the admissibility of evidence. An unlawful interrogation would result in the exclusion of the **testimonial**

evidence obtained as a result of the violation. That evidence could not be used at trial. Without that evidence, the prosecution would have to rely on other evidence and testimony to prove the specific case. Thus, the exclusion of oral statements would not necessarily affect the ultimate outcome of the case.

On the Street

Good Evidence/Bad Evidence

Officer McFee was routinely patrolling his assigned neighborhood. While driving down Roberts Avenue, he heard glass breaking. He quickly realized there was a man break-ing the front window out of Pandora's Pharmacy. The man ran inside and started pulling items off the pharmacy shelves. McFee quickly approached the scene and ordered the burglar to come out of the store with his hands up. He arrested him, searched his pockets, and found **Vicodin** that he had just grabbed out of the phar-macy bins. There was also a large amount of broken glass in the cuffs of his pants. The crowbar he used to break out the front window was on the floor of the store. The officer placed the burglar in the back of the squad car and, without advising him of his *Miranda* rights, asked him why he broke into the store. The burglar said, "I'm stupid. I just needed some Vicodin." Obviously, that was an unlawful interrogation. Does that mean the burglar will go free? Of course not. While the suspect's statement would be inadmissible, the broken glass, the crowbar, the Vicodin in his pockets, and the offi-cer's observations are all still admissible. ▨

Vicodin
A schedule II pain-killing narcotic that is often the subject of criminal abuse or trafficking.

The application of *Miranda* and the Fifth Amendment protection from self-in-crimination extends only to testimonial evidence. Evidentiary issues involving the search and seizure of tangible evidence such as writings, fingerprints, hair samples, and DNA are Fourth Amendment issues and are not affected by the *Miranda* line of cases. Chapter 12 will examine the detailed application of the *Miranda* warnings and the determination of custodial interrogation by law enforcement.

Summary

Incriminating statements made by a criminal suspect certainly provide some of the most critical and compelling evidence in a criminal trial. Those statements are partic-ularly damning when they are considered confessions. After a long history of unfair and, in some cases, abusive interrogation procedures in America, the U.S. Supreme Court provided protections for suspects in the 1966 landmark case of *Miranda v. Arizona*. In perhaps the most recognized criminal procedure case, the Court deter-mined that police officers must advise a suspect of certain rights before conducting a custodial interrogation. The warnings require that the suspects be advised of their right to remain silent, that any statement they make may be used against them in court, of their right to an attorney, and that they may be appointed an attorney if they cannot afford one.

This chapter also addressed the rules surrounding the waiver and invocation of the rights. A suspect who wishes to waive his or her rights must do so voluntarily, knowingly, and intelligently. While this requirement is not cumbersome, it is integral to the spirit of the *Miranda* decision. The U.S. Supreme Court clearly intended to ensure that suspects in a criminal investigation were afforded their Fifth Amendment protections from compelled self-incrimination. Subsequent cases, such as *Maryland v. Shatzer*, have clarified the reinitiating of interrogation once a suspect has invoked the right to remain silent.

Ultimately, the development of the rules surrounding *Miranda* has not prevented criminal suspects from offering their own words as evidence, but it has provided a framework for fairer interrogation procedures.

Review Questions

1. When must the *Miranda* warnings be given?
2. About what facts may a police officer lie during an interrogation?
3. Under what circumstances would a suspect be unable to knowingly and intelligently waive his or her *Miranda* rights?
4. What actions must a suspect take in order to invoke his or her *Miranda* rights?
5. If a suspect invokes his or her *Miranda* rights, under what circumstances may law enforcement renew their interrogation?

Legal Terminology

Invoking

Polygraph

Prophylactic rule

Self-incrimination

Testimonial evidence

Vicodin

Voluntary

Waiver

References

Berghuis v. Thompkins, 560 U.S. 370 (2010)

Brown v. State of Mississippi, 297 U.S. 278 (1936)

Chan, S. (2007, August 9). The Abner Louima Case, Ten Years Later. *The New York Times*. Retrieved from http://cityroom.blogs.nytimes.com/2007/08/09/the-abner-louima-case-10-years-later/?_r=0

Edwards v. Arizona, 451 U.S. 477 (1981)

Maryland v. Shatzer, 559 U.S. 98 (2010)

Miranda v. Arizona, 384 U.S. 436 (1966)

Moran v. Burbine, 475 U.S. 412 (1986)

Oregon v. Mathiason, 429 U.S. 492 (1977)

Chapter 12
The Application of the *Miranda* Warnings

Custodial Interrogation by Law Enforcement

In addition to establishing the *Miranda* warnings, the U.S. Supreme Court also dictated when they applied. The *Miranda* warnings must be given to a suspect prior to any custodial interrogation by **law enforcement**. As indicated in the previous chapter, failure by law enforcement to advise a suspect of the rights may result in the exclusion of any evidentiary statement he or she might make. Thus, it is critical to understand the meaning of the three components: custodial, interrogation, and law enforcement.

The strategy decision as to whether to advise a suspect of his or her rights also turns on the understanding of the three components. The *Miranda* warnings are not required if the components are not present. Some criminal justice professionals argue that since it is a prophylactic rule, officers should take the safe route and always advise the warnings when they arrest or question a suspect. That view, while protective of the suspect, is neither legally correct nor required. To advise of the rights unnecessarily may cost law enforcement a strategic advantage in their efforts to obtain evidence.

In the years since *Miranda v. Arizona* was decided, there have been numerous cases that examined the application of the warnings. They have defined the three components as they apply to the *Miranda* rights.

Custodial

Not all detentions or restraints are considered significant for the purposes of *Miranda*. However, a physical arrest is always considered **custodial**. If a suspect has been placed under arrest it is custodial regardless of the crime for which he or she has been arrested. The concern for the courts is the disadvantage created by the custodial setting. The moment of arrest creates the custodial setting whether it is on the street, in a residence, in the back of a police car, or in a detention facility.

Law enforcement
For *Miranda* purposes, an individual who is an agent of or working on behalf of a government law enforcement agency.

Custodial
A person's freedom of action is restrained in a significant manner.

While it would be clearly a custodial arrest if the officer has informed the suspect that he or she is under arrest, that does not always occur. A suspect would also reasonably believe that he or she is under arrest if he or she has been placed in handcuffs. However, officers may handcuff a suspect who is being temporarily detained but not yet under arrest. The police may do so to safely restrain a suspect during the execution of a search warrant. They might briefly handcuff a suspect during a *Terry v. Ohio* stop and frisk encounter. While these situations are not arrests, officers should inform the suspect that the restraint is temporary and that the suspect is not under arrest.

Detention in a jail or prison is also considered custodial. Investigators often will conduct interrogations within the confines of a detention facility, and those settings are custodial interrogations. Police officers often approach suspects on the street and question them about their conduct. These informal settings are not considered custodial for the purposes of *Miranda* even though the suspect may feel obligated to engage in the conversation. It is legal for an officer to simply walk up to a person and ask him or her questions. Likewise, the individual does not have to talk to the officer. The individual would only have to stop if the officer had reasonable suspicion to temporarily detain him or her.

On the Street

The Cop's Casual Conversation

Early one Sunday morning, Officer Fletcher was on routine patrol. He noticed two men standing on a sidewalk in front of a closed gas station. They were both smoking. The officer pulled his car into the station lot, stepped out of his car, and approached the two men. The officer says, "Gentlemen, the buses have stopped running, everything is closed and it's late, what are you doing out here?" Was Officer Fletcher required to give them their *Miranda* rights before he asked them the question? Do they have to respond to his question?

Stop and Frisk

As discussed previously, police officers may temporarily detain a suspect based on reasonable suspicion and conduct a *Terry v. Ohio* stop and frisk. As part of that procedure, the officer may ask questions in order to determine if the suspect is engaged in criminal behavior or poses a danger to the officer. Officers may ask pointed questions such as, "What are you doing? May I see your identification? Why were you hiding? Do you have any weapons or drugs on you?" These are certainly questions directed at criminal activity, and the suspect is not free to leave. However, the *Terry v. Ohio* stop and frisk is not considered a *Miranda* custody. The detention is only temporary; thus, the suspect is not restrained in a significant manner. Of course, if the stop and frisk results in an arrest, it then becomes a custodial situation and the warning would have to be given before any additional questions are asked.

On the Street

A Drive-Thru Conversation

A state trooper was sitting in her patrol car finishing a report. She noticed a car stopped on the side of a fairly busy road. A van pulled behind the car. A tall man wearing a black and gold running suit stepped out of the car, walked to the rear of the vehicle, and opened the trunk. He handed the driver of the van what appeared to be a flat-screen television box. There was another exchange, but the trooper was unable to see what was involved. As the car pulled away, the trooper followed the car and pulled it over about a half-mile down the road. She approached the car and asked the driver for his proof of insurance and license. After she received it, she asked, "So, are you running a drive-through television store out here on my highway? What are you selling?" The driver responded, "Oh come on, lady. All the cops around here know I sell a little discount merchandise. They don't care if it's a little warm. I gotta make a living, just like you. Tell you what. I can hook you up with a brand new, in the box, iPad2 right now. No charge. Whaddya say, pretty trooper? Or better yet, I have some Oxy that will relieve that headache you seem to have today. You are on board like the other cops, right?" Are the driver's statements admissible? Why or why not? ■

Traffic Stops and Miranda

The police often ask a series of questions during routine traffic stops. The response to those questions may provide incriminating evidence that can be used in court to establish proof of the traffic violation. It is common for an officer to ask a driver if he or she knows why he or she was stopped. The answers such as, "Was I speeding officer? I was only going 48 and I thought the speed limit was 45" may be presented as an admission in court. Officers will ask additional questions when they suspect driving under the influence of alcohol or drugs. Questions might include the following:

■ "Where are you coming from?"
■ "Have you been drinking? How much? How long?"

The answers often provide evidence of the driver's behavior and use of alcohol or drugs. If the driver admits to coming from a bar or a wedding reception, those statements may be indicative of drinking. When officers suspect drunk driving, they may request that the driver submit to a series of cognitive tests such as reciting the alphabet or counting. Obviously, the driver is not allowed to leave during these on-the-street investigations. Are the *Miranda* warnings required? No. In 1984, the U.S. Supreme Court examined the application of *Miranda* during these traffic stops.

BERKEMER v. MCCARTY

468 U.S. 420 (1984)

The Facts: On March 31, 1980, an Ohio highway patrol officer observed the defendant's car weaving in and out of his traffic lane. After following for over two miles on I-270, the officer pulled the vehicle over. After being removed from the car, the driver had difficulty standing. The officer decided that the driver was going to be arrested for a traffic offense but did not inform the driver of such and did not place him in handcuffs or in the police car. He did not physically take control of the suspect at that point. The officer then asked the driver to do a field sobriety test that involved balancing. The driver was unable to balance without falling down. The officer asked the suspect if he had been using any intoxicants. He replied that he had two beers and smoked several joints of marijuana a short time earlier. The officer also testified at trial that the defendant's speech was slurred and difficult to understand. The driver was arrested and transported to the patrol station where he was given a blood test that did not detect any alcohol. He was questioned further and again made incriminating statements including an admission that he had barely drank any alcohol. At no point was he advised of his *Miranda* rights.

McCarty was convicted of operating a vehicle under intoxication. He appealed contesting the admissibility of his statements taken during the initial stop and later during the interrogation at the police station.

The Decision: The Court ruled that the statements made during the initial traffic stop were not the result of a custodial interrogation so they were admissible. Though temporarily detained, McCarty was not restrained in a significant manner as required by *Miranda*. A person in his situation would have reasonably believed that he would be free to go once the traffic stop was completed. The Court stated the following:

> The roadside questioning of a motorist detained pursuant to a routine traffic stop does not constitute "custodial interrogation" for the purposes of the Miranda rule. Although an ordinary traffic stop curtails the "freedom of action" of the detained motorist and imposes some pressures on the detainee to answer questions, such pressures do not sufficiently impair the detainee's exercise of his privilege against self-incrimination to require that he be warned of his constitutional rights. A traffic stop is usually brief, and the motorist expects that, while he may be given a citation, in the end he most likely will be allowed to continue on his way. Moreover, the typical traffic stop is conducted in public, and the atmosphere surrounding it is substantially less "police dominated" than that surrounding the kinds of interrogation at issue in *Miranda* and subsequent cases in which *Miranda* has been applied.

However, the Court excluded the statements obtained at the police station. At that point, the defendant had been placed under arrest and the interrogation was custodial under *Miranda*. Regardless of the nature or severity of the offense, a person subjected to custodial interrogation by law enforcement is entitled to the procedural safeguards enunciated in *Miranda*.

The Field Interview

Police officers seek information in a variety of ways. They often speak to individuals in informal settings such as street corners, living rooms, bars, or offices. While

Field interview
The police questioning of witnesses, victims, or suspects in an informal environment.

these individuals are generally considered witnesses, they may also be persons who the police suspect may be involved in criminal activity. This interview situation is generally referred to as a **field interview**. So long as the person has not been arrested or otherwise restrained of his or her liberty, these situations are not considered custodial and do not require the *Miranda* warnings. A person's home would ordinarily be a less intimidating environment than a police station or squad car. However, if the police arrest an individual in his or her home and then attempt to interrogate the individual, it would be considered custodial. A police officer who knocks on the door of a person's home and asks if they can come in and ask the person a few questions is not required to advise the individual of his or her *Miranda* rights.

In *Beckwith v. United States*, 425 U.S. 341 (1976), Internal Revenue Service agents went to the home of a man whom they were investigating for tax fraud. They arrived at 8:00 A.M. so as to not embarrass him by coming to his place of employment. Beckwith invited them inside. They all sat down at a dining room table. The agents made it clear that they were investigating Beckwith for possible criminal tax fraud. At one point, Beckwith excused himself so he could finish dressing. During the interrogation which the agents described as casual and friendly, Beckwith made several incriminating statements. After a couple of hours, the agents asked if they could examine his records. The documents were housed at Beckwith's workplace that was 45 minutes away, so they traveled in separate vehicles to the site where Beckwith turned the papers over to the agents. Beckwith argued that his statements should have been excluded from trial because they failed to properly advise him of his *Miranda* rights. The Court disagreed and allowed the evidence ruling that the interrogation was not custodial. Given the fact that the agents were invited into Beckwith's home, that the defendant was separated from the agents while he dressed and also during the trip to the workplace, and that at no time was Beckwith restrained, his freedom of action was not deprived in a significant manner. The *Miranda* warnings were not required.

The Police Station Interview

Television and movies often depict scenarios in which the police "take someone in for questioning." Legally the police may take someone to the police station against his or her will only if they are making a valid arrest based on probable cause. It is against the law to take someone in for questioning unless there is legal justification for an arrest. However, the police may ask an individual to voluntarily come to the station for questioning. They can even advise the person that they may arrest the person if he or she will not come voluntarily so long as they have probable cause to do so. Police generally prefer to conduct interviews and interrogations at their station or office. The police station provides the metaphoric home field advantage as well as a safer environment for the questioning. It does raise the issue of whether the *Miranda* rights must be given. Obviously, if the suspect has been placed under arrest, the warnings would be required. However, if the individual has voluntarily agreed to be questioned at the police facility, then it would not be considered custodial. Consider the following case.

OREGON v. MATHIASON

429 U.S. 492 (1977)

The Facts: While investigating a residential burglary near Pendleton, Oregon, an Oregon state trooper asked the homeowner if she had any idea who might have broken into her home. She said she knew Carl Mathiason, an associate of her son, had done some time in prison and was on parole. There was no other evidence that would implicate Mathiason or any other suspect. The trooper made several efforts to contact Mathiason. After about 25 days, he left a business card on Mathiason's door asking him to call him at the police post. When Mathiason called him, the trooper asked him to come to the police station which was only a couple of blocks from Mathiason's apartment. Mathiason came to the police station about an hour and a half later. The Court described the encounter:

> The officer met defendant in the hallway, shook hands and took him into an office. The defendant was told he was not under arrest. The door was closed. The two sat across a desk. The police radio in another room could be heard. The officer told defendant he wanted to talk to him about a burglary and that his truthfulness would possibly be considered by the district attorney or judge. The officer further advised that the police believed defendant was involved in the burglary and [falsely stated that] defendant's fingerprints were found at the scene. The defendant sat for a few minutes and then said he had taken the property. This occurred within five minutes after defendant had come to the office. The officer then advised defendant of his *Miranda* rights and took a taped confession.

The Decision: The Court ruled that the *Miranda* warnings were not required and allowed Mathiason's confession. The case turned on the issue of whether the stationhouse interrogation was custodial under *Miranda*. The Court determined that Mathiason had come to the station voluntarily. During the interrogation, he was not under arrest and the door was unlocked. The Court explained as follows:

> In the present case, however, there is no indication that the questioning took place in a context where respondent's freedom to depart was restricted in any way. He came voluntarily to the police station, where he was immediately informed that he was not under arrest. At the close of a 1/2-hour interview respondent did in fact leave the police station without hindrance. It is clear from these facts that Mathiason was not in custody "or otherwise deprived of his freedom of action in any significant way."

On the Street

The 911 Call

Police Dispatcher: 911, how can I help you?

Caller: Please help me. My wife needs help. I just found her unconscious in the bathtub. Please hurry.

Police Dispatcher: We have dispatched police units and emergency medical personnel. Is your wife breathing? Can you describe her injuries?

Caller: I don't think she is breathing. She hit her head when I pushed her. She fell into the water. In the bathtub. Hurry!

Police Dispatcher: Sir, did you say you pushed her?

Caller: Yeah, but I didn't mean to kill her. I just wanted to teach her a lesson. And that boyfriend of hers. But I don't want her to die.

Police Dispatcher: Sir, answer the door, the police have arrived at your house.

The caller hangs up.

Is the caller's confession admissible? Will the 911 operator be allowed to testify in court and present the audiotape of the call? ▪

Citizens who telephone the police often provide incriminating information. Officers or other support personnel such as dispatchers may ask questions about the caller's involvement in a crime. Those situations do not require the *Miranda* warnings since the caller's freedom of action is not impeded by the police. The police may ask direct questions relating to criminal activity without advising of the *Miranda* rights. In the above bathtub scenario, the caller's statements would be admissible as would any audiotape confirming the content of the call.

Juveniles and School Environments

As addressed previously, age may be a factor in determining whether a person is able to knowingly and intelligently waive his or her rights. In 2011, the U.S. Supreme Court examined an interrogation conducted in a school environment and ruled that age may be a contributing factor in determining whether the setting is custodial.

J. D. B. v. NORTH CAROLINA

131 S.Ct. 2394 (2011)

The Facts: A 13-year-old student, J. D. B. (the initials are used because the defendant is a juvenile) was pulled from his class at the Smith Middle School in North Carolina by a police officer. The student was taken to the administration office where he was questioned by two police officers in the presence of a school administrator concerning a series of house burglaries. The questions were unrelated to any in-school conduct or discipline. J. D. B. was never given his *Miranda* rights or told that he could leave the office and return to class. His guardian grandmother was never contacted. Officer DiCostanzo, a juvenile investigator, conducted the questions. However, at one point, the assistant principal joined in by telling J. D. B. that he needed to do the right thing because the truth always comes out in the end. Ultimately J. D. B. confessed to his involvement in the burglaries.

The Decision: The Prosecution argued that a child's age should have no bearing on the determination as to whether the interrogation setting was custodial. They stressed that this question was conducted in a school as opposed to a police station and that the juvenile had not been arrested. However, the Supreme Court disagreed. Justice Sotomayor, in her majority opinion, stated the following:

> The State and its *amici* contend that a child's age has no place in the custody analysis, no matter how young the child subjected to police questioning. We cannot agree. In some circumstances, a child's age "would have affected how a reasonable person" in the suspect's position "would perceive his or her freedom to leave." *Stansbury*, 511 U. S., at 325. That is, a reasonable child subjected to police questioning will sometimes feel pressured to submit when a reasonable adult would feel free to go. We think it clear that courts can account for that reality without doing any damage to the objective nature of the custody analysis.

She further stated the following:

> Reviewing the question *de novo* today, we hold that so long as the child's age was known to the officer at the time of police questioning, or would have been objectively apparent to a reasonable officer, its inclusion in the custody analysis is consistent with the objective nature of that test.

The court did not create a bright line fixed age requirement and did not suggest that all school interrogations would require the giving of the *Miranda* warnings. They clearly indicated that the police would have to consider age as a factor in determining whether an interrogation was custodial.

Interrogation

Interrogation
An effort to elicit an incriminating response.

The U.S. Supreme Court explained the term **interrogation** in *Rhode Island v. Innis*, 446 U.S. 291 (1980). In January 1975, the police in Providence, Rhode Island, were investigating the shotgun murder of a local taxi driver. Another taxi operator who had been robbed with a shotgun identified his assailant from a wanted poster in the police station. Police suspected the offender might also be involved in the murder. An officer spotted the suspect, Thomas Innis, on the street and arrested him without resistance. Innis was placed in the back of a police car with one officer in the back seat and two others in the front. Prior to being transported to jail, he was advised of his *Miranda* rights three times including once by the officer's captain who was the commanding officer on the scene. He invoked his *Miranda* rights. The captain also stated to the transporting officers that they were not to interrogate Innis. The two officers in the front seat engaged in a conversation about the missing shotgun and how it posed a danger to children in the area. One of the officers stated that there were "a lot of handicapped children running around in this area" because a school for such children was located nearby, and "God forbid one of them might find a weapon with shells and they might hurt themselves." At that point, Innis interrupted the officers and told them he would show them where the shotgun was located. They again advised him of his *Miranda* rights, but he led them to a nearby field where they found the weapon. The issue before the Court was whether the discussion between the officers was simply a genuine dialogue or if it was an interrogation directed at the defendant in order to gain incriminating evidence. The U.S. Supreme Court concluded that it was not an interrogation, thus allowing the shotgun and his statements as evidence:

> We conclude that the *Miranda* safeguards come into play whenever a person in custody is subjected to either express questioning or its functional equivalent. That is to say, the term "interrogation" under *Miranda* refers not only to express questioning, but also to any words or actions on the part of the police (other than those normally attendant to arrest and custody) that the police should know are reasonably likely to elicit an incriminating response from the suspect.

The U.S. Supreme Court addressed the definition of an interrogation in *Brewer v. Williams*, 430 U.S. 387 (1977). In *Brewer*, also discussed in Chapter 4, the Court determined that a lone detective conducted an interrogation by directing a conversation toward a suspect in an effort to obtain an incriminating response. Ten-year-old Pamela Powers had been kidnapped from a YMCA in Des Moines, Iowa, and was still missing. Robert Williams, the suspect in the case, turned himself in to the Davenport, Iowa, police. He was advised of his rights, and he indicated that he was unwilling to make a statement. While transporting Williams from Davenport to Des Moines, police detective Cletus Leaming started talking to Williams. He said he wasn't going to ask him any questions but he wanted him to share some thoughts with him to think about. The detective then delivered what is now infamously known as the "Christian burial speech." He made an emotional appeal in which he talked about the tragedy of a devout family having their daughter kidnapped and murdered during the Christmas season and being unable to even provide a proper Christian burial. Williams then told Leaming where some of the child's clothing was and provided information about where the body was located. However, the Supreme Court ruled that the detective's speech was an interrogation. They stated that Leaming's efforts were the functional equivalent of questioning. Williams had invoked his *Miranda* rights and could not be interrogated so his incriminating statements were excluded. Williams was later convicted at a second trial without the use of his statements.

Unsolicited and Spontaneous Statements

Statements that are not in response to an interrogation are not impacted by the *Miranda* warnings. These unsolicited statements occur in a variety of settings. It is not unusual for an arrestee who is being transported to jail to talk to the officers. This may occur even if the officers try to avoid conversation. The suspect, who is often distraught or anxious, will try to explain his or her situation. Police officers are not required to interrupt the suspect's ramblings to advise of the rights so long as they do not ask the suspect any questions. Just listening is not an interrogation. Witnesses, bystanders, and suspects often spontaneously provide evidentiary statements during a crime scene investigation. "Excuse me officer, I was just in the back alley smoking some crack and this dude came running by me carrying a gun. I thought you oughta know." The police are not required to give the *Miranda* rights to an individual who approaches them and starts talking.

On the Street

Blah, Blah, Blah

Carmen is arrested for stabbing her boyfriend, Jameson. The police arrest her at her mother's house, handcuff her, and place her in the rear of a patrol car. They do not give her the *Miranda* warnings. During the 30-minute ride to jail, the officers ask her for her personal information such as her address, social security number, height, weight, and date of birth. She answers them. About ten minutes into the ride she starts yelling at the officers. They ignore her. She starts screaming louder and tells them that they shouldn't arrest her. She pleads, "You fools have the wrong woman. You should lock up Jameson. I'm glad I stabbed the cheating jerk! If he doesn't die, you should go arrest him for not being able to keep his pants on!" Is her statement admissible? ▦

Conversations of others, though intended to be private, are also admissible and do not require the *Miranda* rights. A police officer who overhears incriminating statements made while sitting in a restaurant is not obligated to interrupt and advise the individuals of their *Miranda* rights. The same premise applies to the overheard cell phone conversation. Most folks have had the unpleasant occurrence of overhearing another's cell phone conversation whether in a shopping mall, on a college campus, or in a restaurant. If the statements are testimonial evidence of a crime, they are admissible. The parties to the conversation have no expectation of privacy and listening to the conversation does not constitute an interrogation.

On the Street

TMI

Bledsoe, a local police officer, is attending a college basketball game with his young son. Unfortunately, there are two obnoxious guys sitting directly behind him. They are complaining about everything and using foul language. Just as Bledsoe is ready to say something to them, one of the men says to the other, "Look, don't worry about this game. In a few hours, you're gonna be rolling in the dough baby. Those idiots at the check cashing place aren't going to know what hit them. So calm down, watch the game, and then we go do our business." Officer Bledsoe didn't say anything. He just listened intently for the rest of the game. It wasn't long before the two men discussed more details about a planned robbery. Are their statements admissible? Should Officer Bledsoe have advised them of their rights? ▦

Law Enforcement

The *Miranda* rights are necessary only if the custodial interrogation is conducted by or on behalf of a law enforcement officer. Across the United States, there are hundreds of government agencies with law enforcement functions. They include local police, sheriff's departments, the Federal Bureau of Investigation, the U.S. Marshals, Military Police, NCIS, and even the Internal Revenue Service. The *Miranda* requirements apply only to interrogations arising from government agencies.

Private Security

They do not apply to individuals working for private businesses such as retail stores, corporations, or private security firms. Those types of firms certainly employ staff who have duties similar to law enforcement but in most cases are not working on behalf of a government entity. Private security personnel are usually charged with protecting the assets of a business, executive protection, or loss prevention. In those capacities, they may conduct interrogations. The *Miranda* rights are required only if the situation involves acting on behalf of government law enforcement.

On the Street

Bagged at the Boutique

Marvella would like to get something special to wear for the upcoming New Year's Eve bash so she goes shopping at Laci's Lingerie Boutique. She finds a beautiful teal camisole that fits her perfectly. Unfortunately, its price exceeds her budget. So, Marvella takes it into the dressing room, stuffs it down her pants, and attempts to walk out of the store. Unknown to Marvella, Laci employs a plainclothes security guard to monitor this type of behavior. He saw Marvella take the camisole into the dressing room and come out without it. He quickly checks to make sure she didn't leave it in the room and then grabs her as she walks out of the front door. The guard then takes Marvella to the office. He begins asking her questions about why she took the merchandise. He never advises her of the *Miranda* rights. Marvella makes a sobbing confession saying that she just didn't have enough money. She also tells him it isn't her first time. Is Marvella's confession admissible? Was the guard required to give Marvella the *Miranda* warnings? ■

Private businesses often hire off-duty police officers to work for them as security personnel. While those officers are off duty and working for the private enterprise, they are still considered law enforcement and would have to advise the *Miranda* rights if they conducted a custodial interrogation. Law enforcement officers are commissioned 24 hours a day.

If a police officer instructs a civilian to conduct a custodial interrogation, the *Miranda* rights would be required. Consider the previous hypothetical scenario involving Laci's Boutique. In all likelihood, the security guard would have contacted the local police to transport Marvella to jail. If the police arrived and the officer directed the security guard to ask Marvella some questions, *Miranda* would be required. At that point, the security guard would be acting on behalf of law enforcement and would thus be required to give the *Miranda* warnings.

Interrogations by Private Citizens

Considering that an interrogation is an effort to elicit an incriminating response, most people have been interrogated at some juncture. It is also likely that most have conducted an interrogation. People are interrogated by girlfriends, boyfriends, spouses, parents, and bosses. Most parents are rather astute at interrogating their teenage children concerning their actions. Are the *Miranda* rights required? Of course they're not. The *Miranda* rights are not required if the interrogator is not a government law enforcement officer.

On the Street

A Personal Note from the Author: Mom

My mother was an excellent interrogator. I certainly recall my mother coming to my downstairs bedroom and questioning me when she had been out of town for a weekend. "Sit down, Roger!" I had a small bedroom and she would sit knee to knee across from me. Then she would use the nuclear mom interrogation technique. She would start crying. "We've tried to raise you better than this." Sobbing now (probably fake), "Did you have a girl in your bedroom while we were gone?" "Did you have a party?" "Do you smoke marijuana?" "Were you drinking?" As I recall, she never advised me of my *Miranda* rights. ■

Non–Law Enforcement Government Officials

The large majority of government employees are not engaged in law enforcement functions. Questioning from these non–law enforcement government employees would not require the *Miranda* rights unless they were acting on behalf of law enforcement and conducting a custodial interrogation. Consider the following.

On the Street

Confessions from an Ambulance

Police respond to a bank robbery in progress. As the robbers exit the bank, they exchange gunfire with the officers who have surrounded the scene. One of the suspects receives a serious gunshot wound to the abdomen. He is arrested and placed in an ambulance where he is handcuffed to the gurney. He is bleeding severely. A police officer sits in the rear jump seat and secures his seat belt. He never says a word as he is only worried about holding on and not throwing up. The ambulance rushes off to the hospital and the emergency medical technician frantically works to save the suspect's life. The EMT is a city firefighter. During the ride to the hospital, the EMT in an effort to try to keep the suspect focused asked him, "Man, why did you guys try to rob that bank?" The suspect mumbled, "Just trying to get some money to get out of this godforsaken town." At no time was the suspect advised of his *Miranda* rights. Is the statement admissible? ■

The Public Safety Exception

When circumstances exist that pose a danger of imminent harm to others, the police may seek answers from a suspect without first giving the *Miranda* warnings. This procedure has been used several times in recent years in order to manage terroristic threats. The exception was first carved out by the U.S. Supreme Court in 1984.

NEW YORK v. QUARLES

467 U.S. 649 (1984)

The Facts: In the early morning hours of September 11, 1980, Officers Frank Kraft and Sal Scarring were patrolling the streets of Queens, New York. They were approached by a young woman who said that she had just been raped at gunpoint. She described her assailant as a black male, approximately six feet tall, wearing a black jacket with the name "Big Ben" printed in yellow letters on the back. She also told them that the man had just run into the nearby A&P supermarket. The officers had the woman get in the patrol car and they drove to the supermarket. As soon as they walked inside, they spotted the suspect, Benjamin Quarles, approaching a checkout counter. He also spotted the officers. He then turned and ran toward the rear of the store. Officer Kraft pursued him with his gun drawn. During the foot chase, Kraft lost sight of Quarles when he ran around the end of an aisle. Once he regained sight of him, he ordered him to stop and place his hands over his head. Though more than three other officers had now joined him, Kraft was the first to reach the suspect. He frisked him and discovered that Quarles was wearing an empty shoulder holster. Kraft handcuffed him and asked him where the gun was. Quarles said, "The gun is over there," and pointed toward some empty cartons. The officers quickly searched the cartons and retrieved a loaded .38-caliber revolver. At that point Kraft read Quarles the *Miranda* warnings from a printed card. Quarles waived his rights and, pursuant to the officer's questions, admitted that he owned the gun and that he had purchased it in Miami, Florida.

The Decision: Quarles was clearly in custody when Officer Kraft asked him where he had thrown the gun. He had been captured and handcuffed at gunpoint. The question, "where is the gun," was certainly an interrogation question designed, in part, to discover the whereabouts of a valuable piece of evidence. If the suspect knew where the gun was, it would link him to the weapon and also corroborate the claims of the victim that she was assaulted at gunpoint. Thus, it was a custodial interrogation by law enforcement and under ordinary circumstances would necessitate the *Miranda* rights. Quarles argued on appeal that the statement as to the location of the gun should have been excluded because he had not been advised of his rights. He also contended that the gun and any subsequent statements should have also been excluded as fruits of the poisonous tree.

However, the U.S. Supreme Court allowed the evidence by establishing the public safety exception to the exclusionary rule. They stated the following:

Kaleidoscopic
Describing a series
of changing phases,
events, or actions.

We hold that on these facts there is a "public safety" exception to the requirement that Miranda warnings be given before a suspect's answers may be admitted into evidence, and that the availability of that exception does not depend upon the motivation of the individual officers involved. In a **kaleidoscopic** situation such as the one confronting these officers, where spontaneity rather than adherence to a police manual is necessarily the order of the day, the application of the exception which we recognize today should not be made to depend on post hoc findings at a suppression hearing concerning the subjective motivation of the arresting officer. Undoubtedly most police officers, if placed in Officer Kraft's position, would act out of a host of different, instinctive, and largely unverifiable motives—their own safety, the safety of others, and perhaps as well the desire to obtain incriminating evidence from the suspect. *New York v. Quarles*, 467 U.S. 649 (1984)

On the Street

The Kidnapper

A seven-year-old boy is snatched from the play area of a fast food restaurant. Two days later, the kidnapper contacts the parents and demands $50,000 for the return of their child. Otherwise, they will kill him. The parents are instructed to place the money in a red cloth bag and leave it in a locker at the airport. The parents must then tape the locker key underneath a specific bus bench located near the airport. The FBI and local law enforcement set up a surveillance of the bus bench and locker. The father places the money as instructed into locker 451 at the airport terminal and then drives to the bus bench where he tapes the key. Two hours later, the man retrieves the key and is driven to the airport by a young woman. She drops him off, and he goes inside to get the money. The police immediately arrest him and the woman driver. They are immediately taken into the security offices at the airport where they are questioned about the whereabouts of the little boy. Neither is advised of their *Miranda* rights. The young woman quickly admits her involvement, blames it all on her boyfriend, and tells the police that the boy is locked in an underground tornado shelter at a farm about 30 minutes away. The police send units to the farm and find the child. Are the statements of the female kidnapper admissible? ▪

Terrorism and the Public Safety Exception

Since the establishment of the exception, it has played a role in several counterterrorism investigations. It was discussed by the news media as a possibility during the investigation of the Boston Marathon bombing. It was successfully utilized in the attempted bombing of an airliner on Christmas Day, 2009. Umar Farouk Abdulmutallab, now infamously known as the "underwear bomber," boarded Northwest Flight 253 from Amsterdam to Detroit, Michigan. During the flight, he wrapped himself in blankets and attempted to detonate explosives hid in his underwear. The explosive failed to ignite properly, but the detonation device burned Abdulmutallab. When the flight landed, U.S. Customs and Border Protection arrested him and transported him to the University of Michigan Hospital. There he was questioned by FBI Joint

Terrorism Task Force Special Agent Timothy Waters. Special Agent Waters had information that Abdulmutallab was operating on behalf of the terrorist organization al Qaeda. The agents, aware of al-Qaeda's involvement in international terrorism, were concerned about additional imminent attacks on aircraft in the United States and internationally. Abdulmutallab was questioned for 50 minutes regarding his actions and other possible al-Qaeda attacks. He provided detailed information concerning other planned terroristic attacks including targeted aircraft and how the attacks may occur. He also provided information about his bomb maker and the procedure he had planned to follow in carrying out his attack. As a result of the interrogation, agents were able to notify appropriate law enforcement officers around the world. Later, in a pretrial evidentiary hearing, Abdulmutallab's attorneys attempted to exclude the statements arguing that they were the subject of a custodial interrogation and Abdulmutallab had not been advised of his *Miranda* rights. The Court, in *United States v. Umar Farouk Abdulmutallab*, 2011 U.S. Dist. LEXIS 104159, determined that the interrogation questions were for the purpose of preventing imminent threats to the lives of others and to prevent further acts of terrorism. Citing the public safety exception established in *New York v. Quarles*, the statements were admitted into evidence.

The public safety exception was applied in another case involving an imminent terroristic attack in 1997. Abdelrahman Mossabah informed the New York Police that his roommates, Gazi Ibrahim Abu Mezer and Lafi Khalil, had bombs in their apartment and were planning on detonating them soon. Mossabah said that Abu Mezer was "very angry because of what happened between Jerusalem and Palestine." Abu Mezer had shown Mossabah pipe bombs in a black bag and indicated that he was going to detonate them in a crowded subway or bus terminal. Mossabah gave the police a key to the apartment, diagrammed the layout, and went with officers on an early morning raid of the building on July 31, 1997. When the officers approached the apartment, they heard "ruffling" noises inside. When they entered, one of the men grabbed the gun of an officer, and the other tried to grab a black bag that the officers believed might contain a bomb. The police officers shot and wounded both men who were then identified as Khalil and Abu Mezer. They were handcuffed and transported to the hospital.

The black bag contained pipe bombs, wiring, and a switch that appeared to have been activated. Concerned that it might explode, officers at the hospital questioned Abu Mezer about the construction of the bombs. Abu Mezer answered the questions and advised the officers there were five bombs and that each would explode when its four switches were flipped. When asked if he was planning on killing himself, he simply responded, "Poof." Later the same day, Abu Mezer was advised of his *Miranda* rights. He then informed the officers that he belonged to Hamas and that he wanted to "blow up a train and kill as many Jews as possible." Khalil and Abu Mezer were charged with threatening to use a weapon of mass destruction. Abu Mezer attempted to exclude his statement concerning killing himself. However, the court allowed the statement pursuant to the public safety exception: "Abu Mezer's vision as to whether or not he would survive his attempt to detonate the bomb had the potential for shedding light on the bomb's stability" *United States v. Khalil*, 214 F.3d 111 (2d Cir. 2000).

Summary

The *Miranda* decision clearly stated that law enforcement was required to advise a suspect of the warnings when conducting a custodial interrogation. However, it was not immediately clear how the concepts of custodial, interrogation, and law enforcement were going to be interpreted. In the years since, there have been a number of cases that offered more defining rules for the application of *Miranda*. The clarifications have instructed that not all detentions by the police fall under the custodial parameters of *Miranda*. *Miranda* custody occurs only when a suspect is deprived of his or her freedom in a significant manner. Temporary detentions such as traffic stops and *Terry v. Ohio* frisks do not require the warnings. In *Brewer v. Williams*, the Court proclaimed that an interrogation did not have to include questions. They defined interrogation as an effort to obtain an incriminating response and allowed that a functional equivalent of questioning must also be preceded by the warnings. The warnings were designed only to protect suspects during custodial interrogations by government law enforcement officials. Interrogations by private persons do not require the warnings.

Also examined was the public safety exception arising from *New York v. Quarles*. The exception, which allows law enforcement to bypass the *Miranda* requirement when there is an imminent danger to the public, has now been applied to a number of situations involving threats of terrorism.

It is certainly clear that the 1963 *Miranda* decision has withstood the test of time. While there have been a number of interpretations, the effort by the U.S. Supreme Court still provides protection from compelled self-incrimination.

Review Questions

1. Why doesn't a police dispatcher have to advise a caller of the *Miranda* rights when the caller is confessing to a crime?
2. Explain the phrase "functional equivalent" of an interrogation.
3. Under what circumstances would a private security guard be required to give a suspect the *Miranda* warnings?
4. Would the public safety exception apply in a situation where the police were trying to determine the location of a dead body? Why or why not?
5. If a private citizen approaches a police officer and starts talking about his involvement in a crime, is the officer required to interrupt him and advise him of his *Miranda* rights? Why or why not?

Legal Terminology

Custodial
Field interview
Interrogation

Kaleidoscopic
Law enforcement

References

Beckwith v. United States, 425 U.S. 341 (1976)
Berkemer v. McCarty, 468 U.S. 420 (1984)
Brewer v. Williams, 430 U.S. 387 (1977)
J. D. B. v. North Carolina, 131 S.Ct. 2394 (2011)
New York v. Quarles, 467 U.S. 649 (1984)
Oregon v. Mathiason, 429 U.S. 492 (1977)
United States v. Khalil, 214 F.3d 111 (2d Cir. 2000)
United States v. Umar Farouk Abdulmutallab (2011) U.S. Dist. LEXIS 104159

Chapter 13
Identification Procedures

> The Prosecutor: Do you see in the courtroom the person who robbed the store?
>
> The Witness: Yes, there he is. Sitting in the suit at the defense table, behind the sign that says he is the defendant. That's the man. That's the man who did it.

A version of the above scenario unfolds in criminal courtrooms every day. An eyewitness to a criminal act identifies the perpetrator in open court. This type of courtroom identification provides damning evidence against a criminal defendant and certainly makes an impression on a jury. However, eyewitness identifications are fraught with problems. While human beings often provide valuable investigative information to law enforcement, they are not always perfect witnesses. There are many influences that affect an eyewitness' ability to accurately identify another person. People do not recall and remember places, people, or events in a consistent and accurate manner. Some folks never forget a face. Some can't remember a name even though they just heard it earlier that morning. Some can't remember where they were earlier that morning. Yet in the criminal courtroom they are often asked to recall details of an event that occurred months earlier.

Have you ever had an event occur right in front of you but you have no idea what happened because you were not paying attention? Have you ever walked up to a person thinking that that person was someone you knew only to embarrassingly discover it was not who you thought it was? Have you ever failed to recognize someone whom you had talked to just a few days earlier? Have you ever described someone's car as being a particular color only to have your friend disagree? Do you remember what color shirt your boss was wearing at work yesterday? Upon winning the 2008 presidential election, Barack Obama made a victory speech in Chicago's Grant Park in front of thousands of people. Television viewers watched from all over the world. What was he wearing? It was November in Chicago. Was the president-elect wearing a coat?

Human fallibility may not be the only problem. In many criminal investigations, witnesses may be asked to identify a suspect prior to the actual trial. The witness may be asked to provide a physical description of a suspect immediately after a crime has occurred. A witness may also be asked to participate in a pretrial identification procedure such as a lineup, photographic array, or showup.

These pretrial identification procedures can result in inaccurate courtroom identifications if they are not conducted properly and in compliance with the law. As a matter of human nature, witnesses are reluctant to change their mind once they have made a decision. If a witness has identified a particular suspect from a lineup, he or she may be unwilling to change his or her selection at trial. After sticking with the identification for months, it is unlikely that the witness would sit in front of a judge and jury and indicate that he or she has chosen the wrong person. "I'm sorry everyone. I picked the wrong guy out of the lineup. It's not the defendant. I'm sorry I put him through all of this and led the police astray. I'm sorry I wasted everyone's time." Yet, the question arises: Is the witness identifying the defendant because it is actually the person who committed the crime? Or was the identification made because the witness had selected the person during a previous police procedure? Witnesses often mentally accept that the person they observe during a pretrial procedure is actually the offender. It is critical that the pretrial identification procedures do not taint the identification process. In this chapter, students will examine the procedures and the requirements set by the U.S. Supreme Court.

Pretrial Identification Procedures

- **Lineup:** Usually conducted in a police facility, a lineup consists of several individuals positioned in a group setting. The witness is asked to observe the individuals and identify a suspect. The traditional lineup usually consists of an arrangement of six people in a line. The participants, other than any potential suspects, are typically other prisoners or law enforcement personnel who match the general description of the suspect. Lineups are conducted at some point after the criminal activity but before the trial. Occasionally lineups are conducted in nonpolice settings. For example, the police might take a witness into a bar and ask if the witness sees the suspect.
- **Photographic array:** In a procedure similar to a lineup, a witness is shown a variety of photographs and asked to identify the suspect. As with lineups, it is recommended that the individuals in the array possess similar physical characteristics in order to diminish suggestiveness. A photo array may be a series of photographs or even one group photograph.
- **Simultaneous or sequential lineup:** Individuals or photographs may be presented in a sequential or simultaneous format. In a simultaneous lineup, the most common, the individuals are viewed at the same time. In sequential lineups or photo arrays, the witness is presented with the individuals one person at a time.

Lineup
Usually conducted in a police facility, a lineup consists of a several individuals positioned in a group setting. The witness is asked to observe the individuals and identify a suspect.

Photographic array
Similar to a lineup, a witness is shown a variety of photographs and asked to identify the suspect if he or she is present in the photo array. The photo array may be a series of photographs or even one group photograph.

Simultaneous lineup
The individuals are viewed by the witness at the same time.

Sequential lineup
In sequential lineup, one individual at a time is viewed by the witness.

■ **Showup:** A showup is a one-on-one identification. The witness observes only one person and is asked to determine if that individual is the correct suspect. A photographic showup would involve the showing of only one person's photograph to the witness.

■ **In-court identification:** The in-court identification occurs when the witness is actually testifying at a hearing or at trial and is asked to identify a suspect. An attorney would ask the witness if he or she sees the suspect in the courtroom.

Lineup Procedures

On the Street

A fair lineup?

Rhonda was assaulted by a man she described as African American, six foot six inches tall, over 300 pounds, approximately 40 years old, and wearing all black clothing. A couple of hours after the attack, the police apprehend Ernie. He was arrested walking near the crime scene and his physical characteristics matched Rhonda's description. The police arranged a lineup and asked Rhonda to see if she saw the man who attacked her. The five-man lineup consisted of four Caucasian men, two of which had red hair, and four of which were quite thin. None of the four men were over six feet tall. Ernie was placed in the center position of the lineup. Problems? ■

Most lineups are not as blatantly unfair as the depiction in the above scenario. However, bias may be manifested in more subtle ways. Arguably, there is a certain amount of suggestiveness inherent in any identification procedure. Witnesses may presume the police would ask them to view a lineup only if the suspect is included.

Whether intentional or not, the police may create a setting in which they encourage the witness to identify a specific suspect. If the procedure is suggestive to a point that it does not meet the requirements of the U.S. Supreme Court, then the identification may be excluded from evidence. The witness may not be allowed to testify as to the identity of the perpetrator of a crime. Showups are certainly the most problematic. If the police ask a witness if they have captured the right suspect, it is natural for the witness to assume the police believe they have.

In *Foster v. California*, 394 U.S. 440 (1969), the U.S. Supreme Court disallowed the courtroom testimony identifying a defendant because the pretrial lineups and showups were unduly suggestive. The police first placed the defendant, Foster, in a three-person lineup wearing a leather jacket similar to that of the robber. The other two men in the lineup were significantly shorter than Foster and wore different clothing. He was not identified. They then placed him in a showup situation by allowing him to sit alone in an office with the eyewitness manager. The manager was still unsure. They conducted a third lineup in which Foster was the only person who had been in the previous lineup. It was only then that the manager was convinced that Foster was the robber.

Fillers
The participants or photographs included in a lineup which are not suspects in the criminal investigation.

Lineups should be conducted in a manner that does not suggest that any specific person is the correct suspect. The individuals who are not suspects, often referred to as **fillers**, should have similar physical characteristics as the primary suspect. There should be minimal variance in height, weight, complexion, and facial hair. They should, of course, be of the same gender and race as the description of the suspect. The police may not have any environmental indicators as well, such as a variance in the size or color of the numbers above the participants. The administrator of the lineup should not provide any assistance to the witness in selecting the correct suspect. As indicated in *Foster*, multiple lineups that include the accused as the only repeated suspect are problematic.

Photographic Arrays

Mugshot
A photograph of a suspect upon arrest by the police or correctional officials.

Photographic arrays may also be unfairly suggestive. The array should, if possible, include photographs of similar tone, color, texture, and size. The police should ensure that the witness is not being encouraged to select a specific photograph. For example, a photo array in which the suspect's photograph was a prison **mugshot** and all of the others were passport photos would be inherently unfair. A mugshot would alert the witness that the individual already has a criminal record. All photographs should be presented in the same manner. For example, an officer should not lay six photographs on a table while placing the suspects in a different position or angle than the others.

Double-blind
A term used in a line-up procedure when the administrator is unaware of the actual suspect.

Some states have enacted legislation that specifically outlines lineup and photographic array procedures. The photo array requirements typically involve a **double-blind** folder system in which the photographs to be viewed are inserted into individual folders and then viewed separately by the witness. The procedures are considered double-blind if the administrator of the procedure has not prepared the folders and is unaware of which, if any, of the photographs are those of a suspect. Some states require blank folders that do not include any photos to be shuffled along with those of the suspect and the fillers. It is, of course, a requirement that the fillers possess similar physical characteristics as the suspect and there are no other identifying marks or notes that would lead the witness to a specific individual or photo.

The View from the Supreme Court

NEIL v. BIGGERS

409 U.S. 188 (1972)

The Facts: The case involved the sexual assault of a Tennessee woman. The assailant grabbed a woman in the kitchen of her home, grappled her to the ground, and threatened her with a butcher knife. When she screamed, her 12-year-old daughter came out of a bedroom, saw the intruder, and also began screaming. The assailant directed the victim, "tell her [the daughter] to shut up, or I'll kill you both." She told her daughter to return to her room. Her attacker then wrestled her out of the house and walked her at knifepoint along a railroad track. Approximately two blocks away from her house, he pulled her into some woods and raped her. She testified later that during the rape, "the moon was shining brightly, full moon." He then ran off into the woods and she returned home. The entire event lasted between 15 and 30 minutes. At trial she testified about the lighting in the house during the initial attack:

A. [H]e grabbed me from behind, and grappled-twisted me on the floor. Threw me down on the floor.

Q. And there was no light in that kitchen?

A. Not in the kitchen.

Q. So you couldn't have seen him then?

A. Yes, I could see him, when I looked up in his face.

Q. In the dark?

A. He was right in the doorway—it was enough light from the bedroom shining through. Yes, I could see who he was.

Q. You could see? No light? And you could see him and know him then?

A. Yes.

When the police arrived, she described her assailant as "being fat and flabby with smooth skin, bushy hair and a youthful voice." She had also indicated that he was between 16 and 18 years of age, between five feet ten inches and six feet tall, weighing between 180 and 200 pounds, and that he had a dark brown complexion. An officer later verified her initial description by testifying from his notes taken at the scene. The Federal District Court who later conducted a habeas corpus hearing characterized her observations as "only a very general description."

For seven months, the police asked her to view suspects at both showups and lineups. During those procedures, some of which were at her home, she was shown between 30 and 40 photographs. Once she indicated that one of the photographed men had similar features to her assailant, but she never identified anyone as being her attacker. After seven months, the police asked her to come to the police station to view the defendant who had been arrested on an unrelated charge. Because of the defendant's unusual physical characteristics, they could not find other similar men to participate in a fair lineup. Having no choice, they conducted a showup. Two detectives walked the defendant past the victim. At the victim's request, the suspect was directed to say, "Shut up or I'll kill you," the same words her attacker had spoken in the house. The victim identified the suspect as her attacker and later testified that she had "no doubt" about her identification. At a subsequent habeas corpus hearing, she elaborated in response to questioning:

A. That I have no doubt, I mean that I am sure that when I—see, when I first laid eyes on him, I knew that it was the individual, because his face—well, there was just something that I don't think I could ever forget. I believe _____

Q. You say when you first laid eyes on him, which time are you referring to?

A. When I identified him—when I seen him in the courthouse when I was took up to view the suspect.

She also indicated in her identification that her assailant had a unique voice. She stated that because she had teenage boys of her own, she recognized that her attacker had a high, immature voice.

The Decision: The Supreme Court allowed the identification testimony of the victim to be presented to the jury. As part of their decision, the Court was very instructive. They identified the factors that must be considered in determining if the pretrial identification would be allowed. The factors included the following:

1. Opportunity of the witness to observe the suspect
2. Certainty of the witness
3. Degree of attention
4. Accuracy of the description
5. Length of time between the crime and the identification

The Court also indicated that the factors must be viewed as a whole by considering the totality of circumstances. Some factors in any given case may be more important than others. In *Biggers*, the Court seemed to give substantial weight to how certain the witness/victim was of her identification. They verified that an identification based on a pretrial identification procedure should be excluded if there is "a very substantial likelihood of irreparable misidentification."

They were clear in their assessment that out of court pretrial identifications may be suggestive; however, after examining all of the factors involved, they allowed the victim's testimony and identification of the suspect. The Court further stated the following:

The victim spent a considerable period of time with her assailant, up to half an hour. She was with him under adequate artificial light in her house and under a full moon outdoors, and at least twice, once in the house and later in the woods, faced him directly and intimately. She was no casual observer, but rather the victim of one of the most personally humiliating of all crimes. Her description to the police, which included the assailant's approximate age, height, weight, complexion, skin texture, build, and voice, might not have satisfied Proust, but was more than ordinarily thorough. She had "no doubt" that respondent was the person who raped her. In the nature of the crime, there are rarely witnesses to a rape other than the victim, who often has a limited opportunity of observation. The victim here, a practical nurse by profession, had an unusual opportunity to observe and identify her assailant. She testified at the habeas corpus hearing that there was something about his face "I don't think I could ever forget."

There was, to be sure, a lapse of seven months between the rape and the confrontation. This would be a seriously negative factor in most cases. Here, however, the testimony is undisputed that the victim made no previous identification at any of the showups, lineups, or photographic showings. Her record for reliability was thus a good one, as she had previously resisted whatever suggestiveness inheres in a showup. Weighing all the factors, we find no substantial likelihood of misidentification. The evidence was properly allowed to go to the jury.

Pretrial Identification Factors

Opportunity of the Witness to View the Suspect

There are many factors that may affect a witness' ability to make an accurate identification. Environmental factors such as lighting conditions, weather, noise, and view obstructions may come into play. In *Neil v. Biggers*, the assailant was first observed with the light from the kitchen in his face. Later, during the sexual assault, it was nighttime but there was light from a full moon which allowed the victim an excellent look at the suspect's face. On the other hand, a suspect running from the back of a store in a dark and rainy night would be quite difficult to identify. The victim's perspective can certainly impact his or her ability to see an event. The distance from the suspect would clearly be an issue.

There may also be issues relating to the condition of the witness that impact the witness's ability to clearly identify a suspect or other events. Is the witness impaired because of drugs or alcohol? Does the witness wear glasses or contacts? A homeowner who wakes up in the middle of the night upon hearing an intruder may not be wearing his or her corrective lenses. Likewise, a person may be groggy upon first awakening. Fear sometimes heightens one's senses, but it also causes some people to freeze up.

Certainty of the Witness

The witness may express certainty or doubt concerning the strength of their identification. In *Biggers*, the victim stated that she would never forget her assailant's face and that she had no doubt. Additionally, she had viewed a number of lineups, photographs, and showups over a seven-month period prior to the time that she identified the defendant, yet she never selected anyone else. It also may be obvious in a witness' testimony that the witness is not sure of his or her identification. Statements such as "I think it is him" or "It looks like the guy" do not indicate a high level of certainty.

Degree of Attention

The lack of attention by the witness is one of the most common causes of misidentification. People are often focused on their own lives and concerns and do not clearly notice the events that are occurring around them. A person texting on a cell phone may briefly notice a person running by them but do not necessarily pay sufficient attention to describe or identify that person. In the *Biggers* case, the victim was totally focused on her assailant. The attack was close and personal, and she was in fear of her own life and that of her daughter. A cashier in a bank robbery would be paying close attention, whereas a passing motorist may not.

Accuracy of the Description

The police will often ask a witness to provide a physical description of a suspect or an event. Ultimately, if a suspect is arrested, the court may consider whether the initial description is consistent with the actual defendant. As previously mentioned, people are often poor at describing others. People see colors somewhat differently. Police often encounter two witnesses who have observed the same person but their descriptions differ wildly. It is difficult to accurately assess another person's weight, height, eye color, and other physical characteristics from a brief encounter. Adding to the problem is the fact that the witness wants to be helpful and may offer information that the witness did not actually observe. For example, a witness might describe a person's height yet only observed the person sitting in a car. In *Biggers*, the physical characteristics of the defendant were rather unusual, and the witness's initial description was reasonably accurate.

Length of Time Between Crime and ID

The Court will consider the amount of time that has passed between the identification and the actual crime. Memories fade with time. Have you ever met someone at a party and then when you encounter them again six months later have no idea who he or she is? It is human nature. However, during a dramatic event such as a crime, the passage of time may not be a critical factor. The Court noted in *Biggers* that even though seven months had passed between the crime and the identification of the suspect, the lengthy time frame was outweighed by the certainty of the witness.

Totality of Circumstances and Showups

Showups are inherently suggestive. If a witness is being shown only one suspect by the police, the witness would presumably think that the police believe they have arrested the correct person. However, while discouraged, showups are occasionally the only available approach to determine if the correct suspect has been apprehended. It may also be the only opportunity to **exculpate** the suspect if the eyewitnesses indicate he or she is not the perpetrator. The U.S. Supreme Court examined such a situation in *Stovall v. Denno*, 388 U.S. 293 (1967). On August 21, 1963, Dr. Paul Behrendt was stabbed to death and his wife was critically injured in a robbery. A shirt and set of keys left at the scene led the police to arrest Theodore Stovall. The police, who were told that Mrs. Behrendt's diagnosis was grave, brought Stovall to the victim's hospital room. At the time, they reasonably believed that this was the last and only opportunity to determine if Stovall was the killer. She identified him as the man who stabbed her and killed her husband. Though the Supreme Court agreed the showup was suggestive, they concluded that considering the totality of circumstances, the police had no choice but to conduct the showup. While it was the only chance that they had to determine whether Stovall was the assailant, it was also the only opportunity for Mrs. Behrendt to exculpate Stovall by stating he was not the killer.

Exculpate
To clear of guilt or blame.

On the Street

Was the lineup so impermissibly suggestive that there was a substantial likelihood of an irreparable misidentification?

The noise was deafening. When the shot rang out, Candace looked out through the window in the kitchen door only to see Sanjay lying on the floor behind the counter. A man was standing at the counter holding a shotgun. He saw Candace, too. He yelled at her and demanded that she come out and give him the money. Candace carefully stepped over her colleague, emptied the cash register, and handed it to the man. The robber then stuck the shotgun up against Candace's face and told her that she should not remember him or he would come back and leave her lying on the floor also. The man then ran out of the side door. Next to the door of the Chuck's Chewy Chicken Hut was a photo of the owner, Charles Davenport. Candace was able to tell the police later that the robber was exactly the same height as the top of the photo. They measure it as six feet tall. Candace also told the police that the robber was a large white man wearing camo pants and a Carolina Panthers sweatshirt. She also said he had a scar cutting through his left eyebrow. When asked about the gun, Candace said, "I know exactly what it was. My Uncle Buford used to take me hunting every Sunday. It was a Remington 870 Wingmaster, likely a .12 gauge because the barrel was pretty big. Walnut stock."

About 30 minutes after the robbery, a deputy pulled over Chris Bottlesworth for speeding about five miles from the restaurant. When the deputy approached the car, he saw a shotgun lying in the back seat. He ordered Bottlesworth out of the car and realized that he fit the description of the robber. He was wearing camo pants and a Panthers T-shirt. The deputy immediately arrested Bottlesworth and transported him to jail. When he searched him, he found a napkin from Chuck's Chewy Chicken Hut.

Two days later, the sheriff arranged for Candace to view a photographic array. She was shown a series of six photographs inserted into separate manila folders. In folder 1 was the full-body photograph of Chris Bottlesworth. He was still wearing his camo pants and Panthers T-shirt. The other men in the lineup had similar physical characteristics with the exception of the scar and the clothing. Their photos were only upper torso and head shots. Candace immediately identified Bottlesworth as being the man who robbed the store and shot her friend. She screamed when she saw his picture, "That's the creep. I would know him anywhere. Anytime. I know he has even been in the restaurant before."

Should Candace be allowed to identify the suspect at trial? Why or why not? Does the procedure pass the U.S. Supreme Court test for determining the admissibility of a pretrial identification? What factors should be considered? ■

Summary

Eyewitness identifications provide some of the most critical evidence in criminal trials. However, as outlined in this chapter, such identifications are not without potential problems. In addition the expected human fallibilities, investigative procedures such as lineups, showups, and photographic arrays may be so suggestive that they taint the accuracy of any subsequent courtroom identification. This chapter has outlined the factors that must be considered when a court examines the impact of a pretrial identification. The U.S. Supreme Court has also determined that an eyewitness identification may be excluded from court if the pretrial identification procedure was "so impermissibly suggestive as to give rise to the substantial likelihood of an irreparable misidentification." After examining the totality of circumstances, a trial court must apply that Supreme Court test.

Review Questions

1. What is the Supreme Court test for determining the admissibility of a pretrial identification procedure?
2. List the factors that may be considered in determining the admissibility of a pretrial identification.
3. Explain the problems associated with a showup identification.
4. Explain the procedure involved in a double-blind photographic array.
5. A criminal defendant has a right to have an attorney present during a photographic lineup. True or false?

Legal Terminology

Double-blind
Exculpate
Fillers
Lineup
Mugshot

Photographic array
Sequential lineup
Showup
Simultaneous lineup

References

Foster v. California, 394 U.S. 440 (1969)
Neil v. Biggers, 409 U.S. 188 (1972)
Stovall v. Denno, 388 U.S. 293 (1967)

Section IV
Constitutional Issues

The previous sections of this book focused primarily on police procedures and their consequences as they related to admissibility of evidence. Section IV takes a slight turn and hones in on how the U.S. Constitutional impacts courtroom-related practices.

Constitutional issues surrounding the right to a fair, speedy, and public trial by jury are presented in Chapter 14. They include impact of media coverage, the considerations for mandating change of venues, and the right to a speedy trial. In addition to the U.S. Supreme Court criteria for the determination of whether the right to speedy trial has been denied, individual states may draft statutory time frames.

Chapter 15 examines the protection from double jeopardy provided by the Fifth Amendment. Included are discussions on dual sovereignty and collateral estoppel and the steps in which jeopardy is attached. In Chapter 16, the reader explores the right of the accused to have access to a lawyer. When is an attorney provided by the courts and why?

The procedures and criteria for determining bail are outlined in Chapter 17. Pretrial detention for the purpose of ensuring public safety is also considered. Chapter 18 takes an extensive look at how punishments are determined and the relationship between sentencing laws and the Eighth Amendment. Of particular note is a discussion of the habitual-offender laws that have been enacted in both state and federal jurisdictions.

The last chapter examines the procedural issues that affect the imposition of the death penalty. The landmark cases of *Furman v. Georgia* and *Gregg v. Georgia,* which defined modern death penalty laws, are presented. The text also discusses more recent cases that barred death as a punishment for nonhomicide cases and for offenders who were minors or mentally incapacitated.

Chapter 14
The Right to Trial

The Sixth Amendment states in part the following: "In all criminal prosecutions, the accused shall enjoy the right to a speedy and public trial, by an impartial jury of the State and district wherein the crime shall have been committed, which district shall have been previously ascertained by law."

Right to a Speedy Trial

The right to a speedy trial addresses the time between the arrest of a criminal defendant and the trial. A long period of time results in a number of possible problems. The memory of witnesses may fade, witnesses may die or become otherwise unavailable, and evidence may be lost. Some will argue that justice delayed is justice denied. The Sixth Amendment gave the right to the criminal defendant. All of these factors may harm a defendant's ability to have a fair trial. The U.S. Supreme Court, in *United States v. Ewell*, 383 U.S. 116 (1966), described the right to a speedy trial as "an important safeguard to prevent undue and oppressive incarceration prior to trial, to minimize anxiety and concern accompanying public accusation and to limit the possibility that long delay will impair the ability of an accused to defend himself." But they also recognized the need for a deliberate pace and that unreasonable speed could also be a detriment.

While the constitutional forefathers created the requirement of a speedy trial, they did not define "speedy." The answer to the question of "how speedy?" is found in two separate but intertwined sources. Some states have drafted statutes that specifically identify the time frames in which a criminal defendant must be brought to trial. The U.S. Supreme Court has also adopted criteria that must be met in the determination of whether the right to a speedy trial has been violated. As a result, a criminal defendant must be brought to trial within the statutory requirements of the jurisdiction, but those time frames must also comply with the criteria set by the Supreme Court. If the trial does not occur within applicable state time lines and in compliance with the Supreme Court criteria, the case must be dismissed, and the defendant is free from prosecution. The Court interpreted the Sixth Amendment right to speedy trial as follows.

BARKER v. WINGO

407 U.S. 514 (1972)

The Facts: In July 1958, an elderly couple was found beaten to death in Christian County, Kentucky. The apparent murder weapon was a tire iron. Shortly after, Silas Manning and Willie Barker were arrested. Both were indicted September 15 and appointed counsel. Their cases were separated, and Barker's trial was originally scheduled for October 21. The prosecution had a stronger case against Manning and was concerned that they could only obtain a conviction against Barker if Manning testified against him; however, at that point, Manning was unwilling to incriminate himself. Therefore, the prosecution wanted to convict Manning first. Prior to the beginning of Barker's trial on October 21, the Commonwealth of Kentucky attorney sought the first of 16 **continuances** over the next five years. Barker made minimal objections during that time. However, there were problems with Manning's prosecution. His first trial resulted in a **hung jury**, meaning the jury was unable to reach a verdict. Manning was convicted at the second trial, but the conviction was reversed on appeal because of a search-and-seizure issue. He was convicted again at his third trial, but that conviction was also overturned because of a failure to change venue. The jury was again unable to make a decision at the fourth trial. In March 1962, Manning was finally convicted of murdering one of the victims. In December, he was found guilty of the murder of the other victim at his sixth trial. During this period of time, Willie Barker never went to trial. He remained in jail for the first ten months after his arrest and then finally posted bail. In the ensuing years, the prosecution requested and received 11 continuances without objection from Barker. Prior to the 12th trial setting, Barker asked that the case be dismissed but the Court granted another continuance to the commonwealth. The case was continued once again in March 1963 because the primary investigator was ill. After two more continuances by the prosecution, Barker was finally brought to trial in October 1963. Silas Manning testified against him, and Barker was convicted and sentenced to life in prison.

The Decision: Barker appealed arguing that his Sixth Amendment right to enjoy a speedy trial had been violated. He had been arrested in the summer of 1958 but had not been brought to trial until more than five years later. The Supreme Court upheld Barker's conviction and ruled that his right to a speedy trial had not been denied. In their opinion, they identified the criteria for determining whether a speedy trial violation has occurred:

1. Length of delay
2. Reasons for the delay

Continuance
A hearing or trial is delayed until a future date.

Hung jury
The members of a jury are unable to reach a verdict.

3. Defendant's assertion of the right to speedy trial
4. Prejudice to the defendant by the delay

Length of the Delay

While the Court recognized that individual states may wish to set specific time requirements, they declined to do so. They agreed that five years between arrest and trial appeared to be an extraordinary length of time. However, they indicated that it was tempered by the fact that the case was tried in a rural area of Kentucky and that the Christian County Circuit Court only held three sessions per year. The time frame would be assessed differently in large metropolitan jurisdictions with numerous courtrooms and judges which were in session year-round. They also recognized that this was a complicated murder case involving multiple victims and multiple defendants. As a result, the preparation for both sides would have been complex. The complexity and seriousness of the offense would certainly impact the length of time necessary to prepare for trial. A simple misdemeanor case would have been viewed differently.

Reason for the Delay

The reason for the granting of continuances by the trial court must be considered. It is certainly reasonable for a trial court to grant a continuance in order for the attorneys to properly prepare for the case. As stated previously, there is a relationship between the complexity of the case and the time necessary for preparation. It is also reasonable to grant a continuance if critical participants such as judges, attorneys, or witnesses are unable to attend because of a legitimate reason. In the Barker case, there were continuances due to the illness of the sheriff. However, a delay for the sole reason of gaining an advantage would not be considered in the delaying party's favor.

Defendant's Assertion of the Right to Speedy Trial

The fact that Willie Barker did not object to most of the prosecution's requests for continuances damaged his argument that his speedy trial was denied. While the right to a speedy trial belongs to the accused, the accused must assert the right in order to reasonably claim that it has been denied. Barker only objected to one continuance in five years and never objected during the first eleven. The Supreme Court noted that the delay in a trial often works in the defendant's favor. That was likely true in Barker's case as well.

Prejudice to the Defendant by the Delay

Barker was released from jail after ten months. Thus, he was free to live his normal life in his community during most of the five years while he was awaiting trial. While the delay could have created a disadvantage, it could also work in the defendant's favor. Witnesses may become unavailable due to death, illness, or relocation. Evidence may have deteriorated or been destroyed. The memory recall of witnesses may have diminished. The circumstances in each case will differ, and the court may consider those factors. A delay that creates an undue disadvantage to the defendant is a strong indicator that the right to speedy trial has been violated. Courts do not want the cloud of criminal charges to be unresolved for an unreasonable amount of time. That is particularly true if the accused is incarcerated during the period of time prior to trial.

Statutory Law

As previously discussed, some states have enacted statutes that identify specific time lines in which a defendant must be brought to trial. Those time lines must, of course, comply with the constitutional criteria set forth in *Barker v. Wingo*. Statutory time lines, while often stricter, usually include language that allows the extension of the time if necessary to the administration of justice. Consider the following statute from the State of Ohio.

O.R.S. 2945.71 Time for trial

(A) Subject to division (D) of this section, a person against whom a charge is pending in a court not of record, or against whom a charge of minor misdemeanor is pending in a court of record, shall be brought to trial within thirty days after the person's arrest or the service of summons.

(B) Subject to division (D) of this section, a person against whom a charge of misdemeanor, other than a minor misdemeanor, is pending in a court of record, shall be brought to trial as follows:

(1) Within forty-five days after the person's arrest or the service of summons, if the offense charged is a misdemeanor of the third or fourth degree, or other misdemeanor for which the maximum penalty is imprisonment for not more than sixty days;

(2) Within ninety days after the person's arrest or the service of summons, if the offense charged is a misdemeanor of the first or second degree, or other misdemeanor for which the maximum penalty is imprisonment for more than sixty days.

(C) A person against whom a charge of felony is pending:

(1) Notwithstanding any provisions to the contrary in Criminal Rule 5(B), shall be accorded a preliminary hearing within fifteen consecutive days after the person's arrest if the accused is not held in jail in lieu of bail on the pending charge or within ten consecutive days after the person's arrest if the accused is held in jail in lieu of bail on the pending charge;

(2) Shall be brought to trial within two hundred seventy days after the person's arrest.

(D) A person against whom one or more charges of different degrees, whether felonies, misdemeanors, or combinations of felonies and misdemeanors, all of which arose out of the same act or transaction, are pending shall be brought to trial on all of the charges within the time period required for the highest degree of offense charged, as determined under divisions (A), (B), and (C) of this section.

(E) For purposes of computing time under divisions (A), (B), (C)(2), and (D) of this section, each day during which the accused is held in jail in lieu of bail on the pending charge shall be counted as three days. This division does not apply for purposes of computing time under division (C)(1) of this section.

In Ohio, felony trials must be held within 270 days from the arrest of the defendant. However, every day that the defendant is incarcerated counts as three days. If a criminal defendant was arrested and could not post bail, then the state speedy trial requirement would be 90 days. The State of New York has a 180-day speedy trial requirement for a felony which is reduced to 90 if the defendant is in jail awaiting trial. The time for the trial may also be extended by the defendant if he or she is willing to waive the statutory requirement. Procedural requirements such as a mandated psychological evaluation may also result in an extension of time.

Right to a Public Trial

The Bill of Rights guarantees the right to a public trial to prevent the abuses of secret proceedings. As a result, criminal trials must be open to the public, family members, and the news media. A trial judge has the right to limit access to a trial if it is in the interests of safety or justice but would have to provide clear reasoning that would stand up to review by appellate courts. Judges have discretion in allowing cameras in the courtroom. While many states allow cameras, the federal system does not.

There are special circumstances in which trials may be held in secret. Secret military tribunals have been used in cases involving enemy combatants held in the U.S. Military Prison in Guantanamo Bay, Cuba. The facility holds prisoners captured during the military conflicts in Afghanistan and Iraq as well as others who have been accused of terrorist actions against the United States. The adjudication of juvenile delinquents may also be held in private.

In 2010, the Supreme Court ruled that the right to a public trial includes the jury selection as well as the actual presentation of evidence. In *Presley v. Georgia*, 130 S. Ct. 721, the trial court judge did not allow the defendant's uncle to be present in the courtroom during jury selection. The Supreme Court overturned Presley's conviction stating that while there may be safety concerns that would justify the closure of a trial to the public, they must be articulated by the trial judge. The Court compared the issue to the same rights that the media has to provide coverage of a criminal trial.

Right to an Impartial Trial by Jury

Petit jury
A jury that hears the evidence and determines guilt or innocence.

The right to jury trial set forth in the Bill of Rights applies to petit juries. A criminal **petit jury** is a collaboration of citizens who hear the evidence presented in a trial and determine guilt or innocence. Grand juries, which determine whether probable cause exists and whether an indictment should issue, are not constitutional required by the Sixth Amendment. The U.S. Supreme Court has also determined that the constitutional requirement of a trial by jury does not extend to all criminal trials. In *Baldwin v. New York*, 399 U.S. 66 (1970), the Court ruled that the constitutional right applies only in cases in which the defendant could be sentenced to more than six months in jail. However, most state constitutions provide for jury trials for any crime in which the defendant faces incarceration.

This chapter examines several issues associated with the right to an impartial jury trial such as the determination of the jury pool, selection of jurors, number of jurors, and requirement of a unanimous verdict. Also considered is the impact of media publicity on the selection of a fair and impartial jury.

Jury Service

Eligibility for jury service is determined by each jurisdiction. Statutory laws determine the criteria for jury duty in the individual states. The majority of states consider motor vehicle registrations, driver's licenses, and voter registration lists, while some also consider real estate and income tax rolls. The identifiers are used in order to establish a pool of prospective jurors which represent a cross section of the community. Citizens who are eligible for federal cases come from motor vehicle and voter registrations, commonly referred to as motor/voter pools. In addition to being identified as a prospective member of the pool, citizens in each jurisdiction must also meet the eligibility requirements set by law. While each state may determine its own qualifications, most are similar to the federal system.

U.S. Juror Qualification Requirements
   U.S. Citizen
   18 years of age or above
   Reside in the judicial district for one year
   Be reasonably proficient in English
   No disqualifying mental or physical condition
   No current felony charges pending
   No felony convictions (unless civil rights legally restored)
   Federal courts also prohibit service by active members of the military,
      firefighters, law enforcement, and other government public officers.

A summons for jury duty is a court order requiring citizens to report and make themselves available to serve. The jury summons should not be ignored. In many jurisdictions, a citizen who is ineligible or unable to serve may be excused or have his or her service rescheduled by contacting the jury commission or filing a request. However, the failure to respond may result in arrest.

Jury Selection

Once summoned for jury duty, citizens will be directed to a specific court where the selection process will unfold. The selection of the jurors who will actually hear a case is conducted by the attorneys and the judge. The selection process is referred to as **voir dire**, an Old French term meaning "to truly speak." Prospective jurors are questioned by the attorneys and in some cases the judge to determine if they have the ability to render a fair and impartial verdict. In many systems, the jurors are first asked to complete a written questionnaire with basic questions that address certain inherent biases. The attorneys may ask jurors about their prejudices, politics, opinions, experiences, and previous involvement with the legal system. In death penalty cases, the attorneys will often explore the prospective jurors' views on capital punishment. Voir dire is also designed to identify if the prospective juror has any connection to the case at hand or a relationship to any of the parties or witnesses. For example, a relative of a defendant would be unable to serve. The prosecuting attorney goes first and then the defense. Not all judges participate in voir dire, but they may if they wish. It is up to the individual judge whether to conduct voir dire before or after the attorneys.

Upon completion of the initial voir dire, attorneys may use challenges to exclude specific jurors. There are two types of challenges: cause and peremptory.

- **Challenge for cause**: An attorney may request the removal of a specific juror because the individual's responses to voir dire have indicated an inability to be impartial. The decision then lies with the trial judge whether to grant the challenge for cause. There are no restrictions on the number of challenges for cause. The prosecution goes first and then alternates with the defense.
- **Peremptory challenges**: A peremptory challenge allows the attorney to exclude a prospective juror without stating a reason. The judge does not rule on a peremptory challenge; however, each attorney is allowed only a fixed number. The number is determined by statutory law. It is often strategically preferred to use a challenge for cause rather than a peremptory challenge. If a judge refuses to remove a juror for cause, the attorney may still utilize a peremptory challenge to exclude the specific juror. The U.S. Supreme Court has barred peremptory challenges based solely on a prospective juror's race, ethnicity, or sex. The Court in *Batson v. Kentucky*, 476 U.S. 79 (1986), disallowed the systematic removal of African Americans from a jury by the prosecutor's use of peremptory challenges.

When the attorneys have completed both the challenges for cause and peremptory challenges, the remaining jurors will constitute the jury. The trial judge will also make a determination if any alternates should be selected. Alternate jurors will sit through the trial and listen to all of the evidence but will only participate in the verdict in the event another juror becomes ill or is otherwise unable to serve. Alternate jurors are also subject to voir dire.

Voir dire
The process in which the judge and the attorneys question prospective jurors in order to determine if the individual would be able to serve in a fair and impartial manner.

Challenge for cause
The request of an attorney to a trial judge to exclude a prospective juror because the juror has indicated an inability to be impartial or to properly serve.

Peremptory challenge
The exclusion of a prospective juror during voir dire by an attorney without indication of a reason. The number of peremptory challenges is limited by statute.

The Jury Verdict

The federal system and most states require unanimous verdicts in criminal jury trials. The statutory law of the jurisdiction dictates the requirement. All members of the jury must agree on the verdict in order for it to be considered unanimous. Until all members have voted either guilty or not guilty, a verdict has not been reached. If the members are unable to reach a unanimous decision, they are considered to be a hung jury and the judge must order a mistrial. A mistrial resulting from a hung jury is not considered double jeopardy, and the case may be retried. There is no limit on the number of retrials based on hung juries.

The U.S. Supreme Court has set some constitutional guidelines relating to the unanimity of juries. If a state allows a criminal jury of only six members, the verdict must be unanimous. Unanimous verdicts are also required in death penalty cases. They have, however, determined that the Sixth Amendment does not require unanimous verdicts in state criminal trials determined by 12 jurors. In *Apodaca v. Oregon*, 406 U.S. 404 (1972), the Court affirmed a verdict vote of nine of twelve jurors in a non–death penalty felony case. Unanimous verdicts are not required in most civil verdicts.

Jury Nullification

Jury nullification
A jury verdict in which the jury ignores the weight of the evidence and renders a verdict of not guilty.

The Fifth Amendment protection from double jeopardy prevents a defendant from being tried for the same offense if the defendant has been found not guilty. **Jury nullification** occurs when jurors render a not guilty verdict even though the facts and evidence indicate guilt. The jurors ignore the evidence, law, or instructions of the judge. Regardless, a verdict of not guilty is final, and the defendant cannot be further prosecuted for that specific crime. Once a verdict has been rendered, the jury is under no obligation to explain their reasoning, and thus, the impetus for jury nullification is seldom known. Nullification may occur because the jurors wish to correct a perceived injustice or an unjust law. For example, a jury might exonerate a defendant out of sympathy or they might find a defendant not guilty of a crime because they did not believe that the law was fair.

Judges try to prevent nullification through voir dire. Ideally, the questioning of the prospective jurors will reveal any prejudices that may be manifested during deliberations. Theoretically, a juror who lies during voir dire could be prosecuted for perjury, but those cases are rare as they are seen as an affront to the jury system and a disincentive to citizens who are asked to serve. Once deliberations have begun, jurors are free to deliberate and make their own decisions. Judges may overturn a guilty verdict that is clearly contrary to the evidence presented but cannot overturn a not guilty verdict.

On the Street

An empathetic jury?

Vanessa's 11-year-old son was brutally raped and murdered by two high school foot-ball players. The assault occurred behind a local convenience store. They left his body in the store Dumpster. The young men confessed to the police, claiming they were drunk at the time and were just messing with the boy because he was nerdy. At trial, the judge excluded the confession because the boys' parents were not present during the interrogation. In spite of the fact there was overwhelming physical evidence, the jury found the defendants not guilty. Two months later, Vanessa saw the two acquitted football players hanging out near the same convenience store. They were obviously smoking marijuana and having a good time. Vanessa turned her car toward them and rammed them both into a concrete wall instantly killing them both. When the police arrived she said only, "They killed my boy, they killed my boy." She was charged with murder. At her trial, the prosecution provided physical evidence matching fabric from the boys' clothes to the grill of Vanessa's car. The jury also viewed a store video that had caught the incident on camera. They also heard her confession. However, the jury found her not guilty. One of the jurors told the court bailiff later that the boys deserved what they got and she would have done the same thing had she been Vanessa. Is this jury nullification? Can Vanessa be retried? ■

Right to Public Trial

When pop singer Michael Jackson faced child molestation charges, the Los Angeles County Courthouse was surrounded by news media from around the world. In 1993, the world watched a slow-speed police pursuit of a white Ford Bronco being driven by former pro football player O. J. Simpson. Many news channels broadcast the verdict live at the conclusion of the Sanford, Florida, trial for shooting of Trayvon Martin in 2013. With the world enamored by the high-profile criminal cases, the intense media coverage of the courtroom procedures will only increase. It is doubtful that the framers of the Sixth Amendment could have imagined such public interest and media coverage that surrounds the criminal justice process today. The original intent of requiring pub-lic trials was to prevent secret procedures by the government. By bringing the criminal justice process to the public's eye, the scrutiny would encourage due process. However, another problem ultimately arose. With so much information available to the public, true or untrue, it may be difficult to ensure that decisions are fair and impartial.

The Impact of Publicity

Judges and jurors are required to examine the evidence presented in court and make fair and impartial decisions based on that evidence. Information that comes from any other source such as friends, family, or the news media may not be considered. Yet, in some cases, it is virtually impossible to insulate jurors and prospective jurors from the information now available online, on television, and in print publications. Opinions abound on social media. It is also within our human nature to form an opinion based on the information of which we are aware. Consider some of the following cases.

On the Street

Did you have an opinion?

State of Florida v. George Zimmerman. February 26, 2012, Trayvon Martin, a 17-year-old African American youth, was shot to death by 28-year-old George Zimmerman, a Hispanic man participating in a neighborhood watch program. Zimmerman was legally carrying a firearm pursuant to a concealed carry permit. The case was tried in Sanford, Florida. The trial was the subject of national news coverage. Zimmerman was found not guilty of murder on July 13, 2013.

State of California v. Conrad Murray. Dr. Conrad Murray was the personal physician for entertainer Michael Jackson. After a six-week trial, he was convicted of involuntary manslaughter for his role in Jackson's death and sentenced to four years in prison. The 2011 trial was the subject of continuous media coverage.

State of California v. Charles Manson. On the evening of August 8, 1969, five people were brutally murdered near Hollywood, California. The victims included Sharon Tate, actress and wife of director Roman Polanski; Abigail Folger, coffee heiress; celebrity hair stylist Jay Sebring; writer Wojciech Frykowski; and a family friend, Steven Parent. The following evening, supermarket executive Leno LaBianca and his wife Rosemary were murdered in a similar fashion. After the longest criminal trial in history, Charles Manson and five of his followers were convicted of first-degree murder on January 15, 1971. Manson was sentenced to death; however, his sentence was commuted a year later as a result of an unrelated Georgia death penalty case. The murders and Manson's continuing parole hearings are still fodder for talk shows, news coverage, and even seminars. The prosecutor, Vincent Bugliosi, resigned and began a career as an author by writing *Helter Skelter*, a book based on the case.

These trials are just three examples of how the national spotlight shines on what may have otherwise been local cases. At the time of the trials, it was rare to find a person who had not already formed an opinion as to the guilt or innocence of the defendants. Why does the public have so much interest?

In some cases it is because of the recognition of the victim. Conrad Murray was prosecuted because of the drugs he gave to Michael Jackson. Had the victim not been famous, it is unlikely that there would have been any media coverage. If someone attempts to harm a famous person such as an entertainer or politician, the case generates a great deal of public interest. The same occurs when the defendant has a high profile. O. J. Simpson's case was certainly the most publicized criminal trial in history at the time. Why? He was a hall-of-fame football star who had also appeared in numerous commercials, movies, and television shows. The murder trial of an all-American icon became the topic of discussion on not just television but also around offices, dinner tables, and bar tops for almost an entire year. The 2013 murder charges against Aaron Hernandez, wide receiver for the New England Patriots, created a national media buzz. In recent years, actor Robert Blake, music producer Phil Spector, and rapper Corey "C-Murder" Miller were all convicted of murder in trials garnering national publicity. The same phenomenon occurs on a local level. While victims or offenders may not have national recognition, they may be well known in their own jurisdiction because of local involvement in business, arts, athletics, or politics. In some places, if a high school basketball star is arrested, it gains a lot of attention in the community in which the case is likely to be tried.

Cases also receive notoriety because of the heinous or unusual nature of the crime. Certainly mass killings such as the 2012 Aurora, Colorado, theater murders demand national attention. But the unusual nature of the crime may also create interest. The names of John Wayne and Lorena Bobbitt are now synonymous with the felonious assault case in which Mrs. Bobbitt cut off her husband's penis. A slang verb evolved from the case. Jeffrey Dahmer is perhaps one of the most well-known serial killers because he dismembered his victims and kept their body parts as sex toys and trophies.

The problem that arises is that it is difficult to select a fair and impartial jury. Prospective jurors may be aware of certain facts concerning the case, yet they must now be able to base their decisions on that which is presented at trial. If a prospective juror is unduly influenced by that pretrial publicity to the point that he or she would be unable to provide a fair and impartial decision, then that person cannot serve as a juror. Imagine if the news media reports that a suspect has confessed to a crime, yet it is later determined that the confession is inadmissible due to a *Miranda* violation. Would a juror who is aware of the confession be able to disregard that information when deliberating the verdict? It should be noted that awareness of the case does not automatically prevent a juror from serving. This happens only in those cases where the information has made it impossible to view the evidence without forming preconceived opinions.

Judicial Management of Publicity

In some cases, the publicity may be so pervasive and prejudicial that the selection of a fair and impartial jury is unlikely. If that occurs, the court may change **venue**.

Venue
The geographical location in which a trial is held.

Venue is the location in which the trial is held. In most states, the trial will be held in the county in which the crime occurred. If the court determines that the venue must be changed, the trial may be moved to another venue so long as it is still within the jurisdiction. If it is a state charge, the venue could be changed to another county within the same state. In federal cases, the United States has jurisdiction, so venue could be moved to any U.S. District Court in the country. The federal murder trial of Timothy McVeigh, the Oklahoma City bomber, was moved from Oklahoma to Denver, Colorado. Either party to a trial may file a motion for the change of venue. The decision belongs to the trial judge. In some cases, the decision may be made after the attempt to select a jury indicates the difficulty in finding a fair and impartial jury pool.

Voir dire also offers an opportunity to examine the impact of pretrial publicity. As the attorneys and judge question the prospective jurors about their prior knowledge of the case, they attempt to determine if the publicity has impacted their ability to listen to the evidence and render a fair verdict. As previously discussed, jurors who portray the inability to make an impartial decision may be removed from the jury via challenges for cause or peremptory challenges.

Judges may also **sequester** the jury. The jury may be isolated during the trial to prevent their exposure to any prejudicial information that might impact their decision. When sequestration is ordered, the jury will usually be lodged in a hotel and be banned from watching any news, reading any publications, or accessing any Internet information regarding the case before them. Judges are generally reluctant to order sequestration because of the hardship on the jurors as well as the expense to the taxpayers. The jurors were sequestered in the aforementioned Manson and Simpson trials. In those situations, the jurors were isolated from their families, jobs, churches, and social networks for months. As with change of venue, either party may move the court for a sequestration order.

At the close of the presentation of evidence and closing arguments, the judge provides instructions to the jury. The **jury instructions** provide information to the jury as to the applicable criminal statutes, legal terminology, and any other procedural information such as the burden of proof, application of defense, and their role in weighing the evidence. For example, if the defendant in an assault case is claiming self-defense, the jury instructions will include an explanation of the law of self-defense. The jury will also be instructed on the rules of **jury deliberation** as well as the verdict forms that they are charged with completing. Deliberations consist of the discussions and the voting on the verdict. The jury will not be allowed to speak with anyone else concerning the case until deliberations are complete. If they have a question concerning the evidence, the question must be directed to the judge only. The jurors are warned to ignore all information they may learn outside of the courtroom and to base their decisions solely on the evidence presented. They are also warned not to conduct any testing or experimentation on their own. In 2011, a jury verdict was overturned in an Ohio murder trial because one of the jurors went home and conducted the juror's own test concerning the length of time it took to air dry after a bath. One of the evidentiary issues in the case involved whether the victim was murdered in a bathtub. The judge ordered a mistrial, and the case had to be retried. The prosecutor and defense attorneys may recommend specific instructions to the judge, but the final instructions are determined by the judge. The attorneys may not speak during the instructions. Once the instructions are completed, the jurors begin deliberations.

Trial court verdicts may be overturned on appeal if the pretrial publicity resulted in an unfair trial. The totality of circumstances will be reviewed to determine whether the trial was conducted fairly and whether the jurors were unduly prejudiced by publicity. The U.S. Supreme Court, in *Florida v. Murphy*, 421 U.S. 794 (1975), stated that, "The constitutional standard of fairness requires that a defendant has 'a panel of impartial, "indifferent" jurors.' Qualified jurors need not, however, be totally ignorant

Sequester
The isolation of a jury during a trial in order to limit exposure to any prejudicial information that might impact their decision.

Jury instructions
A judge's instructions to a jury explaining the applicable law and the rules of deliberations.

Jury deliberation
The discussions and voting in which a jury engages in determining a verdict.

of the facts and issues involved. To hold that the mere existence of any preconceived notion as to the guilt or innocence of an accused, without more, is sufficient to rebut the presumption of a prospective juror's impartiality would be to establish an impossible standard. It is sufficient if the juror can lay aside his impression or opinion and render a verdict based on the evidence presented in court."

Summary

The right to a speedy and public trial guaranteed by the Sixth Amendment has resulted in a considerable number of clarifications through the years by the U.S. Supreme Court. The Court has now identified criteria for speedy trial as well as decisions on the application of public trials and the requirements for a trial by jury. This chapter has examined the question: How fast is "speedy"? The answer comes in two forms. The Supreme Court set criteria in the landmark case of *Barker v. Wingo* where a criminal prosecution unfolded over a five-year period. But individual states have also been able to enact statutory speedy trial requirements so long as they comply with the *Barker* criteria.

The mandate of an impartial jury in criminal cases has also been addressed in this chapter. Like the speedy trial issue, state governments have the right to enact their own laws regarding jury size, unanimity, and selection, so long as they meet the federal constitutional guidelines.

The explosion of public interest and media coverage in recent years has severely tested the concept of a "public" trial. Courts must use voir dire, sequestration, and jury instructions in an effort to ensure that trials are conducted in a fair and just environment.

Review Questions

1. What are the criteria set by the U.S. Supreme Court for determining if an accused right to speedy trial has been violated?
2. What does the term *motor/voter pool* refer to?
3. Define and explain the distinctions between a *challenge for cause* and a *peremptory challenge*.
4. Define and explain *jury nullification*.
5. Describe three methods of managing pretrial publicity in order to protect the right to a fair and impartial trial.

Legal Terminology

Challenge for cause
Continuance

Hung jury
Jury deliberation

Jury instructions   Sequester
Jury nullification   Venue
Peremptory challenge   Voir dire
Petit jury

References

Apodaca v. Oregon, 406 U.S. 404 (1972)

Baldwin v. New York, 399 U.S. 66 (1970)

Barker v. Wingo, 407 U.S. 514 (1972)

Batson v. Kentucky, 476 U.S. 79 (1986)

Florida v. Murphy, 421 U.S. 794 (1975)

Presley v. Georgia, 130 S. Ct. 721 (2010)

Speedy Trial; Time Limitations, New York Criminal Procedure—Article 30—§30.30. Retrieved from http://law.onecle.com/new-york/criminal-procedure/CPL030.30_30.30.html

Time for Trial, Ohio Revised Code 2945.71

United States v. Ewell, 383 U.S. 116, (1966)

U.S. Courts. (n.d.). *Jury Service*. Federal Courts. Retrieved from http://www.uscourts.gov/FederalCourts/JuryService.aspx

Chapter 15
Double Jeopardy

The Fifth Amendment to the U.S. Constitution states in part the following: *No person shall . . . be subject for the same offense to be twice put in jeopardy of life or limb.*

On the Street

True Story: A Murder Triangle

The family of Brenda Sue Schaeffer reported her missing on September 24, 1998. She had left her Louisville, Kentucky, home the previous evening to meet Mel Ignatow, her fiancé. Ignatow later claimed that Schaeffer had dropped him off from their date at 11:00 P.M. During the ensuing investigation, Ignatow continually proclaimed his innocence as well as his outrage that he was a target of accusations. Six months later, he agreed to appear before a grand jury. During his testimony, he mentioned another girlfriend, Mary Ann Shore. Shore ultimately came forward and under the grant of limited immunity led the police to Schaeffer's body. Unfortunately, the body, which was buried in moist soil, had decomposed to the point that all trace evidence had vanished. Buried nearby was a plastic bag containing Schaeffer's clothing. Shore provided detailed testimony that Ignatow had tortured, sodomized, and murdered Schaeffer. She also claimed that she had filmed the torturous murder and participated at Ignatow's request, but she did not have the film. The trial was moved from Louisville to Covington, Kentucky, because of the concern over pretrial publicity. Despite Shore's lurid testimony, Ignatow was found not guilty in 1991.

Meanwhile, Ignatow had sold his home in Louisville. Six months after his acquittal, the couple who had purchased the home hired a heating and air conditioning company to complete some update work. One of the workers pulled up a piece of carpet that covered a heating vent and discovered a bag containing jewelry and 35-mm film. The film contained vivid images of the murder of Brenda Schaeffer and confirmed Shore's testimony. Mel Ignatow had tortured and murdered Brenda.

However, he had already been found not guilty. The Fifth Amendment protection from double jeopardy prevented a retrial on the murder charges. Ignatow was prosecuted for two counts of perjury for his testimony before the grand jury and was sentenced to five years in prison. He was released in 2006 and moved back to Louisville to live with his son. He died in 2008 after falling through a glass table and bleeding to death. ▪

The double jeopardy clause of the Fifth Amendment protects an accused from being prosecuted multiple times for the same offense if the case has already been adjudicated. However, the application of the double jeopardy is complex and often misunderstood. It does, in fact, prevent the retrial of a defendant who has been found not guilty of a specific offense. The above mentioned Ignatow case is a classic example in which a defendant is free though further damning evidence was later discovered. Mel Ignatow could have walked out of the courtroom after his acquittal and announced that he had killed his fiancé and the commonwealth could not prosecute him for the murder.

The protection against double jeopardy applies only to the "same offense." In the Ignatow case, he was subsequently convicted of perjury. That was allowed because he was not charged with perjury at his original murder trial. The perjury charge was a separate and distinct offense. Double jeopardy does bar the retrial on a lesser included offense. For example, if a defendant in a homicide case could be found not guilty of murder but guilty of voluntary manslaughter, that is permissible so long as it was a decision during the same trial. However, if the defendant was found not guilty of murder, he or she could not be prosecuted at a second trial for voluntary manslaughter of the same victim. The finding of guilt on a lesser included offense instead of the initial primary charge infers a not guilty verdict on the primary offense. If a defendant was tried for first-degree murder but was instead found guilty of manslaughter, he or she could not be retried for the murder charge. Double jeopardy also applies to guilty verdicts and the subsequent sentencing. If a defendant is found guilty of a crime and sentenced, the prosecutor cannot retry the defendant in order to obtain a more severe punishment.

The doctrine of **dual sovereignty** permits each jurisdiction to enact its own criminal statutes. A criminal offense in one state is a separate and distinct crime from a similar crime in another. Likewise, a federal crime is separate and distinct from a state crime though the event involves the same conduct by a defendant. If a person kidnapped a child in Montana and transported the victim across state lines to Idaho, the accused could be prosecuted by both states as well as the federal government so long as the elements of the offense were met in their jurisdiction. If the alleged kidnapper was found not guilty of kidnapping in Montana, he or she could still be prosecuted in Idaho. Consider the following case in which a man was convicted of the murder of one victim in two separate states.

Dual sovereignty
The principle that both the federal government and state governments exercise jurisdiction over specific legal issues.

HEATH v. ALABAMA

474 U.S. 82 (1985)

The Facts: In the summer of 1981, Larry Gene Heath hired Charles Owens and Gregory Lumpkin to kill his wife, Rebecca Heath, who was nine months pregnant.

The price was $2,000. In the early morning hours of August 31, Heath left his residence in Phenix City, Alabama, to meet with Owens and Lumpkin in Georgia, just over the Alabama border from the Heath home. He then led them back to his home where Rebecca was sleeping. Heath gave them the keys to the house and family car and drove away in his secret girlfriend's truck. Owens and Lumpkin then kidnapped Rebecca Heath from her home and drove her back to Georgia. Police later discovered the Heath's car, with Rebecca Heath's body inside, on the side of a road in nearby Troup County, Georgia. The cause of death was a gunshot wound in the head. The estimated time of death and the distance from the Heath residence to the spot where Rebecca Heath's body was found were consistent with the theory that the shooting took place in Georgia. Investigations were conducted by both Georgia and Alabama law enforcement officials.

The following February, Larry Gene Heath was charged with first-degree murder in the State of Georgia. Facing the death penalty, he agreed to plead guilty in exchange for a sentence of life imprisonment. As a result of the plea bargaining, Georgia did not pursue the death penalty. However, three months after his sentencing in Georgia, the State of Alabama indicted him for the capital murder of his wife. Heath argued that Alabama could not prosecute him because he had already been convicted in Georgia for the killing. He was tried in Alabama, convicted, and sentenced to death.

The Decision: The Court upheld his Alabama convictions. Larry Gene Heath had met the elements required for murder in both states. Each state has the power to enact their own criminal laws and determine their own punishment. The doctrine of dual sovereignty allowed each state to pursue the prosecution of Larry Gene Heath for the crimes committed in their state. The death sentence was upheld. Larry Gene Heath was executed in Holman Penitentiary electric chair on March 20, 1992.

On the Street

What about that movie?

A discussion about double jeopardy often leads to a mention of the 1999 movie by the same name, starring Tommy Lee Jones and Ashley Judd. In the film, the main character is convicted of killing her husband. She allegedly stabbed him to death on a boat and dumped his body in the ocean, never to be found again. However, during her prison stay, she figured out that her husband may have faked his own death and framed her. On her release from prison, she tracked him down in an effort to regain custody of her young son. The premise of the plot was that she could kill him again because she had already been convicted and punished. She could not be prosecuted for killing him a second time. However, the movie's legal theory was inaccurate. She was originally convicted in the State of Washington. However, she tracked him down in New Orleans where she shot him to prevent him from killing her parole officer. Had she unlawfully killed him in Louisiana, she could have been prosecuted under the doctrine of dual sovereignty. Double jeopardy would not have applied.

Mistrials and Double Jeopardy

A retrial is not prohibited unless jeopardy has attached. The attachment occurs when there has been an adjudication of guilt or innocence. If a trial is terminated because of a ruling other than a verdict or a dismissal with prejudice, the case may be retried. A mistrial that is a result of a hung jury does not constitute jeopardy, and there is also no limit to the number of times that a defendant can be retried if the trial has resulted in a mistrial due to the inability of a jury to reach a verdict. Should the judge declare a mistrial because of a courtroom event that prevents the trial from continuing in a fair and impartial manner, the case may be retried. For example, if one of the attorneys became ill and was unable to continue, the judge might have to terminate the trial. A mistrial might be ordered because of a disruption in the courtroom which would bias the jurors. In a previous chapter, a case was discussed in which a juror engaged in misconduct by conducting an unauthorized scientific test in a bathroom murder. The jury's verdict was vacated, a mistrial was declared, and the case was retried several months later, ultimately resulting in a conviction. In those cases, jeopardy has not attached. In rare cases, a judge might dismiss a case with prejudice because of prosecutorial misconduct. If that occurs, the dismissal has the same weight as an acquittal, and the case cannot be retried.

The Impact of an Appeal

Double jeopardy does not prevent a retrial when it is ordered as a result of a request by the defendant. Criminal defendants may ask for a new trial by either filing a motion for reconsideration or via the appeals process. Occasionally, once a verdict has been rendered, a criminal defendant will ask the trial court to vacate the verdict and order a new trial. This may occur because new evidence has been discovered that would exculpate the defendant. The prosecutor does not have the right to do this, however. The protection against double jeopardy belongs to the accused, not the state. Criminal defendants may, of course, also appeal a conviction. On appeal, they are requesting a new trial. Since the appellant is requesting the new trial, double jeopardy does not apply.

Probable Cause and Double Jeopardy

There are several stages in the criminal justice process in which a determination of probable cause is made. In some jurisdictions, preliminary hearings are held within a few days of arrest in order to determine if probable cause exists. If the judge determines that there is probable cause to believe the defendant has committed a crime, the case will be bound over to a grand jury. If the judge, presiding at the preliminary hearing, rules that probable cause does not exist, the charges are dismissed and the defendant will be excused from court. However, the finding at a preliminary hearing does not constitute jeopardy. Since it is not an adjudication of guilt, the defendant's case could still be examined independently by a grand jury. If the police gained additional information or were able to provide more evidence, the accused could be arrested again on the same charge and processed through the system. Double jeopardy does not apply to probable cause determinations. The same premise occurs with the grand jury. The grand jury is a body of citizens charged with examining the existence of probable cause. A decision of no true bill also does not constitute jeopardy; therefore, a case could be presented to a grand jury more than once. As a practical matter, that seldom occurs unless the prosecution has discovered additional evidence.

Collateral Estoppel

Collateral estoppel
An accused cannot be tried if the ultimate issue of fact has been determined at a previous trial.

The defense of **collateral estoppel** is an extension of the concept of double jeopardy. A defendant cannot be tried for an offense if the ultimate issue of fact has already been determined in a previous trial. Double jeopardy only protects an accused from being prosecuted for the same offense, but collateral estoppel extends the protection.

ASHE v. SWENSON

397 U.S. 436 (1970)

The Facts: In the early morning hours of January 10, 1960, six men were playing poker in the basement of a home in Lee's Summit, Missouri. Three or four men came into the home and robbed the six poker players at gunpoint. In addition to taking their cash and valuables, the robbers stole a car belonging to one of the victims. The stolen car was discovered abandoned in a field. Three men were arrested walking along a highway not far from the abandoned car. Swenson was arrested by a Missouri state trooper some distance away. All four men were charged with the robberies of the six different victims as well as the auto theft. The court separated the trials by crime victim. In the first trial, Swenson's only defense was that he was not one of the robbers and that the eyewitnesses were wrong. He was found not guilty. He was then tried for the robbery of another victim and found guilty.

The Decision: The U.S. Supreme Court overturned Swenson's conviction on the basis of collateral estoppel. In the first trial, the jury determined that Swenson was not one of the robbers. If he was not one of the robbers, then it would have been impossible for him to have robbed the other victims. His presence on the scene was the ultimate issue of fact, and it was determined at his first trial that he was not there.

On the Street

Crash and Dash

Sean "Crash" Sterling earned his nickname because of his affection for fast cars and inability to keep them under control. He was admittedly a bit of a wild character who liked to drink a bit and drive fast. He was arrested while using a public telephone booth at 1:00 A.M. and charged with receiving stolen property. About 40 minutes earlier, a young couple was waiting at a red light about a mile from where Crash was arrested. They were struck in the rear by another car, and the driver ran from the scene. They were able to give the police a physical description of the driver. When the police ran a computer check on the hit-and-run vehicle, they discovered it had been stolen about an hour earlier. Thus, when the cops found Crash, they thought they had their guy.

At trial, Crash claimed only the defense of alibi arguing that it could not have possibly been him who caused the wreck because he had been drinking in a local bar at the time the accident occurred. He was found not guilty. The prosecutor and the police were not happy. So they filed misdemeanor traffic charges against him for following too closely. Can these charges be brought or are they barred because of collateral estoppel?

While a crime is not considered the same offense if each crime contains an element that the other does not, prosecution in a separate trial may be barred because of collateral estoppel.

Summary

The protection from double jeopardy was born from the Fifth Amendment's language that an accused could not be "twice put in jeopardy of life or limb" for the same offense. Double jeopardy does not bar the prosecution of a defendant for a separate offense. This chapter has also examined dual sovereignty that confirms each state's right to enact its own criminal laws. A crime against the law of one state is considered a separate and distinct offense from a similar act in another state. Double jeopardy does not bar prosecution in both states. Likewise, federal crimes constitute separate offenses.

Jeopardy only attaches when the defendant has been exposed to a decision of guilt or innocence. Preliminary issues such as probable cause hearings, grand jury, and the suspension of cases due to mistrials do not constitute jeopardy, so the defendant may be retried. The chapter has also examined collateral estoppel, an extension of double jeopardy. Collateral estoppel prevents prosecution when the ultimate issue of fact has previously been determined in an earlier trial.

Review Questions

1. If a criminal defendant is tried for burglary but the jury finds him not guilty of burglary but guilty of a lesser included offense of theft, can he be retried for the burglary? Why or why not?
2. Explain the doctrine of dual sovereignty.
3. Why doesn't a hung jury prevent the retrial of a criminal case?

4. If a criminal defendant is found guilty of robbery and appeals her conviction, is it a violation of the double jeopardy protection for the court to order a new trial? Why or why not?

5. Describe an example of collateral estoppel.

Legal Terminology

Collateral estoppel   Dual sovereignty

References

Ashe v. Swenson , 397 U.S. 436 (1970)

Burgin, S. (October 30, 2012). *FBI releases files on Mel Ignatow investigation.* WLKY. Retrieved from http://www.wlky.com/news/local-news/wlky-investigates/FBI-releases-files-on-Mel-Ignatow-investigation/-/9705322/17185756/-/item/1/-/mpwkj1z/-/index.html

Heath v. Alabama, 474 U.S. 82 (1985)

Chapter 16
The Right to Counsel

Indigent
A criminal defendant who is unable to afford an attorney.

The Sixth Amendment states in part: *In all criminal prosecutions, the accused shall enjoy the right to . . . have the Assistance of Counsel for his defence.*

In our modern criminal justice systems, federal, state, and local courts provide appointed counsel for most **indigent** criminal defendants. However, the right to counsel did not immediately apply when the Sixth Amendment was ratified in 1791. In order to understand how the Sixth Amendment right to counsel applies to today's criminal justice system, one must examine its history and development. As the due process discussions in Chapter 3 indicated, the individual rights set forth in the Bill of Rights did not always apply to state criminal proceedings. Likewise, the interpretation and application of the rights by the U.S. Supreme Court evolved over many years. Today, federal, state, and local jurisdictions provide appointed counsel for most indigent criminal defendants.

The Landmark Case: *Gideon v. Wainwright*

The 1963 case involving Earl Gideon provided the foundation for the current public defender systems. Robert Kennedy, the late attorney general of the United States, stated: "If an obscure Florida convict named Clarence Earl Gideon had not sat down in his prison cell . . . to write a letter to the Supreme Court . . . the vast machinery of American law would have gone on functioning undisturbed. But Gideon did write that letter, the Court did look into his case . . . and the whole course of American legal history has been changed."

GIDEON v. WAINWRIGHT

372 U.S. 335 (1963)

The Facts: Clarence Earl Gideon was described as a drifter who had spent much of his life in and out of jail for committing nonviolent crimes. He had an eighth-grade education and had run away from home when he was in junior high. In June 1961, he was charged with breaking into the Harbour Bay Pool Room in Panama City, Florida. At the time he lived in a boarding house across the street from the pool hall and was an occasional customer. He was accused of breaking in to steal money from the vending machines, a noncapital felony in the State of Florida. Facing trial, Gideon asked the court to appoint an attorney as he was too poor to afford one. The Florida trial judge denied his request. The court's transcript indicated the following dialogue:

The COURT: *"Mr. Gideon, I am sorry, but I cannot appoint Counsel to represent you in this case. Under the laws of the State of Florida, the only time the Court can appoint Counsel to represent a Defendant is when that person is charged with a capital offense. I am sorry, but I will have to deny your request to appoint Counsel to defend you in this case."*

The DEFENDANT: *"The U.S. Supreme Court says I am entitled to be represented by Counsel."*

In 1961, in the State of Florida counsel was only appointed counsel in capital cases. Since Gideon was not facing the death penalty and could not afford to hire an attorney, he had to represent himself. The Supreme Court suggested that he did as well as could be expected from a nonattorney. He made opening statements to the jury, cross-examined witnesses, presented witnesses in his own behalf, and made a closing argument. He did not testify on his own behalf. In spite of his efforts, he was convicted and sentenced to five years in prison. From prison, Gideon filed a Writ of Habeas Corpus against the Florida Department of Corrections and a Writ of Certiorari to the U.S. Supreme Court. The Writs were handwritten on prison stationary. The Florida Courts denied his petitions. However, the U.S. Supreme Court agreed to review the case. They also provided counsel for him to pursue his appeal before the Supreme Court. His appointed counsel for the Supreme Court review was Abe Fortes, who became a U.S. Supreme Court Justice years later.

The Decision: The U.S. Supreme Court overturned Gideon's conviction and held that in a criminal prosecution for a felony, the defendant has a right to counsel and if indigent, must be provided an attorney by the government. The Court also ruled that the failure to provide counsel was a denial of due process of law. They explained as follows:

> That government hires lawyers to prosecute and defendants who have the money hire lawyers to defend are the strongest indications of the widespread belief that lawyers in criminal courts are necessities, not luxuries. The right of one charged with crime to counsel may not be deemed fundamental and essential to fair trials in some countries, but it is in ours. From the very beginning, our state and national constitutions and laws have laid great emphasis on procedural and substantive safeguards designed to assure fair trials before impartial tribunals in which every defendant stands equal before the law. This noble ideal cannot be realized if the poor man charged with crime has to face his accusers without a lawyer to assist him. A defendant's need for a lawyer is nowhere better stated than in the moving words of Mr. Justice Sutherland in *Powell v. Alabama*:

"The right to be heard would be, in many cases, of little avail if it did not comprehend the right to be heard by counsel. Even the intelligent and educated layman has small and sometimes no skill in the science of law. If charged with crime, he is incapable, generally, of determining for himself whether the indictment is good or bad. He is unfamiliar with the rules of evidence. Left without the aid of counsel he may be put on trial without a proper charge, and convicted upon incompetent evidence, or evidence irrelevant to the issue or otherwise inadmissible. He lacks both the skill and knowledge adequately to prepare his defense, even though he have a perfect one. He requires the guiding hand of counsel at every step in the proceedings against him. Without it, though he be not guilty, he faces the danger of conviction because he does not know how to establish his innocence." *Powell v. Alabama* 287 U.S. 45 (1932) at 68-69.

The case was remanded to Florida for a new trial. At the retrial, Gideon's attorney convinced the jury that the witness against his client was actually a lookout for the real burglars. Gideon was acquitted.

The *Gideon* Impact

The case changed the American legal system. As a result of the landmark decision, every state had to revise its procedures regarding the appointment of counsel for indigent criminal defendants. Prior to *Gideon*, most states, like Florida, limited the type of cases in which they would provide an attorney. But with the *Gideon* decision in March 1963, all states had to at least provide an attorney for every indigent defendant charged with a felony offense.

Several years later, the ruling was extended to most misdemeanors in the Florida case of *Argersinger v. Hamlin*, 407 U.S. 25 (1972). Jon Richard Argersinger was convicted of a state weapons charge and sentenced to 90 days in jail. Though indigent, he was denied appointed counsel. At that point, Florida did not provide counsel for indigent defendants unless they were facing more than six months of incarceration. *Gideon* had only required the appointment of counsel in felony cases. Argersinger ultimately appealed to the U.S. Supreme Court. Though the Court did not automatically extend the right to appointed counsel to all misdemeanors, they ruled that a criminal defendant could not be incarcerated as a result of a criminal offense if he or she had been denied the right to counsel:

> Under the rule we announce today, every judge will know when the trial of a misdemeanor starts that no imprisonment may be imposed, even though local law permits it, unless the accused is represented by counsel. He will have a measure of the seriousness and gravity of the offense and therefore know when to name a lawyer to represent the accused before the trial starts.
>
> The run of misdemeanors will not be affected by today's ruling. But in those that end up in the actual deprivation of a person's liberty, the accused will receive the benefit of "the guiding hand of counsel" so necessary when one's liberty is in jeopardy.

The Court clarified the rule a few years later in *Scott v. Illinois*, 440 U.S. 367 (1979). In *Scott*, the defendant was prosecuted for shoplifting, a state misdemeanor for which the possible sentence was a year in jail and a $500 fine. The defendant asked for appointed counsel, but his request was denied. After a bench trial, he was convicted and fined $50. The Supreme Court upheld his conviction stating that he was not incarcerated so he was not entitled to appointed counsel.

Self-Representation

There is a common proverb in law which states that a man who represents himself has a jackass for a lawyer and a fool for a client. Many judges will provide this caution to criminal defendants who wish to go forward without an attorney. However, in spite of the warning, a criminal defendant has the constitutional right to refuse representation and represent himself or herself. In those situations, the trial court judge will usually question defendants to ensure that they understand they have a right to counsel and that they are giving up that right voluntarily. In some cases involving serious offenses, judges will appoint an attorney to observe the trial in the event the defendant changes his or her mind. The act of a person representing himself or herself without an attorney is referred to as **in pro persona** or **pro se**. Representing one's self, while allowed, is often discouraged. A defendant's lack of legal expertise and knowledge often creates an awkward and cumbersome trial process since the defendant is not versed in proper procedure or trial techniques. Additionally, a criminal defendant who voluntarily and intelligently waives representation may not later claim ineffective assistance of counsel as a reason for appeal.

In pro persona/pro se Latin terms referring to a criminal defendant who is representing himself or herself without the assistance of an attorney.

On the Street

Famous Defendants Who Represented Themselves

Nidal Malik Hasan was the lone gunman who attacked the Soldier Readiness Center on the Fort Hood Army base near Killeen, Texas, on November 5, 2009. Hasan, a former U.S. Army psychologist and medical officer, refused counsel and represented himself. During his trial he admitted that he was the shooter but claimed that the shootings were justified because he was defending the Islamic faith. He was convicted of 13 counts of murder and 32 counts of attempted murder and sentenced to death. He is currently incarcerated at the federal prison in Fort Leavenworth, Kansas.

John Allen Muhammad, the Beltway Sniper who masterminded the 2002 shootings that terrorized citizens in the Washington, D.C., area was sentenced to death. He represented himself until late in his trial when he brought back the team of attorneys originally assigned to the case. He was executed in Virginia by lethal injection November 10, 2009.

Charles Manson, the mastermind of the 1969 killing spree that resulted in the death of seven victims, fired his lawyers and represented himself. During the trial he had to be shackled and removed from the courtroom several times because of his disruptive conduct. His death sentence was ultimately commuted, and he is serving multiple life terms in the California prison system.

The infamous serial killer, Ted Bundy, represented himself on three murder charges in the State of Florida. Bundy, a former law student, attempted to use his law school skills and charm to sway the jury. He failed and was convicted of all three murders. In prison, he confessed to over 30 killings but was suspected of many more. He died in Florida's electric chair in 1989. ▪

Determination of Indigency

Trial court judges have the duty of determining if an accused is eligible for appointed counsel. The determination of whether a defendant has the financial ability to afford an attorney depends on a variety of factors that include income, assets, the complicated nature of the pending case, community economics, reasonable attorney compensation and costs in the jurisdiction, and the ability of the accused to support himself or herself and provide for his or her own needs and obligations.

The National Legal Aid and Defender Association has developed a set of guidelines for determining the eligibility for appointed counsel. Those guidelines include the following criteria:

Financial Eligibility Criteria

Effective representation should be provided to anyone who is unable, without substantial financial hardship to himself or to his dependents, to obtain such representation. This determination should be made by ascertaining the liquid assets of the person which exceed the amount needed for the support of the person or his dependents and for the payment of current obligations. If the person's liquid assets are not sufficient to cover the anticipated costs of representation as indicated by the prevailing fees charged by competent counsel in the area, the person should be considered eligible for publicly provided representation. The accused's assessment of his own financial ability to obtain competent representation should be given substantial weight.

(a) Liquid assets include cash in hand, stocks and bonds, bank accounts and any other property which can be readily converted to cash. The person's home, car, household furnishings, clothing and any property declared exempt from attachment or execution by law, should not be considered in determining eligibility. Nor should the fact of whether or not the person has been released on bond or the resources of a spouse, parent or other person be considered.

(b) The cost of representation includes investigation, expert testimony, and any other costs which may be related to providing effective representation.

A refusal to appoint counsel could have the consequence of denying an accused's right to due process. Thus, courts take great care in evaluating a criminal.

The Attachment of the Right to Counsel

When does an accused have the right to counsel? A suspect may claim his or her right to an attorney at any point. As discussed previously, the police may not interrogate a suspect if the suspect has requested a lawyer. The police do not have to immediately provide a lawyer for a suspect during an interrogation; they just cannot continue the questioning. A suspect may, of course, contact his or her attorney at any time so long as it does not interfere with public safety. For example, the fact that a suspect requests an attorney when he or she is arrested does not prevent the police from taking the measures to effect the arrest and transport the suspect to jail. However, once a suspect is booked and secured in the detention facility or police station, he or she has a right to speak with his or her attorney. Generally, the court will not appoint counsel for an indigent defendant until the first court appearance. Many jurisdictions have **public defenders** available to handle the initial appearance and arraignments. If not, cases are generally continued until the defendant has a reasonable opportunity to obtain counsel.

A criminal defendant has the right to counsel at almost all court hearings including arraignment, pretrial conferences, motions, trial, and sentencing. The right to counsel applies to the first right of appeal in a criminal cases. In the rare event that a defendant is subpoenaed to testify before a grand jury, the defendant does not have the right to have his or her attorney present in the hearing room. The defendant may, however, refuse to make a statement and even ask to step outside the hearing room to consult with his or her attorney after every question.

A suspect also has the right to counsel at all critical stages of a criminal proceeding. In *United States v. Wade*, 388 U.S. 218 (1967), the Supreme Court held that a lineup conducted after a suspect had been indicted constituted a critical stage. Failure to provide or allow counsel at such a lineup violated the Sixth Amendment. In *Wade*, the defendant and two others were indicted and arrested April 2, 1965, for a bank robbery that was committed the previous September. Wade was appointed counsel on April 26. Two weeks later, the FBI conducted a lineup that included Wade, but they did not allow him to have an attorney present. He was identified by the witnesses as being one of the bank robbers. The Supreme Court ultimately overturned his conviction. Even if a defense attorney is present at a lineup, the attorney's role is simply to observe so as to be able to address the issues of fairness and suggestiveness at a later time.

The right does not apply, however, to pre-indictment investigatory lineups or photographic arrays. A criminal suspect also does not have the right to counsel during the taking of evidence such as blood samples or handwriting exemplars.

Selection of Appointed Counsel

An accused in a criminal case is not entitled to the perfect or best lawyer. Winning is not required, only that the attorney zealously represents his or her client in an effective

Public defender
An attorney appointed by the court and paid by the government to represent a criminal defendant who is unable to afford an attorney.

and appropriate manner. In order to successfully claim ineffective assistance of counsel, a defendant must prove that his or her attorney failed to provide reasonable professional assistance in compliance with the prevailing professional standards and that the attorney's conduct impacted the ultimate outcome of the case. In most circumstances, an impact on a collateral issue does not give rise to an ineffective assistance of counsel claim. For example, if an attorney failed to tell his or her client that a conviction might also result in a job loss, that issue would be considered collateral to the criminal case and not ineffective assistance of counsel. However, in *Padilla v. Kentucky*, 130 S.Ct. 1473 (2010), the Supreme Court ruled that a defense attorney's failure to warn his immigrant client that he would be deported if he pled guilty was ineffective assistance of counsel. Though the immigration issue was collateral consequence, it was significant enough that the defendant should have been apprised. The defendant was allowed to withdraw his plea and go to trial.

An indigent criminal defendant who is going to be provided appointed counsel does not generally have the right to select the specific lawyer. That decision belongs to the judge and the applicable court system. In most systems, the attorneys either work as staff lawyers for a public defender officer or they have volunteered to provide services for the fees set in that particular county. However, in extraordinary circumstances, a judge may consider the request of the defendant for a specific lawyer if the case requires unique knowledge or skills.

Public Defender Systems

The appointment of counsel for indigent defendants is usually administered by some type of public defender system in the county or state in which the case will be tried. Public defender offices are usually run by state or county governments in collaboration with the judicial system. In some local systems, the individual judges may appoint private attorneys who are then paid by either the state or county government. Some public defender offices employ staff attorneys who are on salary and are assigned the indigent cases. Public defender offices are often criticized because of low-paid, inexperienced attorneys and excessive caseloads. However, in many jurisdictions, the attorneys who agree to handle indigent criminal defendants are the most experienced in criminal defense strategies. A criminal defendant may, of course, retain an attorney of his or her choice if the defendant is willing to pay his or her own attorney fees.

Summary

In this chapter, you examined the constitutional right to counsel which derives from the Sixth Amendment that states that a criminal defendant shall "enjoy . . . the right to assistance of counsel in his defense." In the 1963 case of *Gideon v. Wainwright*, the U.S. Supreme Court interpreted the clause to mean that states must provide an attorney for those defendants who could not otherwise afford one. A few years later, they extended their decision by barring a sentence of incarceration for any defendant who had been denied counsel. As a result of the landmark case, court systems throughout the country provide some type of public defender system in order to comply with the Sixth Amendment. As discussed in Chapter 11, the right has also been incorporated into the *Miranda* warnings. Other issues discussed in this chapter include the impact of the *Gideon* series of decisions as well as the fact that defendants have the right to refuse an attorney so they can represent themselves.

Review Questions

1. How does the Fourteenth Amendment's due process clause impact the Sixth Amendment right to counsel?
2. A criminal defendant has the right to counsel at which of the following stages:
   a. Preliminary hearing
   b. Grand jury
   c. Arraignment
   d. Sentencing
3. What are the responsibilities of an attorney in complying with the right to effective assistance of counsel?
4. Under what circumstances could a trial judge deny right to appoint counsel for an indigent defendant?
5. Under what circumstances would an indigent criminal defendant be allowed to select his or her appointed counsel?

Legal Terminology

Indigent

In pro persona/pro se

Public defender

References

Argersinger v. Hamlin, 407 U.S. 25 (1972)
Gideon v. Wainwright, 372 U.S. 335 (1963)
National Legal Aid and Defender Association. (1976). *Guidelines for Legal Defense Systems. History of the Right to Counsel*. Retrieved from http://www.nlada.org/About/About_HistoryDefender
Padilla v. Kentucky, 130 S.Ct. 1473 (2010)
Scott v. Illinois, 440 U.S. 367 (1979)
United States v. Wade, 388 U.S. 218 (1967)

Chapter 17
Bail and Pretrial Detention

Bail
An amount of money
or another security that
is designed to ensure
a criminal defendant's
return to court if released
from jail.

Own recognizance
The pretrial release of
a defendant without
the requirement of
money or property as
bail. The defendant is
released based upon
their own reputation and
circumstances.

The Eighth Amendment states in part: *Excessive bail shall not be required.*

Bail is the surety provided to the court in order to ensure that a person who has been arrested will return to court as required. The surety may be money, property, or the defendant's **own recognizance**. A defendant may be released on his or her own recognizance (also referred to as an O.R. Bond) without posting any money or property if the court believes the circumstances of the case and the defendant's background make it likely that the defendant will return as ordered. The term *bond* is commonly used interchangeably. However, bond is a fee that is paid to guarantee the payment of bail. If a defendant is unable to post the entire amount of bail, he or she may pay a fee, usually a percentage of the bail amount, to a bondsman who then guarantees to the court the payment of the bail if the defendant fails to appear. Bail bonds have been outlawed in a few states.

On the Street

Set the Bail

After a lengthy investigation, Zak was arrested for involuntary manslaughter and leaving the scene of an accident. The police allege that he was driving a vehicle that hit a bicyclist who was riding along a rural highway. The evidence against him includes an eyewitness who was sitting on the porch of a nearby house. Zak owns a small trucking business that handles local deliveries. He is married with two adult children; however, he is currently undergoing divorce proceedings. He stated in his pretrial questionnaire that he had $6,000 in the bank and earns about $40,000 a year from his business. However, he makes no money if he can't drive. Zak also has two previous drunk driving convictions. One was 20 years ago but the last one was only a year ago. Both involved traffic accidents. He had work driving privileges during the license suspension. The court records indicate that he failed to appear in court twice on his first DUI charge. He is begging for a low bail so he can continue to work and swears he didn't remember hitting anyone.

OK, your honor, what's the bail? ▦

Determination of Bail

The U.S. Constitution and the Eighth Amendment does not guarantee the right to bail; rather it protects criminal defendants from the requirement of excessive bail. There are circumstances in which a trial judge may deny bail altogether in order to ensure the safety of the community. However, those occurrences are rare. The presumption of innocence is a basic tenet of the American criminal justice system; therefore, the denial of reasonable bail results in the detention of an accused before he or she has been found guilty. The need to ensure a defendant's return to court and the protection of society must be balanced against the presumption of innocence.

The determination of bail usually occurs during the first court appearance of a criminal defendant. In addition to the reading of charges, entering of pleas, and designation of counsel, judges will decide bail. However, bail can be addressed at any time subsequent to the initial appearance. Either the defense or prosecution may file motions to increase or decrease bail. This may occur because of the discovery of new information or simply because a party is asking the court for reconsideration of bail. The purpose of bail is to ensure that the defendant will return to court as required. At a bail hearing, the parties will present information to the court which will assist the judge in the bail determination. Those factors are as discussed below.

Criminal Record of the Defendant

The court may consider if the accused has a past history of criminal activity. While that may not specifically address a defendant's likelihood of returning to court, it may be an indication of his or her behavior if released. Since judges consider criminal records in sentencing, it may also indicate that the defendant is now facing more serious punishment if convicted, thus increasing his or her incentive to run. In some cases, defense attorneys will argue that the defendant, while facing several previous criminal charges, always returned to court as directed. The defendant's criminal record may provide insight into whether he or she has failed to appear in the past.

Nature of the Crime

An accused may be more likely to leave the jurisdiction when facing a long period of incarceration. A defendant would be much less likely to walk away from a misdemeanor charge than a serious felony. The nature of the offense might also indicate the danger to the community. A defendant charged with serial offenses would certainly be considered a continuing threat if released.

Community Connection

The judge may consider the defendant's ties to family and community. The premise is that a defendant who has significant connections to family, jobs, and other community factions is less likely to escape the jurisdiction of the court. Factors such as involvement in church and school activities, attending college, and career employment all indicate a likely return to court. The need for a defendant to provide care and support for his or her family may also be considered.

Defendant's Resources

The ability of the defendant to pay bail must be considered. A thousand dollars might be impossible for one defendant to post, while it would mean very little to a wealthier person. Certainly many criminal defendants are poor and would have difficulty in posting minimal bail. Appellate courts frown upon the imposition of bail which makes it impossible for an indigent defendant to obtain release. However, the court might impose a much higher bail on a drug dealer who had access to more resources. In that case, the judge might believe that a higher bail was necessary to ensure the defendant returned to face the charges.

The Evidence

A bail hearing is not a setting in which the judge hears evidence relating to the charges. However, attorneys may argue the strengths or weaknesses of the case in arguing bail. While the defendant is considered innocent until proven guilty, the likelihood that a defendant will be convicted may weigh against minimal bail. Likewise, if the case appears to be weak, the judge may be concerned about continuing to detain a defendant who may ultimately be found guilty.

Excessive Bail

After a judge considers the above factors, the question becomes the following: When is bail excessive? The law does not provide a fixed chart identifying the correct amount of bail for each criminal offense. Judges must make reasonable decisions after considering the circumstances of each individual defendant's case. Some local jurisdictions may offer bail guidelines for misdemeanor cases in order to provide instant release for arrestees, but even those may be reconsidered when the defendant makes his or her personal court appearance. How does the Eighth Amendment impact bail?

The U.S. Supreme Court took an early look at that question in the historic case of *Stack v. Boyle*, 342 U.S. 1 (1951). In *Stack*, 12 men were arrested for a violation of the **Smith Act**, a crime involving advocating the overthrow of the government. Initially, they were granted bails ranging from $2,500 to $100,000, but then the U.S. District Court changed it to $50,000 for each defendant. The prosecution presented no evidence other than a reference to defendants in another district who had failed

Smith Act
A federal offense directed at individuals advocating the overthrow of the U.S. government.

to return to court when facing Smith Act charges. The defendants had submitted information concerning their financial resources, family relationships, health, and prior criminal records. The Supreme Court, on a habeas corpus appeal, instructed the trial court to hold a hearing in order to determine reasonable bail. The Court stated, "Like the ancient practice of securing the oaths of responsible persons to stand as sureties for the accused, the modern practice of requiring a bail bond or the deposit of a sum of money subject to forfeiture serves as additional assurance of the presence of an accused. Bail set at a figure higher than an amount reasonably calculated to fulfill this purpose is 'excessive' under the Eighth Amendment." The Court also reprimanded the lower court for not conducting a reasonable hearing that considered all of the factors for the defendants.

Pretrial Detention

Bail Reform Act of 1984
Federal legislation that, in part, allowed the denial of bail if the conditions of release could not ensure the safety of the community.

Pretrial detention
The incarceration of a defendant prior to the determination of guilt.

The U.S. Congress enacted the **Bail Reform Act of 1984** in order to identify rules and procedures for addressing bail in federal criminal courts. There were concerns that prior legislation, while identifying factors that encouraged reasonable bail, also prevented the **pretrial detention** of dangerous and elusive criminal defendants. The new act allowed the denial of bail for defendants who posed a threat to society. Pretrial detention, the incarceration of a defendant prior to the determination of guilt, was certainly permissible if necessary to ensure the return to court. However, the Bail Reform Act also allowed the detention to protect the public. If the safety of another person or the community could not be ensured by the conditions of the release, the court was required to detain the accused. In a landmark case, the Supreme Court upheld the new law and clarified when a defendant could be denied bail.

UNITED STATES v. SALERNO

481 U.S. 739 (1987)

Racketeer Influenced and Corrupt Organizations Act (RICO)
RICO is a federal law that provides criminal punishment for those engaged in racketeering, an organized criminal enterprise. Racketeering often involves crime networks that engage in gambling, prostitution, drug trafficking, and illegal firearms.

The Facts: Anthony Salerno and Vincent Cafaro were arrested on March 21, 1986, upon a 29-count indictment alleging violations of the **Racketeer Influenced and Corrupt Organizations Act (RICO)**. The indictment included charges of racketeering, mail and wire fraud, extortion, criminal gambling, and conspiracy to commit murder. Salerno was described by the government as the boss of the Genovese crime family of the La Cosa Nostra and Cafaro as a captain. At the bail hearing, the prosecution presented evidence that the defendants had engaged in wide-ranging conspiracies to aid their criminal enterprises through violent means. The evidence included wiretaps and testimony from witnesses who were also expected to testify at trial. There was evidence that Salerno had been involved in two murder conspiracies. Salerno presented no evidence at his bail hearing but argued that his statements on the wiretaps were just "tough talk" and that the witnesses were not credible. In denying bail, the District Court stated:

> The activities of a criminal organization such as the Genovese Family do not cease with the arrest of its principals and their release on even the most stringent of bail conditions. The illegal businesses, in place for many years, require constant attention and protection, or they will fail. Under these circumstances, this court recognizes a strong incentive on the part of its leadership to continue business as usual. When business as usual involves threats, beatings, and murder, the present danger such people pose in the community is self-evident.

The District Court concluded that no condition of release would ensure the safety of the community and denied Salerno bail.

The Decision: Upon appeal of the bail decision, Salerno argued that the provisions in the Bail Reform Act of 1984 which allowed the denial of bail based on the likelihood that the defendant would commit additional crimes if released was unconstitutional. The defense also argued that the denial of bail violated the Eighth Amendment's bar of excessive bail as well as the Fifth Amendment's due process requirement. They contended that denying release of bail constituted punishment before trial.

The Supreme Court affirmed the denial of bail and upheld the pretrial detention section of the Bail Reform Act. They indicated that Congress had not drafted the bill with the motive of pretrial punishment but rather to address the evolving societal problem of continual criminal harm while awaiting trial. They stated, "There is no doubt that preventing danger to the community is a legitimate regulatory goal." In their concluding words, they reiterated their decision:

> The Act authorizes the detention prior to trial of arrestees charged with serious felonies who are found after an adversary hearing to pose a threat to the safety of individuals or to the community which no condition of release can dispel. The numerous procedural safeguards detailed above must attend this adversary hearing. We are unwilling to say that this congressional determination, based as it is upon that primary concern of every government—a concern for the safety and indeed the lives of its citizens—on its face violates either the Due Process Clause of the Fifth Amendment or the Excessive Bail Clause of the Eighth Amendment.

Summary

The Eighth Amendment language regarding bail is arguably quite simple; excessive bail shall not be required. But, of course, the constitutional forefathers did not give further advice on what constituted excessive bail in 1791, much less today. Subsequent cases from the courts have provided some guidance, but local trial court practices have impacted the imposition of bail just as much. This chapter outlines the criteria that courts consider in determining bail.

The purpose of bail is to ensure that a criminal defendant returns to court as directed. The denial of bail or the imposition of a high bail cannot be for the purpose of punishment. In 1984, the U.S. Congress passed a bail reform act that provided for bail to be denied in cases where the accused posed a threat to public safety. This type of pretrial detention was approved in *United States v. Salerno* in 1987.

Review Questions

1. What is the purpose of bail?
2. When is pretrial detention permitted?
3. What impact might a defendant's prior criminal record have on the determination of bail?
4. What is the role of a bail bondsman in the American bail system?
5. Why is the denial of bail considered a due process problem?

Legal Terminology

Bail
Bail Reform Act of 1984
Own recognizance
Pretrial detention

Racketeer Influenced and Corrupt
    Organizations Act (RICO)
Smith Act

References

Stack v. Boyle, 342 U.S. 1 (1951)
United States v. Salerno, 481 U.S. 739 (1987)

Chapter 18
Sentencing and Punishment

Legislators, law enforcement and corrections officials, criminal justice researchers, social workers, and community leaders continually search for ways to prevent criminal behavior. The pursuit, of course, gives rise to a great deal of debate over the most effective and humane models. Added to the difficulty of the task are the tremendous economic and social costs to society. With over two million people incarcerated in America's prisons and jails, governments struggle with overcrowding and budget constraints. The onus falls on legislators to enact criminal statutes that provide effective and constitutional punishments for crime. This chapter addresses the models, methods, and constitutionality of those punishments.

Models of Punishment

The consequence of criminal behavior is punishment of the offender. The objectives of such punishment include retribution, rehabilitation, incapacitation, and deterrence. In recent years, many criminologists have also stressed restoration.

- **Rehabilitation:** Proposes that offenders will become more productive citizens and less likely to continue criminal behavior if provided with treatment, education, and training. Rehabilitation programs are designed to assist offenders in developing employment skills and attaining education. Treatment for addictions and behavioral issues is included in the rehabilitation model.
- **Deterrence:** Infers that an individual is less likely to engage in criminal behavior when threatened by incarceration and other punishments. The concept of **general deterrence** suggests that the fear of conviction and punishment will discourage others from criminal behavior. **Specific deterrence** inhibits a specific defendant from committing future offenses.
- **Incapacitation:** Restricts an individual offender's ability to commit additional criminal behaviors. The model argues that if an offender is incarcerated, he or she

Rehabilitation
A model of punishment proposing that an offender who undergoes treatment, education and training will be less likely to reoffend.

General deterrence
A theory of punishment proposing that the fear of conviction and punishment prevents others from committing crime.

Specific deterrence
A punishment theory proposing that the penalty discourages a specific individual from committing future offenses.

is unable to engage in other criminal acts. A murderer who is executed is no longer able to kill.

■ **Retribution:** Adopts the concept that the punishment fits the crime. This model provides vengeance for the criminal act. Retribution is sometimes described as the "just desserts" model.

■ **Restoration:** Focuses on the victims of crime. This model is designed to engage offenders in restitution to the victims and community. In a sense, the objective is to restore the victim, offender, and community to their status prior to the commission of the crime. Restorative justice combines elements of restitution and rehabilitation. Many advocates encourage apology by the offender as well as interaction between the victim and offender.

Sentencing

Legislators must determine the appropriate penalties for criminal behavior and draft statutory law that provides the parameters of such punishment. Those penalties must also comply with the U.S. Constitution. There are a variety of penalties that are provided in criminal statutes, as discussed below.

Incarceration

Incarceration is imprisonment in a detention facility such as a prison or jail. Prisons are facilities that house inmates who have been convicted of felonies and are usually managed by state or federal jurisdictions. A few jurisdictions have contracted with private corporations to provide incarceration services. Prisoners who have been convicted of misdemeanors or who are awaiting trial are usually incarcerated in local jails. In some situations, felony offenders may be housed in jails if serving short-term sentences. Juvenile offenders who have been **adjudicated delinquent** are typically housed in facilities specifically designed for minors. The determination of guilt for a person under age 18 who has not been prosecuted as an adult is referred to as adjudication.

The U.S. prison systems consist of a variety of security and architectural models. Many institutions are designed and operated consistent with a security level. Maximum security facilities provide the most secure and controlled environments. Inmates in those institutions usually have limited interaction with other inmates and high-level restrictions on their physical movement within the facilities. Prisoners assigned to low-level security facilities often have opportunities to interact with other inmates and even participate in less-restrictive activities such as farming or manufacturing.

Sentencing statutes that include incarceration may provide for either a **determinate sentence** or an **indeterminate sentence**. Indeterminate sentences call for a period of incarceration that falls within a range of time. The judge will indicate a minimum and maximum period of confinement such as two to ten years. Indeterminate sentences apply to felony convictions and the release date is determined by the parole board. Some state statutes allow for parole opportunities prior to the minimum date if certain

---

Retribution
A model of punishment that imposes penalties to punish the offender for their behavior.

Restoration
A model designed to restore the victim, offender, and community to their status prior to the commission of the crime. Restorative justice combines elements of restitution and rehabilitation.

Incarceration
Imprisonment in a jail or prison.

Adjudicated delinquent
The determination that a juvenile offender has committed a criminal offense.

Determinate sentence
A sentence that provides for a fixed incarceration period.

Indeterminate sentence
A sentence that calls for a period of incarceration that falls within a range of time. The parole board determines the release date.

conditions are met. Parole decisions are based on a number of factors including the nature of the crime, the inmate's behavior in prison, and the inmate's efforts to improve himself or herself through rehabilitation programs. Victims, police, and prosecutors often testify at parole hearings. Advocates of the indeterminate sentence argue that it provides incentives for good behavior while incarcerated and thus results in a safer institutional environment. Such sentences also encourage inmates to engage in rehabilitation efforts.

A sentence that provides for a fixed period of incarceration is determinate. In contrast to an indeterminate sentence, there is no range of time. When the inmate serves the time, he or she is released without parole and without consideration to behavior while imprisoned. Determinate sentences are very common for misdemeanors. For example, a defendant might be sentenced to serve 30 days in jail. However, a number of states now include determinate sentence in their felony sentencing structures. Proponents of determinate sentencing laud the financial savings as a result of the reduced role of parole boards. They also argue that it provides a more effective deterrent to criminal behavior as the offender knows exactly how much time will be served for a specific crime.

Concurrent sentence
When a judge orders multiple sentences, the terms of incarceration run simultaneously. The entire sentence is complete when the defendant has served the longest sentence.

Consecutive sentence
When a judge orders multiple sentences, the defendant must serve one period of incarceration before beginning the next.

When a defendant is convicted of multiple offenses, the trial judge has the discretion to impose a **concurrent sentence** or a **consecutive sentence**. Sentences run concurrently if the incarceration period for each crime is served at the same time. For example, if a defendant received ten years for robbery and three years on a weapons charge concurrently, the defendant would serve both at the same time. As a result, the inmate would be released upon serving ten years since the three were served at the same time. Sentences are consecutive if one must be served before the other one. Thus, in the earlier example, the inmate would serve a total of 13 years. Consecutive sentences are often referred to as "stacked" sentences.

Probation

Probation involves the suspension of all or part of a sentence of incarceration. An offender who receives probation in lieu of incarceration must comply with the conditions ordered by the court. The failure to comply may result in the imposition of the original sentence. For example, a defendant may be convicted of misdemeanor assault and sentenced to six months in jail. However, the judge suspends the sentence, thus allowing the defendant to go free unless he violates the conditions of probation. If the defendant fails to meet the conditions, then he would be charged with a probation violation, and the judge could reinstate the original six month sentence of incarceration. A violation usually occurs if an offender commits additional crimes while on probation. Conditions of probation may also include drug or alcohol treatment, completion of behavior modification programs such as anger management, payment of fines and restitution, driver's training, employment, and community service. Offenders must also work with a probation officer. Probation officers serve a dual role. As officers of the court, they must act as law enforcement officers to ensure the probationer is complying with the court-ordered conditions. However, they also encourage and assist the probationer to successfully meet the conditions.

Parole

Parole involves the early release of a felon from prison contingent upon complying with specific conditions. The determination of if and when parole is granted is governed by a parole board rather than the trial judge. The parole board also sets the conditions for the release. Parole officers monitor the postrelease conduct of parolees to ensure their compliance with the conditions. Violations of parole conditions likely result in the offenders' return to incarceration. Conditions of parole are similar to those of probation.

In many jurisdictions, a prisoner's period of incarceration may be reduced as a result of good behavior while imprisoned. Credit or "good time" is granted per a formula. Good behavior reductions are usually available for determinate sentences.

Community Control

Alternative sentencing that dictates specific behaviors and partial restriction of freedom for convicted defendants is often referred to as community control. In a sense, these controls fall between complete freedom and incarceration. They are usually imposed as conditions of parole or probation, and if a defendant fails to comply with the requirements incarceration will result. Community controls include halfway houses, work release programs, house arrest, electronic monitoring, and treatment or rehabilitation programs. Halfway houses allow inmates to live in a housing environment that is less restrictive than prison. Defendants under house arrest may live in their own homes but may not leave without the court's permission. Electronic monitoring utilizes technology by fastening a monitoring device on the inmate's body which allows law enforcement officials to track the inmate's movements. If the inmate leaves his or her prescribed area, officials will be notified, and it may result in a probation or parole violation. These community control programs have provided many local governments with cost-effective options.

Monetary Fines

A fine is an amount of money that the defendant is ordered to pay to the court as part of the punishment. Many criminal statutes specifically identify the range of fine for a particular offense. A statute might provide for a definite sentence of up to 60 days in jail and a maximum fine of $500. The judge would have the discretion to order a fine less than the maximum amount but not more. Minor offenses such as traffic violations and minor misdemeanors often identify fines as the only punishment. A criminal defendant may also be required to pay court costs. Court costs are not considered part of the punishment but rather a civil requirement to reimburse the courts for administrative expenses. Court costs may be made a condition of probation.

In a controversial practice, some jurisdictions incarcerate offenders who fail to pay court-ordered fines or costs of prosecution. Critics argue that the practice constitutes a debtor's prison and that it violates the constitutional prohibition against imprisonment for being unable to pay a debt. However, government officials contend that the practice is legal because it is not an enforcement of a civil debt but rather one imposed by the criminal courts.

Restitution

Judges may also have the discretion to order restitution as a condition of probation. Restitution is the payment from the defendant to the victim to cover actual expenses incurred as a result of the criminal activity. Those expenses may include medical bills, the value of stolen property, or the repair costs of damage to property. Restitution may not be ordered for intangible harm such as pain and suffering. A victim would have to file a civil lawsuit in order to recover intangible damages. The payment of restitution is separate and apart from court-ordered fines. Restitution is paid to the victim, and fines are paid to the court.

Revocation of Rights or License

Individuals who are convicted of criminal offenses may lose certain rights and privileges. Some jurisdictions specifically mandate the revocation of certain rights and privileges such as suspension of driving privileges, the right to possess firearms, or the right to seek public office. In many states, a convicted felon may no longer vote in governmental elections. Yet others restore voting privileges upon release from incarceration. It is common to restrict driving privileges as a result of serious traffic offenses, but in some jurisdictions a drive-off theft of gas will also result in a suspension. In addition to the mandated statutory restrictions, trial judges have the discretion to place reasonable limitations as conditions of probation. Defendants convicted of assault or domestic violence are often ordered to stay away from the victims during the term of probation. Michael Vick, the NFL quarterback for the Philadelphia Eagles and the Atlanta Falcons, was prohibited from owning a dog as a condition of his probation. Judges may also bar a probationer from using alcohol.

Criminals who have committed specific sex offenses may be required to document their status and residence with state and local sex offender registries. In addition to informing the public of the location of registered sex offenders, the statutes may restrict the offender from contact with minors or residence within designated areas such as school zones.

Death Penalty

The death penalty may be imposed in approximately two-thirds of the states as well as the federal system. It is only an acceptable penalty for those crimes that result in the loss of another human being. Each state has the authority to determine whether it is an appropriate penalty in their jurisdiction. The constitutionality and application of the death penalty is examined in detail in Chapter 19.

Considerations in Sentencing

A number of factors must be considered in the determination of a sentence. As previously discussed, the sentence must fall within the mandates of the criminal statute that the defendant has been found guilty of violating. In some instances, criminal statutes may provide for mandatory incarceration. Some states allow the jury to make sentencing recommendations. Judges may generally accept or reduce jury recommendations but may not impose a more severe sentence. In the federal system and some states, judges must impose sentences that fall within structured guidelines. Those guidelines provide for reduced incarceration when certain **mitigating factors** exist. In most cases, however, the trial judge has considerable discretion in determining the appropriate punishment for the offender and will consider the aggravating and mitigating circumstances that impact the case. **Aggravating factors** are those issues that would suggest an elevation of the penalty. The issues that would lead the judge to reduce the punishment are described as mitigating factors. If a criminal statute identifies an aggravating factor that would mandate a more severe penalty, that factor would have to be proved at trial or agreed to as part of the guilty plea.

Mitigating factors
Circumstances that would lead a judge or jury to impose a less severe punishment.

Aggravating factors
Considerations that would lead a judge or jury to impose a more severe punishment.

Criminal Record

A judge may consider the past criminal activity of the defendant. Offenders who have engaged in previous criminal activity may be viewed as a recurring threat to the community. Continued criminal behavior may also be considered as an indicator that the offender has not responded to past punishments. Conversely, in many cases, the lack of a prior criminal record usually leads to a less severe penalty. First-time offenders may argue that their behavior was a one-time error in judgment and that they are less likely to reoffend. However, an offender who continues to offend and elevate the seriousness of his or her criminal behavior is likely to be treated more severely by the court. Some states have criminal statutes that elevate the severity of the penalty based on prior criminal behavior. For example, a first-time theft conviction might be a misdemeanor, while a second offense would be elevated to a felony. The most dramatic example involving the statutory elevation of penalty is found in jurisdictions with habitual offender statutes. Those statutes, discussed in detail later in this chapter, elevate the penalty for multiple offenses beyond the punishment for any single offense.

Nature of the Crime

When a crime is considered particularly cruel or heinous, the punishment is generally more severe. For example, a violation of a state's felony assault statute might occur if an assailant struck a victim with a deadly weapon. However, a judge might consider the torture of a victim with a fireplace poker more severe than one strike in the leg with a baseball bat. A judge would certainly consider the amount and method of harm in addressing the length of incarceration. The commission of multiple offenses or serial offenses would also constitute aggravating factors. An offender's malicious intent could also be taken into consideration. In recent years, there have been a number of assaults involving the "knockout" game in which an offender punches a random victim with the sole purpose of knocking the victim unconscious. That action would certainly be considered more malicious than a typical barroom fight. Offenders who use firearms to commit an offense are often punished more severely as they are viewed as more dangerous to society. Many states have enacted statutes that mandate additional incarceration if a firearm was used.

Status of the Victim

Often related to the nature of the offense is the status of the victim. Many states have enacted statutes that elevate the penalty when the victim of the offense is a child or is elderly. These elevations are common with sexual offenses, assault, theft, and homicide statutes. Many states provide for increased penalties in theft-related cases where the offender has taken advantage of a disabled or elderly victim. Some first-degree murder statutes specifically address the killing of a child. It may also be considered a special circumstance that would qualify for the death penalty. Society generally takes a harsh view toward offenders who victimize the young, the elderly, the mentally impaired, and the disabled. As a result, judges certainly consider those factors even in cases where the statute doesn't specifically address the victim.

Victim's Impact

Judges may also include the viewpoint of the victim in the sentence decision. In some cases, the victim may actually request leniency. It is not unusual for victims to express their desire for a reduced sentence in cases where there is a family or romantic relationship with the offender. They may also testify as to the nature and degree of harm that the offender has caused. Information from the victim may be presented in an open sentencing hearing or may be provided as part of a presentence investigative report.

Offender Status

Defense attorneys often argue that the circumstances of an offender's childhood should be considered in mitigation. Difficult situations such as poverty, family dysfunction, abuse, and lack of education may contribute to an individual's criminal behaviors. Growing up in neighborhood environments that include gang and other criminal activities often produce peer pressures that lead to offending. Courts may view these as factors in their penalty decisions. Judges may also take an offender's diminished mental capacity into consideration. Though a person's low intelligence or mental health issues may not reach the threshold to which it would relieve them from criminal liability, those issues may have impacted their decision making. An offender's ignorance of a law does not generally provide a defense to criminal liability. However, the fact that an offender is unaware that he or she is committing a violation may be considered in mitigation.

Age

Juvenile
A person less than 18
years of age.

The age of the offender may be considered. In some situations, a judge will take into account that criminal behavior was a result of an immature and youthful mistake. Every jurisdiction provides specific court procedures for the adjudication of **juvenile** offenders. Criminal offenders under 18 years of age are usually sentenced to facilities or programs that provide treatment and rehabilitation. However, an offender under 18 may also be subject to prosecution as an adult if his or her offense meets the state's statutory criteria. Juveniles may be tried as adults for serious crimes such as murder, robbery, and rape. The statutory criteria vary from state to state. Advanced age may also be considered as a mitigating factor. Judges may be reluctant to incarcerate an elderly adult.

Offender Remorse

An offender who accepts responsibility for his or her criminal behavior and the consequences is generally viewed more favorably by a sentencing judge. This may be manifested both through a voluntary guilty plea as well as a courtroom apology. Remorse is certainly considered a mitigating factor. On the other hand, judges frown on convicted defendants who deny their guilt or who show no remorse or consideration for the harm imposed on the victim.

Provocation by the Victim

Provocation by the victim may be considered as a mitigating factor. Common in assault cases, the offender may have assaulted the victim as a result of some type of provocative behavior. The provocation does not relieve the offender of criminal liability, but it may be considered in determining the severity of the sentence. For example, a man calls a woman a derogatory racial slur. The woman slaps the man. The slur does not create a defense to the crime of assault, but a sentencing judge might consider the provocation in determining the sentence. In some homicide crimes, the provocation may actually impact the crime. The killing of another as a result of a serious provocation combined with sudden passion or a fit of rage may reduce a homicide to voluntary manslaughter.

Intoxication

Criminal behavior is often impacted by drug and alcohol intoxication. Addiction to drugs and alcohol may result in not only errant behavior but also misguided motivation. Burglars may steal in order to obtain drugs or money for drugs. Violence is often fueled by alcohol. Offenders are often using drugs or alcohol at the time of their crime. As a result, it is not unusual for defense attorneys to argue in mitigation for reduced punishment or alternatives to incarceration due to their client's addictions. Many court systems provide treatment programs in lieu of incarceration. Drug and alcohol rehabilitation programs may be ordered as a condition of probation. Some systems have created drug courts specifically designed to encourage the treatment of addictions for offenders. Treatment programs are often available in correctional facilities as well in order to prepare inmates for more productive lives upon release. The successful completion of such programs is viewed favorably by parole boards. Except in rare circumstances, intoxication or addiction does not relieve an offender from responsibility for his or her crime but may be considered in mitigation. The level of intoxication could be an aggravating factor in offenses that specifically address alcohol or drug abuse such as drunk driving. Judges often impose more severe penalties for repeat offenders and for those with high blood alcohol content.

On the Street

You Are the Judge

Scenario One: Morgan was in a tither. It was 5:30 P.M. and she was still stuck at her desk. It was her five-year-old son's birthday, and she had a big party planned for him at 7:00 P.M. Her boss, Big Ed, was well aware of the party. She had even asked him if she could take off work an hour earlier so she could get home and prepare. Heck, she even invited him. Instead, Big Ed threw a bunch of contracts on her desk and told her she needed to finish them before she could leave. She reminded him of her son's birthday, but he said, "Do you want a job or do you want to play birthday party all day?" Frazzled, she picked up a stapler and threw it at him as he walked away. The stapler struck him in the back of the head causing a two-inch laceration in his scalp. He went to the doctor the next morning and received three stitches. He also fired Morgan.

    Scenario Two: Heather despised Taylor. Taylor had recently been hired to act in a television commercial for a local heating and air conditioning company. Heather really wanted that gig. It seemed like everyone liked Taylor, and Heather was just sick and tired of it. So she planned her revenge for weeks. She found out where and when they were filming the commercial. Just as Taylor was delivering her lines, Heather rushed onto the set and threw drain cleaner into Taylor's face. "Take that, Miss Perfect. See how the rest of your life works out!" Taylor was severely burned, and Heather was arrested. The police later testified that Heather had been drinking prior to the assault.

    Both Heather and Morgan would be guilty of felony assault. If the state statute provides for possible punishments of one, two, three, four, or five years in prison, what penalty would you impose for each offender? Why? What other information would you like to know before imposing sentence? ■

The Impact of the Eighth Amendment

The Eighth Amendment: Excessive bail shall not be required, nor excessive fines imposed, nor cruel and unusual punishments inflicted.

    The punishment for criminal conduct is determined by state, federal, and local legislative bodies. When legislators draft criminal statutes, they also designate the appropriate penalties for a violation of those laws. Each state has the right to enact their own statues, thus determining the penalties so long as the sentencing structure falls within the bounds of the Eighth Amendment's prohibition against cruel and unusual punishment. As a result, the penalties for similar criminal conduct may differ across jurisdictional lines. Some states proscribe death as a possible penalty for first-degree murder. Others do not. For example, if a person commits premeditated murder in Texas, that person could be executed for the crime. However, the same act in Wisconsin would only warrant life in prison. Disparities in sentencing occur on the lower spectrum of punishment as well. For example, in Colorado, the possession of less than one ounce of marijuana is not considered a criminal offense, if the possessor is at least 21 years of age. The same conduct in Tennessee is a misdemeanor with the possibility of a year's incarceration. Both state statutes comply with the U.S. Constitution. However, if a state legislature decided to proscribe life in prison as a punishment for possession of a small amount of marijuana, it is likely that the U.S. Supreme Court would consider that excessive and a violation of the Eighth Amendment.

While the language in the Eighth Amendment provides minimal specific guidance, the U.S. Supreme Court has addressed the issue in a number of cases. In interpreting the cruel and unusual language, they have indicated that the punishment cannot be grossly disproportionate to the offense. In other words, the punishment must fit the crime. In an early historical case, the Court addressed the disproportionate punishment issue.

WEEMS v. UNITED STATES

217 U.S. 349 (1910)

The Facts: Paul Weems, an officer in the U.S. Coast Guard, was convicted of falsifying government documents and sentenced to 15 years of hard and painful labor. While serving as a disbursing officer in the Philippines, he falsely documented the pay of two lighthouse employees. He indicated they had been paid a total of 612 pesos when, in fact, they had not. Prosecuted by the Philippine courts, he was sentenced to **"cadena temporal."** The Supreme Court described it as follows:

Cadena temporal
A punishment under the Laws of the Commission of the Philippine Islands, mandating imprisonment at hard and painful labor for 12–20 years.

> By other provisions of the Code we find that there are only two degrees of punishment higher in scale than cadena temporal—death and cadena perpetua. The punishment of cadena temporal is from twelve years and one day to twenty years, which "shall be served" in certain "penal institutions." And it is provided that "those sentenced to cadena temporal and cadena perpetua shall labor for the benefit of the state. They shall always carry a chain at the ankle, hanging from the wrists; they shall be employed at hard and painful labor, and shall receive no assistance whatsoever from without the institution."

The Decision: The U.S. Supreme Court concluded that the punishment, 12 to 20 years at hard labor, constituted cruel and unusual punishment in violation of the Eighth Amendment. Thus, they overruled Weems' sentencing indicating that the punishment was disproportionate to the criminal behavior.

While it may seem obvious in modern times that 12 to 20 years for a petty theft was disproportionate, there are still occasions in which fairly minor criminal conduct could result in harsh punishment.

Habitual Offender Laws

The federal government and several states have enacted laws providing elevated penalties for offenders who have committed multiple crimes over a period of time. Commonly called "Three Strikes" laws, the statutes determine a threshold for the number of specified crimes. An offender who reaches the threshold number of offenses may then receive a harsher sentence than the specific penalty for the last convictions. For example, in the federal system, an offender who has previously been convicted of two serious violent felonies or drug offenses could receive a life sentence if convicted for a third such offense. The statute reads in part as follows:

18 USC §3559—SENTENCING CLASSIFICATION OF OFFENSES

(c) Imprisonment of Certain Violent Felons.—

(1) Mandatory life imprisonment.— Notwithstanding any other provision of law, a person who is convicted in a court of the United States of a serious violent felony shall be sentenced to life imprisonment if—

(A) the person has been convicted (and those convictions have become final) on separate prior occasions in a court of the United States or of a State of—

(i) 2 or more serious violent felonies; or

(ii) one or more serious violent felonies and one or more serious drug offenses; and

(B) each serious violent felony or serious drug offense used as a basis for sentencing under this subsection, other than the first, was committed after the defendant's conviction of the preceding serious violent felony or serious drug offense.

California's Habitual Offender was once considered even more stringent than the federal law. It provided for a mandatory sentence of 25 years to life for a third felony conviction if the offender had previously been convicted of two violent felonies. The third offense did not have to be a violent felony. The U.S. Supreme Court examined California's law in 2003.

EWING v. CALIFORNIA

538 U.S. 11 (2003)

The Facts: On March 12, 2000, Gary Ewing walked out of the El Segundo Golf Course clubhouse with three golf clubs worth $1,200 concealed in the leg of his pants. He was convicted of grand theft. However, Ewing had a long criminal history involving robbery, burglary, and theft convictions. At the time of the theft of the golf clubs, he was on parole. The Supreme Court's opinion details the numerous convictions, some of which involved weapons violations as well. The prior convictions included at least two violent felonies under California law. Because Ewing had two or more violent felony convictions, he fell under California's Habitual Offender Statute and was sentenced to 25 years to life for the most recent theft.

The Decision: Ewing argued that the severe sentence for a nonviolent theft offense violated the Eighth Amendment's protection from cruel and unusual punishment. The Supreme Court disagreed. In their opinion, they discussed the public safety issues that gave rise to such laws and their concerns about felony recidivism. They upheld his sentence and California's sentencing statutes. However, in November 2012, voters in California approved a reform law that limited the three strikes penalty to those cases in which the third felony was serious and violent.

The Supreme Court has displayed reluctance to interject their interpretations into state legislative decisions as to the appropriate sentence for crimes that occur in the respective states. However, they did so in a case involving the life imprisonment of a juvenile.

Cruel and Unusual Punishment of Juveniles

Chapter 19 includes a discussion of a 2005 case in which the U.S. Supreme Court barred death as a penalty for offenders who were under 18 years of age at the time of murder. Five years later, the U.S. Supreme Court addressed the imposition of a life sentence for a juvenile convicted of a crime not involving a homicide.

GRAHAM v. FLORIDA

130 S. Ct. 2011 (2010)

The Facts: In July 2003, Terrance Jamar Graham, along with several accomplices, entered an unlocked door in the rear of a Jacksonville, Florida, barbeque restaurant. The door was left unlocked by an accomplice who was an employee at the restaurant. They entered wearing ski masks and struck the manager in the head with a steel bar in an attempt to rob the restaurant. When he started yelling, they ran out without obtaining any money. Graham, then 16, entered into a plea agreement to the adult charge of attempted robbery and armed burglary with assault and battery. At the time, he told the judge, "I made a promise to God and myself that if I get a second chance; I'm going to do whatever it takes to get to the NFL." Adjudication of guilt was held, and Graham was sentenced to concurrent three-year terms of probation. He was required to spend the first 12 months in county less the time he served awaiting trial. However, six months after his release he was arrested during a police chase following a home invasion. Though Graham denied the home invasion, he pled guilty to the probation violation. The judge also decided during the probation sentencing hearing that Graham had participated in the home invasion. Though both the defense and prosecution had suggested lower sentences, the judge sentenced Graham to life in prison. According to Florida law at the time, parole was not available for a life sentence, so Graham's sentence was effectively life without parole.

The Decision: The issue before the court on appeal was whether a state could sentence a juvenile offender to life imprisonment without the possibility of parole for a nonhomicide crime. The Supreme Court wrote a lengthy opinion discussing the impact of the four models of punishment, retribution, rehabilitation, incapacitation, and deterrence, on the imposition of a life sentence without parole. They also examined data concerning the availability and use of such punishments for juveniles around the country. In the end, they concluded that while a juvenile convicted as an adult could be sentenced to life in prison, it was a violation of the Eight Amendment to deny any opportunity for future release. They stated the following:

> A State is not required to guarantee eventual freedom to a juvenile offender convicted of a nonhomicide crime. What the State must do, however, is give defendants like Graham some meaningful opportunity to obtain release based on demonstrated maturity and rehabilitation. It is for the State, in the first instance, to explore the means and mechanisms for compliance. It bears emphasis, however, that while the Eighth Amendment forbids a State from imposing a life without parole sentence on a juvenile nonhomicide offender, it does not require the State to release that offender during his natural life. Those who commit truly horrifying crimes as juveniles may turn out to be irredeemable, and thus deserving of incarceration for the duration of their lives. The Eighth Amendment does not foreclose the possibility that persons convicted of nonhomicide crimes committed before adulthood will remain behind bars for life. It does forbid States from making the judgment at the outset that those offenders never will be fit to reenter society.

Graham's case was remanded to Florida for a new sentencing hearing consistent with the Supreme Court's ruling. In February 2012, Terrance Jamar Graham was sentenced to 25 years in prison for his crimes.

In the same year, the U.S. Supreme Court held that mandatory life sentences were unconstitutional for juveniles who committed homicide offenses. They did not rule out the possibility that a state could still impose a life sentence without parole but barred statutory sentences that precluded judicial discretion [*Miller v. Alabama,* 357 U.S. __ (2012)].

Criminalization of Disease or Addiction

It is unconstitutional to enact legislation that punishes a person for a disease or addiction. A government may criminalize specific behaviors but cannot penalize a citizen for the status of alcoholism or drug addiction. In 1962, the Supreme Court addressed the issue in *Robinson v. California*, 370 U.S. 660. California had enacted a criminal statute prohibiting a narcotics addiction. The Supreme Court, in ruling the statute unconstitutional, stated the following:

> This statute, therefore, is not one which punishes a person for the use of narcotics, for their purchase, sale or possession, or for antisocial or disorderly behavior resulting from their administration. It is not a law which even purports to provide or require medical treatment. Rather, we deal with a statute which makes the "status" of narcotic addiction a criminal offense, for which the offender may be prosecuted "at any time before he reforms." California has said that a person can be continuously guilty of this offense, whether or not he has ever used or possessed any narcotics within the State, and whether or not he has been guilty of any antisocial behavior there.
>
> It is unlikely that any State at this moment in history would attempt to make it a criminal offense for a person to be mentally ill, or a leper, or to be afflicted with a venereal disease. A State might determine that the general health and welfare require that the victims of these and other human afflictions be dealt with by compulsory treatment, involving quarantine, confinement, or sequestration. But, in the light of contemporary human knowledge, a law which made a criminal offense of such a disease would doubtless be universally thought to be an infliction of cruel and unusual punishment in violation of the Eighth and Fourteenth Amendments.

The case did not inhibit a state's right to criminalize the sale, possession, and manufacture of illegal drugs. A state may also penalize behaviors that result from the use of drugs or alcohol such as drunk driving or disorderly conduct.

Detention Facilities

The protection from cruel and unusual punishment also applies to the treatment of prisoners during their period of incarceration. It is a violation of the Eighth Amendment for a correctional facility to deprive inmates of basic necessities such as food, clothing, medical treatment, shelter, and other sanitary needs. Those rights have been enacted into statutory law by many state legislatures either through direct statutes or administrative laws affecting correctional facilities. The Eighth Amendment has also been interpreted to bar corporal punishment. With the exception of the death penalty, it is unlawful for officials to physically harm a prisoner to enforce discipline or any form of punishment. That does not, of course, prohibit the reasonable use of force in self-defense or to control an inmate.

Prisoner civil rights lawsuits have resulted in significant improvements in prison treatment and conditions. However, frivolous prisoner lawsuits have also clogged the court systems. The U.S. Congress enacted the Prison Litigation Reform Act of 1995 (PLRA) in order to restrict the influx of frivolous suits without affecting courts' ability to address substantial claims. The act included a provision that the defendant, usually a government correctional facility, could file a motion for an automatic stay and termination of relief in order for the court to make a determination if the claim was reasonable. The mandatory stay would last for 30 days but could be extended to 90 days.

The act also required an indigent prisoner to prepay court costs for civil lawsuits if he or she had previously filed three frivolous complaints. In most civil rights lawsuits, a losing defendant would be required to pay the attorney fees of the plaintiff. However, the PLRA limited those fees for prisoner lawsuits. As a result, lawyers became reluctant to pursue those suits.

Summary

Punishments imposed for criminal behaviors fall within the following models: retribution, rehabilitation, incapacitation, restoration, and deterrence. The efforts by legislators and judges to control crime and determine appropriate sentencing are guided by these models. As legislators draft and enact laws, they must also ensure that the punishments fall within the guidelines of the Eighth Amendment's prohibition against cruel and unusual punishment. Punishments that are grossly disproportionate for the crime committed are considered unconstitutional.

This chapter has outlined the various methods of punishment that are typically utilized by the nation's courts as well as the criteria that judges often consider in determining sentence. Habitual offender laws were examined as well. Punishments for juvenile offenders and those individuals involved in addictive behaviors such as drug and alcohol abuse were also addressed. The next chapter specifically examines the death penalty.

Review Questions

1. Describe the theory of general deterrence.
2. Explain the difference between a mitigating factor and an aggravating factor.
3. How might drug and alcohol addiction impact a judicial sentencing decision?
4. Explain the differences between probation and parole.
5. How do the penalties prescribed in habitual offender statutes differ from traditional criminal statutes?

Legal Terminology

Adjudicated delinquent
Aggravating factors
Cadena temporal
Concurrent sentence
Consecutive sentence
General deterrence
Incapacitation

Incarceration
Juvenile
Mitigating Factor
Rehabilitation
Restoration
Retribution
Specific deterrence

References

Ewing v. California, 538 U.S. 11 (2003)

Graham v. Florida, 130 S. Ct. 2011 (2010)

Miller v. Alabama, 357 U.S. __ (2012)

Robinson v. California, 370 U.S. 660 (1962)

Roper v. Simmons, 125 S. Ct. 1183 (2005)

Scanlan, D. (February, 2012). Man's life sentence changed to 25 years, *Florida Times Union.* Retrieved from http://members.jacksonville.com/news/crime/2012-02-24/story/law-disorder-young-man-gets-45-years-shooting-over-10-disagreement

Sentencing Classification of Offense, U.S. Code 18 U.S.C. 3559

Susskind, J. (November, 2012). Changes in three strikes law reform California Prison System. IVN. Retrieved from http://ivn.us/2012/11/09/changes-in-three-strikes-law-reform-california-prison-system/

Weems v. United States, 217 U.S. 349 (1910)

Chapter 19
The Death Penalty

The imposition of the death penalty as a punishment for criminal activity is certainly the most controversial issue relating to the Eighth Amendment's prohibition against cruel and unusual punishment. Not only has the death penalty given rise to a number of landmark Supreme Court decisions, it continues to feed a national political and social debate. The U.S. Supreme Court has decided that the punishment of death is not barred by the Eighth Amendment, but the Court has developed a number of restrictions on the manner in which it may be imposed. However, even though the U.S. Supreme Court allows the death penalty, each state legislature has the right to determine if it is permissible in their particular state. As a result, some states allow the death penalty and others do not. The same murderous conduct in one state may give rise to the death penalty but may not in another. The infamous serial killer Jeffrey Dahmer was not sentenced to death for his heinous crimes. He was convicted of killing, raping, and dismembering 15 men and boys in Wisconsin and yet was sentenced to 15 life terms. Why not death? The State of Wisconsin did not have the death penalty. Had Dahmer committed his crimes in a state with the death penalty such as Texas or Florida, it is likely that he would have been sentenced to death.

According to the Death Penalty Information Center, 32 states have death as a possible criminal punishment. Connecticut repealed the death penalty statute in 2012 but did not render it retroactive, so there are still 11 inmates on death row. Likewise, New Mexico repealed the death penalty in 2009 but did not bar it for inmates already sentenced to death. Since 2007, New York, New Jersey, and Illinois have also abolished their death penalty statutes. Both the U.S. military and the federal system allow death as a punishment. In 2001, in one of the most publicized executions, Timothy McVeigh was put to death by lethal injection at the Federal Correctional Complex in Terre Haute, Indiana, for the Oklahoma City bombings.

Lethal injection is the primary means of execution in the death penalty jurisdictions though a small number of states still allow electrocution, hanging, and the gas chamber as alternatives. Until the mid-2010s, a couple of states allowed the firing squad.

The Supreme Court Review of the Modern Death Penalty

When criminal justice professionals discuss executions, they often refer to the "modern" death penalty. That common description refers to the imposition of the death penalty after the 1976 case of *Gregg v. Georgia*. In order to understand the current status of the death penalty, it is necessary to review the historical decisions that occurred in the 1970s.

In the years prior to 1972, death was identified as the only penalty for defendants convicted of some specific crimes. Some state murder statutes dictated that a person convicted of crimes such as the purposeful murder of a law enforcement officer or a child would be sentenced to death. Such statutes did not allow the sentencing court to consider any alternative punishments. Additionally, some state statutes included death as a punishment for rape cases that did not result in homicide. The U.S. Supreme Court determined that the death penalty in certain applications was unconstitutional in the 1972 case of *Furman v. Georgia*.

FURMAN v. GEORGIA

408 U.S. 238 (1972)

The Facts: The *Furman* case was actually a combination of three death penalty cases: two from Georgia and one from Texas. In the primary case from Georgia, William Henry Furman was sentenced to death for killing a homeowner during a burglary. The conduct violated Georgia's felony-murder statute because he killed someone during the commission of a felony. In the companion case of *Jackson v. Georgia*, Lucious Jackson, Jr., an escaped convict, raped a female victim while holding a pair of scissors to her throat. The victim was not physically harmed other than bruises and abrasions. At the time, a forcible rape was punishable by death in Georgia. The Texas case, *Branch v. Texas*, involved the forcible rape of a 65-year-old woman. The assailant, Elmer Branch, forced the victim to submit by holding his forearm against her throat. The victim was not otherwise physically harmed.

The Decision: The Court overturned death as a penalty in all three cases. Five of the justices agreed that the death penalty was unconstitutional as it was applied to the cases, but they failed to agree on their reasoning. The ruling indicated that as applied, the death penalty violated the Eighth Amendment prohibition against cruel and unusual punishment. All five justices, Marshall, Stewart, White, Douglas, and Brennan, wrote separate concurring opinions. Likewise, all four dissenting judges wrote separate opinions. While the majority's reasoning was diverse, the case resulting in the determination that the procedures used to determine if death was the appropriate penalty in the *Furman* case was unconstitutional as it did not give the judge or jury the right to consider alternative sentences. The Georgia statute eliminated judicial discretion and failed to consider the aggravating and mitigating circumstances involved in each death penalty case. As for the rape cases, the court, though not unanimously, indicated that death was an inappropriate penalty in a rape case. Several years later, the Supreme Court clarified that decision rule in *Coker v. Georgia*.

While the *Furman* decision did not offer states definitive guidance on capital punishment, it did result in the abolishment of the death penalty in the United States for four years. As a further result of the decision, all inmates who had been sentenced to death in the United States had their sentences commuted to life imprisonment. Perhaps the most famous commutation applied to Charles Manson. Manson had been convicted and sentenced to death for his involvement in seven murders in southern California in 1969. The murders and his subsequent trial were immortalized in the book, *Helter Skelter*. As a result of the *Furman* decision, Manson's death penalty conviction was reduced to life imprisonment.

The U.S. Supreme Court addressed the death penalty again in 1976.

GREGG v. GEORGIA

428 U.S. 153 (1976)

The Facts: On November 21, 1973, Troy Gregg and Floyd Allen were picked up while hitchhiking in northern Florida by Fred Simmons and Bob Moore. A short time later, another hitchhiker, Dennis Weaver, was also picked up, but he was dropped off in Atlanta, Georgia. The next day, the bodies of Moore and Simmons were found in a ditch near a rest area north of Atlanta. Weaver, after hearing about the slayings on the news, told the police of his encounter with the men. Ultimately, Allen and Gregg were arrested driving the car stolen from the victims. They also had a pistol which resulted in a ballistic match to the bullets that were used in the murders. They ultimately admitted killing Moore and Simmons as they were attempting to rob them. Moore was shot in the eye, and Simmons received a gunshot wound to the face and the back of the head.

Both men were charged with **felony-murders** and armed robberies. Both were found guilty by a jury. The judge then conducted a separate sentencing hearing before the same jury. The prosecution offered little evidence other than the facts that had already been established. The defense focused on the appropriateness of death penalty for the crimes in question. The judge instructed the jury to decide between life in prison or death. The jury was also instructed to consider the aggravating circumstances: (1) murder committed during the commission of another capital felony—armed robbery; (2) murder committed for the purpose of stealing the victim's property and vehicle; and (3) murder was "outrageously and wantonly vile, horrible and inhuman, in that they [sic] involved the depravity of the mind of the defendant." The judge instructed the jury that they could only recommend the death penalty if at least one of the aggravating circumstances was proven beyond any reasonable doubt. The jury found that the aggravating circumstances in the first two circumstances had been met and sentenced both men to death.

Felony-murder
A murder that occurs during the commission or attempt to commit a separate felony.

The Decision: The *Gregg* decision revisited the death penalty. Immediately after the *Furman* decision in 1972, a number of states had enacted new death penalty statutes and were now asking the Supreme Court to determine if the new statutes and procedures met the constitutional requirements of the Eighth Amendment. While each state's new statute differed slightly, each case involved defendants who had been convicted of first-degree murder. The Supreme Court first answered the critical question of whether the death penalty was cruel and unusual on its face. They said no. "First, the punishment must not involve the unnecessary and wanton infliction of pain. Second, the punishment must not be grossly out of proportion to the severity of the crime." By doing so, they ruled that the death penalty could be imposed in some cases and, if administered properly, would not cause unnecessary and wanton infliction of pain.

Once they had indicated that the death penalty was not unconstitutional, they addressed the statutory and procedural requirements.

States should limit death penalty crimes. State legislatures should only designate death as a possible punishment for crimes involving special circumstances. By limiting those circumstances to the most heinous of offenses such as the killing of a law enforcement officer, the murder of a child, multiple killings, contract killings, murders committed during other serious felonies, or murders committed by offenders with prior murder convictions, the pool of offenders subject to the death penalty would be reduced. Those special circumstances are often referred to as specifications in many state death penalty statutes. The Court agreed that Georgia, in rewriting its statutes, had narrowed the class of murders subject to death by specifically identifying the aggravating circumstances that had to be proven.

The death penalty could not be imposed unless the trial court had the opportunity to weigh the aggravating and mitigating circumstances in each individual case. The mandatory imposition of the death penalty was a key element addressed in *Furman*. Death penalty statutes that did not allow the trial court the discretion to examine the factors in each case would be considered unconstitutional. The new law in Georgia not only required proof of the aggravating factors, it also allowed a jury to recommend life if they believed the mitigating factors warranted it. Thus, even though the aggravating factors had been proven, a jury could still decide not to impose the death penalty.

Bifurcated process
The two-step process required in death penalty cases. The trial that determines guilt must be completed separately from the sentencing hearing in which the punishment is determined.

The Supreme Court also determined that the sentencing hearing should be separated from the determination of guilt. The **bifurcated process** first required a trial for the determination of guilt followed by a second and separate sentencing phase. It is at the sentencing phase in which the jury considers the aggravating and mitigating circumstances.

As with all criminal trials, the judge imposes the sentence. In death penalty cases, if the jury recommends death, the judge would still have the discretion to impose a life sentence instead. However, in most death penalty states, if the jury recommends life imprisonment, the judge cannot impose the more severe penalty of death.

In the aftermath of *Gregg v. Georgia*, 37 states enacted death penalty statutes modeled after Georgia's, though several have since repealed those statutes. While the U.S.

Supreme Court has clearly upheld the constitutionality of the death penalty, its applications and the methods of execution continue to be reviewed. In recent years, death penalty states have faced a number of lawsuits and appeals attacking the drug protocols used in executions. After *Gregg* upheld the death penalty, the Court examined a number of other related issues including the imposition of death in nonhomicide cases and in murders involving juveniles or intellectually challenged defendants.

The Death Penalty and Nonhomicide Cases

It is unconstitutional to execute an individual for a crime that does not involve the loss of a human life. The death penalty is reserved for homicide offenses and those crimes such as treason, which by their nature would result in the death of others. The Court addressed the issue in *Coker v. Georgia* in 1977. Almost 20 years later, they revisited the issue in a case involving the rape of a child.

COKER v. GEORGIA

433 U.S. 584 (1977)

The Facts: On September 2, 1974, Ehrlich Anthony Coker escaped from the Ware Correctional Institution near Waycross, Georgia, where he had been serving multiple sentences for murder, rape, kidnapping, and aggravated assault. Around 11:00 P.M., he broke into the home of Allen and Elnita Carver by entering an unlocked door. After threatening them with a board, Coker tied up Allen Carver in the bathroom. He then found a knife in the kitchen and forcibly raped Mrs. Carver. Coker also took money and car keys from the kitchen and escaped the scene in the family car. He was ultimately captured and convicted of rape, kidnapping, armed robbery, auto theft, and escape. Per Georgia law at the time, a defendant could be sentenced to die for rape if it was committed in conjunction with other violent felonies and if the offender had prior serious felony convictions. Coker was sentenced to death by electrocution.

The Decision: At issue was whether death was a grossly disproportionate penalty for the crime of rape. The Supreme Court vacated Coker's death sentence and held that death was only appropriate in crimes where another human life had been taken. The Court stated:

> Rape is without doubt deserving of serious punishment; but in terms of moral depravity and of the injury to the person and to the public, it does not compare with murder, which does involve the unjustified taking of human life. Although it may be accompanied by another crime, rape by definition does not include the death of or even the serious injury to another person. The murderer kills; the rapist, if no more than that, does not. Life is over for the victim of the murderer; for the rape victim, life

> may not be nearly so happy as it was, but it is not over and normally is not beyond repair. We have the abiding conviction that the death penalty, which "is unique in its severity and irrevocability," *Gregg v. Georgia*, 428 U.S., at 187, is an excessive penalty for the rapist who, as such, does not take human life.

Coker's death sentence was overturned, and the case was remanded to the Georgia trial court where he was sentenced to multiple life sentences. The case also resulted in the vacation of death sentences for other prisoners who had been sentenced to die for rape or other nonhomicide crimes.

In *Kennedy v. Louisiana*, 554 U.S. 407 (2008), the Court once again addressed the application of the death penalty in a nonhomicide crime. Patrick Kennedy was convicted of brutally raping his eight-year-old stepdaughter. The rape was so vicious that the Supreme Court stated that they could not accurately recount the "hurt and horror" that the victim had undergone. Her injuries, while not fatal, required extensive emergency invasive surgery. In 1995, the Louisiana legislature had enacted an Aggravated Rape statute that provided for the death penalty for the rape of a child less than 12 years of age. Kennedy was convicted and sentenced to death. However, the U.S. Supreme Court, citing its language in *Coker*, once again disallowed death as a penalty for crimes which did not result in the loss of human life.

Juveniles and the Death Penalty

In *Roper v. Simmons*, 125 S. Ct. 1183 (2005), the U.S. Supreme Court ruled that the execution of an offender who was under 18 years of age at the time of the offense was a violation of the Eighth Amendment's protection from cruel and unusual punishment. In that case, Christopher Simmons conspired with two other youths to kill Shirley Crook. One of the co-conspirators abandoned the plan before they carried it out. Simmons, along with Charles Benjamin, broke into Ms. Crook's home, bound her hands, and covered her eyes. They then took her to a state park in St. Louis County, Missouri, and threw her off of a railroad trestle into the Meramec River. At the time of the murder, Simmons was 17. However, the Missouri trial court sentenced him to death.

In 1988, the Supreme Court had barred death for offenders under 16, but one year later they had upheld death as a penalty for offenders 16 or 17 years of age in the 1989 case of *Stanford v. Kentucky*, 492 U.S. 361 (1989). In overturning their own opinion in *Stanford* and remanding Simmons sentence back to the Missouri trial court for further sentencing, the Court cited overwhelming international opinion against the death penalty for juvenile offenders.

Mental Illness and the Death Penalty

In the 1986 case of *Ford v. Wainwright*, 477 U.S. 399, the Supreme Court addressed the issue of whether a mentally ill inmate could be executed. Alvin Bernard Ford had been sentenced to death in the State of Florida in 1974. He did not claim insanity as a defense and there was no indication of mental illness during the trial. However, during his years of incarceration, his mental state deteriorated. He became delusional and developed an obsession with the Ku Klux Klan. He believed there was a conspiracy to kill him and that the prison guards were killing people and hiding their bodies inside the prison walls. He claimed that prison officials had taken 135 of his friends and family, including U.S. Senator Kennedy, hostage. He also referred to himself as "Pope John Paul III." After extensive psychological evaluations, Dr. Jamal Amin concluded in 1983 that Ford suffered from "a severe, uncontrollable, mental disease which closely resembles Paranoid Schizophrenia with Suicide Potential"—a "major mental disorder . . . severe enough to substantially affect Mr. Ford's present ability to assist in the defense of his life." Another physician, Dr. Harold Kaufman, determined that Ford had no understanding of why he was being executed or the connection between the death penalty and his crime. The Supreme Court, in agreeing with the common law description of executing a mentally insane person as savage and barbaric, ruled that the Eighth Amendment barred use of the death penalty. On a side note, the appellee, Wainwright, was the Secretary of the Florida Department of Corrections, the same as in *Gideon v. Wainwright.*

In 2002, the Supreme Court also ruled that an inmate who was mentally retarded could not be executed. In *Atkins v. Virginia*, 536 U.S. 304, the Court examined the case of Daryl Renard Atkins who had been convicted and sentenced to death for the murder of a U.S. Air Force airman during a robbery. Psychological evaluations at trial indicated Atkins I.Q. as 59 or mildly retarded. In holding that the execution of Daryl Atkins would have been cruel and unusual punishment, the Court stated, "We are not persuaded that the execution of mentally retarded criminals will measurably advance the deterrent or the retributive purpose of the death penalty."

Summary

In the 1976 case of *Gregg v. Georgia*, the U.S. Supreme Court determined that death as a punishment for the taking of the life of another was not prohibited by the Eighth Amendment. Additionally, the Court affirmed the bifurcated sentence process that is now utilized in all states that provide for death as a possible punishment. This chapter outlined the historical development of the modern death penalty laws as well as the criteria and procedures that must be followed in order to comply with the U.S. Constitution. Subsequent to the *Gregg* decision, the Court also disallowed the death penalty for crimes that did not result in the unlawful death of another including the rape of a child. The Court has also now ruled that the death penalty is unconstitutional for an offender who was a minor when he or she committed the murder or if the offender was mentally incapacitated. While constitutional, the death penalty continues to be controversial. Many states are now reviewing the drug protocols that are currently used for lethal injections. Those issues will likely face further review by the Supreme Court.

Review Questions

1. Why did the U.S. Supreme Court decision in *Furman v. Georgia* result in the commutation of death penalty sentences in other states?
2. Explain the bifurcated hearing process as required by *Gregg v. Georgia*.
3. Determine if your home state has the death penalty. If so, have there been any executions since the 1976 ruling in *Gregg v. Georgia*?
4. Why can death not be imposed for the rape of a child?
5. A serial killer who committed murders in several states might be sentenced to death in some states but not others. Why?

Legal Terminology

Bifurcated process   Felony-murder

References

Coker v. Georgia, 433 U.S. 584 (1977)
Atkins v. Virginia, 536 U.S. 304 (2002)
Death Penalty Information Center. (n.d.). Death penalty in 2012: Year end report. Retrieved from http://deathpenaltyinfo.org
Ford v. Wainwright, 477 U.S. 399 (1986)
Furman v. Georgia, 408 U.S. 238 (1972)
Gregg v. Georgia, 428 U.S. 153 (1976)
Kennedy v. Louisiana, 554 U.S. 407 (2008)
Sentence of Death, U.S. Code 18 U.S.C. 3591
Stanford v. Kentucky, 492 U.S. 361 (1989)

Abandoned property: Property in which the original possessor has disposed of in a manner which indicates that their privacy interest has been abandoned.

Acquittal: The determination by a judge or jury that a criminal defendant is not guilty of a crime.

Adjudicated delinquent: The determination that a juvenile offender has committed a criminal offense.

Aeronautical drones: Unmanned aircraft used primarily in military operations to conduct surveillance or deliver weapons.

Affidavit: A legal sworn document used in warrant requests stating the facts establishing probable cause.

Aggravating factors: Considerations which would lead a judge or jury to impose a more severe punishment.

***Alford* plea:** A criminal defendant pleads guilty to an offense while contending that they did not commit the act constituting the crime.

Alimentary canal smuggler: One who smuggles drugs by swallowing condoms filled with the narcotics and passing them through their digestive system upon arrival at their destination.

Appellate court: A court that is charged with reviewing the decision of a lower court is acting as an appellate court.

Arraignment: The court hearing in which the formal charges are read to the defendant and the defendant enters a plea.

Arrest: The physical seizure of a person with the intention of accusing them of a criminal offense.

Arrestee: A person who has been placed under arrest.

Articulate: Clearly explain.

Bail: An amount of money or another security designed to ensure a criminal defendant's return to court if released from jail.

Bail Reform Act of 1984: Federal legislation that, in part, allowed the denial of bail if the conditions of release could not insure the safety of the community.

Bifurcated process: The two-step process required in death penalty cases. The trial, which determines guilt, must be completed separately from the sentencing hearing, in which the punishment is determined.

Bill of Rights: The first ten amendments to the U.S. Constitution. Ratified in 1791.

Biometric tecnology: Technology used to detect and recognize human physical characteristics.

Burden of proof: The amount of proof necessary to prove a case. In a criminal case, the required burden is proof beyond any reasonable doubt.

Cadena temporal: Referred to in *Weems v. United States,* a punishment under the Laws of the Commission of the Philippine Islands, mandating imprisonment at hard and painful labor for 12–20 years.

Capital offense: A crime that carries the possible punishment of death.

Challenge for cause: The request of an attorney to a trial judge to exclude a prospective juror because he or she has indicated an inability to be impartial or to properly serve.

Civil law: The laws and procedures that regulate non-criminal issues such as contracts, domestic relations, real estate, and personal injury civil lawsuits. Violations of civil law do not lead to incarceration.

Closed-circuit video: Cameras that broadcast, monitor, or record events and transmit to another receiving source.

Coercion: The use of force, threats, or intimidation to encourage another to engage in an action.

Collateral estoppel: An accused cannot be tried if the ultimate issue of fact has been determined at a previous trial.

Collateral use exception: Allows the use of illegally seized evidence in court settings that do not result in the determination of guilt or innocence.

Commutation: An order by a governor or the U.S. president reducing the sentence of a convicted criminal defendant.

Concurrent jurisdiction: When a criminal behavior is a violation of the laws of more than one jurisdiction at the same time.

Concurrent sentence: When a judge orders multiple sentences, the terms of incarceration run simultaneously. The entire sentence is complete when the defendant has served the longest sentence.

Consecutive sentence: When a judge orders multiple sentences, the defendant must serve one period of incarceration before beginning the next.

Continuance: A hearing or trial is delayed until a future date.

Contraband: An item that is illegal to possess.

Courts of record: A trial court that officially records its proceedings and renders final decisions.

Criminal procedure: The body of laws and rules that determine how police, lawyers, judges, and courts enforce and apply criminal law.

Curtilage: Buildings in close proximity to a dwelling, which are continually used for carrying on domestic employment; or such place as is necessary and convenient to a dwelling, and is habitually used for family purposes.

Custodial: A person's freedom of action is restrained in a significant manner.

De facto arrest: An individual would reasonably believe he or she was under arrest even though it was not the intention of the officer to arrest.

Determinate sentence: A sentence that provides for a fixed incarceration period.

Deterrence: The theory that an action by law enforcement or the courts will discourage another from engaging in criminal activity.

Discovery: The process in which the prosecutor and defense attorney disclose evidence impacting the case.

Double jeopardy: The legal principle that prohibits a criminal defendant from being tried twice for the same offense.

Double-blind: A term used in a line-up procedure when the administrator is unaware of the actual suspect.

Drug courier profile: A compilation of behaviors typical of drug smugglers

Drug interdiction program: A law enforcement program designed to detect and apprehend offenders engaging in illegal drug activities.

Drug paraphernalia: Tools and items used to manufacture or use illegal drugs. Examples include bongs, pipes, scales, and hypodermic needles.

Dual sovereignty: The principle that both the federal government and state governments exercise jurisdiction over specific legal issues.

Dual sovereignty: Each individual jurisdiction has the authority to enact its own criminal laws. The commission of an offense in one jurisdiction is a separate crime from the same action in another. Each state may prosecute separately so long as the elements of the offense are committed in their state jurisdiction.

Due process clause: The Fourteen Amendment guarantees that all citizens of the United States cannot be denied life or liberty without due process of law.

Dumdum bullets: A slang term referring to bullets that are either designed or altered to expand upon striking their target, resulting in fragmentation and more serious damage or injury.

En banc: All of the judges on an appellate court review a case.

Evidence: An item or information that could be used to prove or support a fact.

Exclusionary rule: Evidence that is illegally obtained is inadmissible in court.

Exculpate: To clear a person of guilt or blame.

Exigent circumstances: Extraordinary and emergency circumstances that allow the police to conduct a search for persons or evidence without first obtaining a warrant.

Extradition: The legal procedure in the state where the arrest is made which determines the validity of the warrant and whether to transfer the arrestee back to the originating state.

Felony: A criminal offense for which the possible punishment is incarceration of one year or more.

Felony-murder: A murder that occurs during the commission or attempt to commit a separate felony.

Field interview: The police questioning of witnesses, victims, or suspects in an informal environment.

Field sobriety test: A test conducted on the street to determine if a motorist is intoxicated. It usually evaluates the suspect's motor and cognitive skills through tests such as walking a straight line or counting backwards.

Fillers: The participants or photographs included in a lineup that are not suspects in the criminal investigation.

Frisk: A pat down of the outer part of a suspect's clothing.

Fruit of the poisonous tree doctrine: An extension of the exclusionary rule that excludes evidence discovered as a result of a previous illegality.

Fruits of a crime: Benefits derived from the commission of a crime.

General deterrence: A theory of punishment proposing that the fear of conviction and punishment prevents others from committing crime.

Glassine: A thin water resistant, translucent paper product that is often used to transport illegal narcotics.

Global positioning system (GPS): A navigational system that uses satellite technology to determine a geographic location.

Grand jury: A body of citizens selected to examine evidence in a criminal case and determine if probable cause exists to issue an indictment.

Habeas corpus: A legal proceeding in which a government agency responsible for detaining an individual must appear in court to show cause as to why the detention is legal.

Herbicide: A chemical compound that poisons and kills plants.

Hung jury: A jury that is unable to reach a verdict.

Immigration checkpoint: A roadblock established to determine the immigration status of passing motorists and pedestrians at or near the U.S. border.

Impeachment: The discrediting of a witness. The term also refers to the procedure that attempts to remove a government official from office.

Implied consent law: Statutes associated with drunken driving offenses in which by operating a motor vehicle, the driver has given an implied consent to a test to determine blood alcohol levels.

Impound: The procedure in which police tow and store a vehicle in a secure facility until it is released to the owner. The area in which the vehicle is stored is referred to as an *impound lot*.

In pro persona/pro se: Latin terms referring to a criminal defendant who is representing himself or herself without an attorney.

Incapacitation: A model of punishment designed to restrict an offender's ability to commit future crimes.

Incarceration: Imprisonment in a jail or prison.

Indeterminate sentence: A sentence that calls for a period of incarceration that falls within a range of time. The parole board determines the release date.

Indictment: The formal charging instrument issued by a grand jury in a felony criminal case.

Indigent: A criminal defendant who is unable to afford an attorney.

Information: A written charging document prepared and presented by the prosecutor.

Instrumentalities of a crime: An item used to commit a crime.

Interlocutory appeal: An appeal made in a criminal case before the verdict. It occurs when there is a critical legal issue that must be decided before the trial continues.

Interrogation: An effort to elicit an incriminating response

Inventory search: A search conducted by law enforcement to determine the contents of a vehicle that is being towed and impounded.

Invoking: In *Miranda* situations, the suspect who invokes his rights is accepting his or her rights and refusing to respond to police questioning.

Jurisdiction: The authority of a court system to hear cases and a government's power to enact laws. Jurisdiction is determined by geographical areas or subject matter.

Jury deliberation: The discussions and voting that a jury engages in determining a verdict.

Jury instructions: A judge's instructions to a jury explaining the applicable law and the rules of deliberations.

Jury nullification: Occurs when a jury ignores the weight of the evidence and renders a not guilty verdict.

Juvenile: A person less than eighteen years of age. (Also see *minor*)

Kaleidoscopic: A series of changing phases, events, or actions

Knowingly: Understanding the nature of one's actions. A person consenting to a search must understand that he is granting permission for the police to search a particular area or property.

Law enforcement: For *Miranda* purposes, an individual who is an agent of or working on behalf of a government law-enforcement agency.

Lineup: Usually conducted in a police facility, a lineup consists of several individuals positioned in a group setting. The witness is asked to observe the individuals and identify a suspect.

Mandatory minimum: Criminal statutes that require mandatory sentences, thus taking discretion on sen-tencing away from the judge. If the defendant is convicted for an offense in which there is a mandatory minimum, the judge must impose at least that amount of punishment.

Misdemeanor: An offense considered less serious than a felony.

Mitigating factors: Circumstances that would lead a judge or jury to impose a less severe punishment.

Mugshot: A photograph of a suspect taken on arrest by police or correctional officials.

Open fields: Open space and land that does not immediately surround a person's home.

Operating after revocation: Driving with a revoked driver's license.

Own recognizance: The pretrial release of a defendant without requiring money or property as bail. The defendant is released based on their own reputation and circumstances.

Pardon: An order by a state governor or U.S. president forgiving the conviction of a criminal defendant or excusing a criminal act that may have been committed by an individual.

Pen registers: Technology that records the outgoing numbers called or texted on a communication device such as a phone.

Peremptory challenge: The exclusion of a prospective juror by attorney without indication of a reason during voir dire. The number of peremptory challenges is limited by statute.

Petit jury: A jury that hears the evidence and determines guilt or innocence.

Photographic array: Similar to a lineup, a witness examines photographs and attempts to identify a suspect present in the photo array. The array may be a series of photographs or a group photograph.

Plainclothes: Common description of a police officer working without wearing a uniform.

Plea bargaining: Negotiation between the defense and prosecution in a criminal case.

Plurality opinion: In a case in which a majority of the justices are unable to agree on the holding or reasoning, a plurality opinion represents the reasoning of the highest number of judges.

Polygraph: A device that measures and records several physiological indices such as blood pressure, pulse, respiration, and skin conductivity to determine if a subject is giving truthful responses to prescribed questions. The device is often referred to as a *lie detector*.

Precedent: A decision on a legal issue that has been previously determined. Also see *stare decisis*.

Preliminary hearings: Held to determine if sufficient probable cause exists in order to bind the case over to the grand jury.

Preponderance of evidence: The burden of proof required in most civil cases. A fact is proven by a preponderance of evidence if it is considered more likely than not to be true.

Pretextual stop: The legal justification for using a traffic violation stop to conduct an investigation for other criminal activity.

Pretrial detention: The incarceration of a defendant prior to the determination of guilt.

Probable cause: Facts and circumstances that would lead a reasonable person to believe that a crime has been committed and a particular person committed it. Probable cause is the standard of proof required for an arrest or the issuance of an arrest or search warrant. It is also the legal justification for a search under specific circumstances.

Prophylactic rule: A rule designed to protect the rights of everyone facing a specific issue.

Prosecutor: The lawyer who represents the government in a criminal case. The prosecutor is responsible for presenting evidence and arguing a case in court. The prosecutor might be working on behalf of a county, state, municipal, or federal jurisdiction.

Protective sweep: A quick search of a premises to determine the presence of individuals who might cause harm to officers.

Public defender: An attorney appointed by a court and paid by the government to represent a criminal defendant who is unable to afford an attorney. Some public defenders work directly for a government agency while others may be private attorneys who are compensated on a case-by-case basis.

Racketeer Influenced and Corrupt Organizations Act (RICO): RICO is a federal law that provides criminal punishment for those engaged in racketeering, an organized criminal enterprise. Racketeering often involves crime networks that engage in gambling, prostitution, drug trafficking, and illegal firearms.

Reasonable suspicion: Facts and circumstances that would lead a reasonable police officer to believe that criminal activity is afoot.

Rehabilitation: A model of punishment proposing that an offender who undergoes treatment, education, and training will be less likely to reoffend.

Release on own recognizance: A criminal defendant is released from jail while awaiting trial without the requirement of posting bail.

Remand: When an appellate court rules on a case and refers it back to the lower court with instructions to correct the error.

Respondent: The party responding to an appeal.

Restoration: A model designed to restore the victim, offender, and community to their status prior to the commission of the crime. Restorative justice combines elements of restitution and rehabilitation

Retribution: A model of punishment that imposes penalties to punish the offender for their behavior.

Search incidental to arrest: A search conducted as part of a lawful arrest.

Self-incrimination: The act of a defendant making a statement that could be used as incriminating evidence against them in a criminal prosecution.

Sequential lineup: In sequential lineup, one individual at a time is viewed by the witness.

Sequester: The isolation of a jury during a trial in order to limit exposure to any prejudicial information that might impact their decision.

Showup: A one-on-one identification in which a witness observes one person and is asked to state if that individual is the correct suspect.

Simultaneous lineup: In a simultaneous lineup, the individuals are viewed by the witness at the same time. In sequential lineups or photo arrays, the witness is presented with the individuals one person at a time.

Smith Act: A federal law directed at individuals advocating the overthrow of the U.S. government.

Sobriety checkpoint: A police roadblock in which motorists are randomly stopped and investigated for the offense of driving while intoxicated.

Specific deterrence: A punishment theory proposing that the penalty discourages a specific individual from committing future offenses.

Standing: The authority to consent to search.

Stare decisis: The legal doctrine used in common law in which a court follows the legal precedent set in earlier opinions.

Statutory law: Laws written and enacted by legislative bodies such as state legislature or the U.S. Congress.

Suppress: To exclude evidence from a trial.

Testimonial evidence: An oral statement that may be used to prove a fact in a court of law.

Thermal imaging device: A device that detects the heat emitted from a person or object.

Trace evidence: Evidence that occurs when there is contact or transfer of fluids, tissue, or other tangible substances. Examples include blood, fibers, semen, tissue, paint, and lipstick.

Trafficking: Sale or distribution of a product usually in reference to illegal drugs or other contraband. In some jurisdictions, trafficking also includes possession with intent to sell or manufacture contraband.

Trap and tap: Technology that records the numbers received by a communication device such as a phone.

Trial: The hearing in the criminal process in which guilt or innocence is determined.

True bill: The determination by a grand jury that probable cause exists to issue an indictment.

Venue: The geographical location in which a trial is held.

Vicodin: A schedule II pain-killing narcotic that is often the subject of criminal abuse or trafficking.

Voir dire: The process in which the judge and the attorneys question prospective jurors in order to determine if the individual would be able to serve in a fair and impartial manner.

Voluntary: A requirement for many legal actions. An individual acts voluntarily if the action is of his or her own free will and absent of coercion.

Waiver: Waiving one's rights means that a person is giving up their rights. In *Miranda* situations, the suspect who waives his or her rights may agree to talk to the police without an attorney present.

Writ of certiorari: A petition asking an appellate court to review a case. When an appellant wants the U.S. Supreme Court to review their case, they would file a writ of certiorari.

Table of Cases

Principal cases are indicated by italics.

Index

Continued